To Ron & I

With Best Wishes

Ray McManus

Activate the mind and
let the spirit roam free

# Book Reviews

"Who Dares is an exceptional book written by an exceptional man. Ray Matthews shares his remarkable achievements with the reader who 'joins' him on his journey. It is a reflective and deeply personal book that takes the reader on a roller-coaster of emotions. You will be moved, inspired and motivated to be the best you can become, just as Ray has done. This book tells us much more about the young Ray, his mentors and his recent incredible 150-mile run in 38 hours! In his book Who Dares, Ray shares his expertise and knowledge about ultra running that will benefit and support anyone taking on a challenge, at any age."

*Marina Tune*
*Child and Adolescent Psychotherapist*

"Another wonderful look into the life of Ray Matthews. Looking back at Ray's childhood memories and his boxing days, Ray takes you back to where and how it all began as well as some new adventures. The book is alive and warm and captures your imagination. You will not want to put it down, each page has you gripped and wanting to know what happens next."

*Helen Woodburn*

"For most people, running a marathon is a major achievement; but running 150 miles in one go when you are already past three score years and ten? In his new book Ray Matthews demonstrates how it is possible to give no concessions whatsoever to getting older. He explains with wonderful clarity, how single mindedness and incredible mental toughness can overcome the most daunting of challenges. Much of this mental strength and depth of personality were gained as a young lad in his boxing career and it is fascinating to see how life skills gained nearly six decades earlier still supported him in his truly awesome run.

Ray is a great storyteller and he tells it how it is, in his gritty, no-nonsense South Yorkshire way – but with great warmth and humour as well. Read his book and be inspired; Ray makes achieving the seemingly utterly unattainable, so straightforward."

*Ian Hopper*
*Pinpoint Adventure*

"This new book by Ray Matthews should come with a health warning! The readers of this infectious new book will need enough willpower to harness the desire to go out and achieve something great after reading this most enthralling story of a man who doesn't know the meaning of failure.

Ray is satisfying his dream which comes from decades of learning about himself from coaches who provided the guidance and knowledge of how to fulfil ambitions; sadly they are no longer around to see the fruits of their patient efforts, but it is evident that they are Ray's constant subconscious companions when called upon.

I can think of few people who have demonstrated the mental ability and physical awareness of how the body works to overcome the trauma of running 150 miles in such a short space of time the way this man does . Ray's new book provides an intimate relationship between himself and the reader, I felt that I was there alongside him as he brilliantly describes, blow by intriguing blow, as a young boy, then shall we say mature man, taking on seemingly impossible challenges.

A thoroughly good read from start to finish. There must surely be more to come, can't wait."

*Mike Thompson*
*Life coach and fitness instructor*

## About the Author

A true Yorkshire man, born at a time when a certain Mr. A. Hitler was still slinging bombs at England, took advantage of freedom that allowed him to develop the strong character which would take him through the drama and trauma of his three score and ten years.

# Dedication

This book is dedicated to Maureen, my wife and best mate in appreciation of over fifty-five years of unselfish support, and encouragement. She has continually provided the platform behind the scenes for me to take on these extreme events, without her my challenges would never have been possible. Thank You!

Ray Matthews

# WHO DARES

AUSTIN MACAULEY
PUBLISHERS LTD.

A CIP catalogue record for this title is available from the British Library.

ISBN 978 1 78554 052 3 (Paperback)
ISBN 978 1 78554 054 7 (Hardback)

www.austinmacauley.com

First Published (2015)
Austin Macauley Publishers Ltd.
25 Canada Square
Canary Wharf
London
E14 5LQ

Printed and bound in Great Britain

# Acknowledgments

Massive thanks to my granddaughter Holly who once again set the pendulum in motion. To my good friends who made the 150 mile challenge achievable, for believing in me and just being there --, Brian Harney, John Clarke, Helen Woodburn and Kevin Doyle, Glynn Hookbody, Tony, Ray and Margaret Silcock, Phil Haigh, Adel Morris & Richard Hawley, Rose & Norman Grimley. Sean Rodgers, Nick Stubley, Mat Harvey, Fiona Burkinshaw, Elly Woodhead, Fay Bird and her young daughter Niamh. Dominic Hurley and his daughter Nina.

Thanks to my friends who were there to welcome me back, my daughter, Karen, and son-in-law Chris, Glynn and his wife Lynn, and how lovely to see his grandchildren, Regan and Reece, Vonnie and Andrew, Mick and Sue, with their son, Matt, and daughter, Vanessa, Together with Sean and Maria and my old friend, Ken Chapman.

For the feedback and comments from the 100k London to Brighton Challenge group Kerry Levins, Jo Newton, Vonnie Brodie, Bernadette Franklin & Jane. Thank you guys, I am sure you all have greatly benefited from the experience.

Also a thank you to Michele Vincent for all her editorial help with this book.

# INTRODUCTION

"Three score years and ten!" When I first heard that phrase of life expectancy as a young boy, I figured it was just something that grown-ups worried about, it seemed insignificant and nothing for me to be concerned about because at the age of ten, well, after all it was another 60 years ahead of me, which seemed like hundreds of years away into the future at that time.

So fast forward and boy oh boy, the years certainly have flown by. They have also provided me with plenty of incredible memories.

At three score years and ten, and even a good bit more, what does the future hold for me now? First of all, I figure that it's a great privilege to be growing old, many people don't! And I often wake up with aches and pains, but I do keep waking up! Which is a good job, or this book would have come to an abrupt end. How often was I told that I should respect my elders, today I find it increasingly more difficult to find one? But should I die whilst attempting one of my self-inflicted challenges, then the ultimate climax to growing old, would be that people would no doubt say, "Well, at least he died doing the things he liked best", whereas if anything had gone amiss whilst my family were young and growing up, people would probably have said, "Selfish sod, he's gone doing his thing", therefore the ultimate goal is to die young, but in a long time from now.

Should this be the time when I am expected to start planning for my funeral arrangement, burial or cremation? Well I am having none of that, my friend, because there's a load more to come yet, grab hold of life by the short and curlies and just do it.

What are my expectations for the future? Well, having passed the age that my parents and most of my schoolmates reached, I feel blessed and privileged to be strong enough mentally and bodily to be able to continue with the demanding, self-inflicted challenges that I have set for myself over the years. By having the courage not only to believe in my own capabilities and mental strength to put dreams into reality, I will, before long, satisfy that hunger inside and find that ultimate challenge.

My determination to take on even greater challenges that will not be restricted by the biological clock which brings my birth date into the equation is a passionate target. I vowed and declared many years ago that I would never allow my age to become an influence when it came to setting challenges for myself, The big secret to life is to fit somewhere in between, mentally become ageless and overcome the negative setbacks by embracing my strengths.

There have been times when it's been scary, especially just after deciding to take on distances that most athletes wouldn't even dream of attempting. On reflection of late, it's when the realisation of what I have talked myself into doing kicks in. Fear is fine and I am happy to admit that, which goes some way to proving that I am human, but I never fear failure, because after all that is my ultimate goal. I am still searching for that one extreme challenge which will take me to the edge of my capabilities. Hopefully when I finally reach that situation it will provide me with the satisfaction of having finally fully exhausted all my expectations. With luck and the prevailing wind, before time runs out and leaves me with just great memories of the past.

As the years have passed, it would have been easy to slip into the sedentary world of fewer activities and succumb to what is generally expected of someone my age rather than pushing my reasonably willing but progressively more difficult to train body into achieving increasingly more demanding extreme challenges, in fact, believe me, just standing still is harder to achieve these days, it's probably called "Old Age". But with the help and understanding I get from my local physician Dr Kahn, who probably thinks I am a complete lunatic, but he does nevertheless, with enthusiasm, provide me with the necessary health checks and certified paperwork to allow me to enter some of the most demanding events. I am also blessed to have on hand the great services of a most talented physiotherapist, Phin Robinson, who practises in Rotherham, and always comes up with ways of putting me back together after the abuse of much-used muscles and tendons. These guys keep the old engine serviced and running, but will I know when enough is enough?

It's a sad observation I make that we often limit our achievements only by the ridiculous fear of the embarrassment of failure. Fear and the inability to believe that we can overcome obstacles often stands in the way of doing so much in our lives. Not only fear of failure but also fear of what other people might think or say about failing and then to be judged on the failure. We need to harvest the courage and rely on our own capabilities, remembering the fact that usually the one who is judging is probably the person who has never taken on a challenge in the first place and the person who has never failed is generally the one that's never had a go anyway. It's also a fact that you simply can't fail if you don't try in the first place.

What makes me so different and why do I take on these challenges? That question is levied at me more times than any other and is best answered by going back in time to where it all started. But it is true to say that I have always "dared" to take on seemingly impossible challenges.

Whilst preparing for the current challenge that I am about to take on, I will generally have the next one formulating in my mind. That way, before the end of this challenge there is always something new to look forward to, rather than suffering the low mental dips of the moment when an event is concluded, a time when there's normally a flat period.

My life today is so closely linked to my early years in more ways than one, by people who were instrumental in moulding me and teaching me the values that I would need in life. These values have provided me with the strength to withstand the ups and downs, the highs and lows of my 70-odd years of living up to now. Even today during tough endurance events, I am constantly subconsciously reminded of the powerful set of life skill rules that I was patiently taught by my two early boxing coaches and this goes some way in answering the question that I am most frequently asked.

Those early days, so full of many memorable incidents and moments, have provided the foundations of my life. Hopefully, passing on some of the knowledge I gained during those informative years will prove to be interesting enough to make a lasting impression and maybe change at least one person's life for the better.

So let's make a start and backtrack in time to where it all began.

Hi, I am Ray, the eldest of four brothers, my three sibling brothers being Alan, Peter and David. I was born at a time when a certain Mr Adolf Hitler was still throwing bombs at us. Yes, that old.

I was born in Wath-Upon-Dearne, and brought up at No 5 Holland Place, a terraced house in Masbrough, Rotherham, South Yorkshire, England.

The 1940s were a great time for a young boy like me. All I could ever want, I suppose, with a freedom that we youngsters took for granted during those days. We had an almost unrestricted, simple but happy life, in a time when neighbours were a big part of life's day-to-day existence, a time when we all had almost identical wants and needs, no-one had any inkling of outdoing anyone else or any need to do so.

I believe that the Second World War had become the catalyst for forging each local community into a sort of commune, bringing everyone closer together in a common cause. Neighbours became members of your extended family; people spoke to one another with genuine warmth and were actively interested in each other's welfare. I can't ever remember hearing about anyone being burgled or anything being stolen from houses that were never locked.

My memories of our local bobby, who seemed to know us all by our first names, always seemed to be around when we had been doing something wrong. One of the worst crimes in those days, scrumping apples from trees out of the orchards of the big houses up Clough Road, seemed to be an offence worse than any full-scale crime of today. I always managed to outrun the on-duty policeman by vaulting over garden walls all the way down Brown Street and I knew when he was ready to give in when he would shout "I'll catch you next time you little bugger," in an extended, out-of-breath sentence that tapered to a whisper. A clout around the ear would be administered for any disrespectful act for anyone caught.

We were being brought up more or less as the war was coming to an end and men whom I had never seen before had suddenly started arriving back home from "the War." I met my dad's brother, Uncle Arnold, who had been involved and was wounded during the ill-fated Arnhem Bridge invasion on the outskirts of the Dutch town. Almost three quarters of the 1st Airborne Division were lost. At least he did get back home and back to sign-writing for a living, but it's a wonder he didn't go into the scrap business with all the shrapnel he came home with.

Adolf Hitler was the main topic of conversation and was always the bad guy we shot our arrows and catapults at. Even as young boys, my mates and I were prepared to defend our country against Adolf's soldiers if need be, using our pretend, home-made rifles.

My home town of Rotherham, a major steel manufacturing area, heavily involved in providing steel products for the war effort, was a constant worry regarding air strikes. The local factories, working to full capacity had led a fortunate existence during the war years, escaping the onslaught of the German Luftwaffe bombing. It seems that during one of the German bombing raids, Steel, Peech and Tozer, the massive steel manufacturing plant, together with the surrounding main industrial works, were targets. The river and canal, which meanders its way alongside these factories from Sheffield through Rotherham, usually visible from the air, should have provided a clear guide for the raid, but were so densely covered by fog that night, that the targets became invisible and escaped the heavy bombing. The Luftwaffe's main targeted factories did escape, but unfortunately the bombs were released further up the flight path on the city of Sheffield. Mainly houses and shops around the city bore the brunt of the bombing, causing untold damage and a great loss of life around the city centre.

Our toys were almost always a home-made version of what we had seen some rich kid playing with and anyone who owned a ball was your best mate. My first ball was, in fact, a pig's bladder and was one almighty smelly problem when it came to blowing it up, the taste didn't help much either. It was far from being round and always seemed to have a mind of its own as to which drunken direction it rolled. My first bike was made from butchered scrap parts of maybe half a dozen different discarded bikes.

We seemed to have simple needs and the toys we did have were sufficient and greatly valued. What more could we kids need?

# CHAPTER 1

## Luck of the Irish

During my time at the then Steel, Peech and Tozer boxing club, "Steelo's", there were many incidents and memorable moments that I recall from my time as a young amateur boxer, which often spring into my mind, even after all these 60-odd years. I can now vividly recall this part of my life and the gruelling training I was involved in, taking up a massive part of my life.

It would have been around my 14th birthday and a few months before I was due to defend my Yorkshire Schoolboy boxing title or, to be strictly true, I would be fighting in a higher weight category for a new title because of my increase in weight over the year. These were the representative stepping stones leading up to the Northern Counties championships and then ultimately the ABA junior championships again.

I had been encouraged by my coach, Jacky Pearson, and was even eager myself, to be honest, to have the opportunity to train and spar with a visiting professional featherweight champion fighter from Ireland. This professional boxer had been invited to train at the gym, as had so many other professionals over my time in the few years before that, but this was the first visiting fighter within my own size profile to make it a practicality for me to train and spar with. Little did I realise at that first meeting, how much my life was about to change as I was being introduced to Danny, this very laid back, easygoing character with the broadest of Irish accents. I found it difficult to understand what the hell he was saying to me as we shook hands for the first time. How could I have known at that first meeting what a massive difference this man would make to my advancing amateur boxing career?

I was about to be introduced and inducted into the real world of a true professional fighter, and oh boy what a complete disaster my first encounter in the ring with this stocky Irishman turned out to be.

My first sighting of Danny in training gear a few days after our first meeting was to bring home feelings of a strange kind of fear that I hadn't felt before, not terrifying, just a sort of trepidation, wondering what I was about to encounter for the very first time in the ring with a professional boxer.

Danny, who was heavier but only slightly taller than I was, looked almost barrel-like, comical really, with the dark brown, sweat-stained leather kidney belt he was wearing around his waist. The padded belt, fastened by leather straps to the outside of his track suit bottoms, looked a bit like a nappy as the leather straps passed between his legs.

As we were being gloved up inside the ring that very first time, I couldn't take my eyes off my sparring partner, who was dancing about in the far corner of the ring looking comically overdressed, wearing an old, well-washed, faded vest over a mucky white T-shirt, black shorts over the top of cut off track suit bottoms and what looked like well-worn boxing boots. On his head was what resembled an old brown padded leather cage! The head guard made up his training attire. Did he need to protect himself that much from me, I wondered, although to be honest he didn't seem to have any concern at all about me as I was having the 8oz sparring gloves shoved on to my hands and carefully laced up for me. The final instructions by Jacky, keep on my toes and move fast with the emphasis on fast, as he left the ring, shouting "Time!" and leaving me to face the unknown.

This professional boxer had been invited to train at our gym on Sheffield Road at Ickles on the outskirts of Rotherham, South Yorkshire, with me in mind, I later found out, to enhance his fitness in readiness for his next championship fight in Ireland. My reputation, it seems, had spread and if I had known that at the time it would have been a terrifying act to fulfil, the tremulous fear I had felt would have been more than justified, what a lot for a young lad to live up to. But why would a professional fighter wish to train with an amateur, and a young one at that? Never did get the answer to that one.

I was pretty much on edge, but the fear had gone, leaving me with butterflies in my stomach for the first time in ages. To say I was excited at the prospect of a few rounds in the ring with this "professional boxer" is a massive understatement.

I recall being asked if I fancied a sparring session with Danny during our initial introduction and I had agreed without hesitation. Maybe I should have taken time to consider the consequences, but at nearly 14 and well on top of my game, what harm could there be, I was fearless and always willing and ready to try new training ideas. "Would there really be that much difference in our abilities?" I remember I had immaturely thought. Well I was about to find out, wasn't I, the hard way.

Even today, I can remember from all those years ago that utter sinking feeling right from the start of that first round. The ring immediately seemed to drastically shrink in size as Danny completely dominated every square foot of the canvas. There was nowhere for me to go or hide, making it impossible to settle into my normal way of fighting. I was being knocked from pillar to post and getting a real spanking, as we say up north. This man was a machine, his work rate phenomenal; he worked me over with so much ease, punching with both hands at speed that I had never encountered before. My reactions to guard against the speed and ferocity of his punches were nowhere near fast enough to fend off his relentless attacks. I was unable to land one punch on him at all, which was something that I was definitely not accustomed to in those days.

The feeling of utter despair and skills inadequacy was bringing back memories from my earlier days and that very first evening at the Red Lion Gym in All Saints' Square, Rotherham, when as a raw 11-year-old I had encountered Cloggy Clarke, a very proficient amateur boxer, on my very first episode in a ring. It was there that I was introduced into the world of boxing by my first coach, Benny Kemp, where talent and the proficient skill in the noble art were always going to make a young scrapper like me look a proper inadequate novice.

This Irishman was so fast and fit, almost to the extent of not having to stop for breath. Even when I was not being hit, I was being tied up on the ropes or closed down enough for me to be unable to deliver any punches. He seemed to have far more arms than I possessed as punches were being rained on me from every direction. In effect, it was a feeling of being suffocated, as I was cleverly being stripped of my power and speed. Even when I was able to launch a punch, my arms felt as though they were trapped to the sides of my body. I was unable to peel myself away from him; even though I wasn't being hammered or hit hard enough to be damaged, I did get the impression that should he wish to punch me with the power which he quite clearly possessed, then it would have been a very different kettle of fish.

This very over-powering Irishman was making it impossible for me to use any of my natural speed, skills or power as I did my best to dance out of reach and defend.

Danny hovered so close that I could smell the stale sweat of his clothes and almost taste his breath, which gave me a feeling of being attacked by a deadly predator of immense skill. Now this is proper fear, because no matter how fast I moved or where I moved to, he seemed to be there waiting for me. With an almost panic-like feeling of losing total control of the situation, I was lashing out trying to land a massive punch that would stop this relentless onslaught, only to find that I was putting myself further in bother as he expertly dealt with my feeble attempts at equalling this one-sided sparring session.

What a massive difference there was between my amateur and his professional abilities. I felt as though I had been sparring for hours, pulling in breath for all I was worth at the end of each round.

This so-called fit me was well and truly knackered well before the end of each round and even when I did get a punch away my elusive target was never there.

My question about our differences had been dramatically answered in the little more than nine minutes of our first encounter in the ring. But you know what: in a sadistic way I had enjoyed the experience, because it brought home to me just how much there was for me to learn, making me even more determined to take advantage of skills this man could teach me. I knew it would be harder than anything I had ever done before, even just the experience would benefit me greatly, but this was the opportunity I needed to take me out of the normal amateur club level skills and into a much higher league. I figured that there would be few young boxers who would ever get this level of experience during their amateur careers.

By his absence and the lack of instructions at the end of each round, I felt that Jacky was leaving me to come to terms with this new experience and find my own answers. Dealing with my feelings at the end of each round was certainly a new experience for me.

I looked back and remembered all the hours of being taught by Benny and then Jacky about how to mentally dig in and find the answers that would always be there if I looked hard enough. It was all about having the courage to be self-critical, to be able to analyse and work out the solution from my own autopsy of this first encounter.

I had been taught by both Jacky and Benny my first coach, how to conduct an autopsy at the end of every tournament and sparring session. There was much to analyse about tonight's sparring master-class. It would be a mountain to climb, I had no doubt, but with the hyper competitiveness which I had learnt to control over these past few years, it was a challenge that I was determined to take on and master.

I made myself a promise there and then as Danny lifted the middle rope for me to step out of the ring: "I am having you, mate, sooner rather than later." Did I have the guts and determination?

I knew that I would have to work hard to turn things round within little more than the three months he would be available for me to spar with before heading back to Ireland.

Danny put a gloved hand on my shoulder and said: "Thanks, that was the best workout I have had for some time," commenting that he had enjoyed the sparring session. I didn't know how to take that comment - was he was just telling me what I might like to hear and being easy on my feelings? - later telling me that he felt that we could work well together.

My Dad, on one of his infrequent visits to the gym had witnessed that evening's one-sided master-class of boxing in which I was subjected to the biggest lesson of skill and domination. I believe that my Dad was probably more stressed than I was as he had watched my three rounds of sparring, well, in reality, me back-pedalling and defending.

I watched in horror, as my Dad walked across the gym floor, making a beeline for Jacky and then confronting him by complaining with raised voice. I can vividly recall my Dad's concerned look as he commented about the one-sided three-round demolitions of his "boy," so to speak. This would not be allowed to happen again to me, I was not going to be a punch bag for this professional to practise on. He was fuming. "Oh hell!" I felt a real sense of embarrassment as heads turned to look at me in sympathy. Not what I needed at this stage in my career!

On our way home from the gym that night, during lengthy discussions and after much pleading about the merits of my training and sparring with Danny, I managed to persuade my Dad that this was just what was needed and could greatly benefit my advancement. I knew that Danny could teach me more all-round boxing skills than I could ever get from sparring with my amateur club-mates.

I had already made my mind up anyway before getting out of the ring.

We discussed what I had planned and how I could reap the rewards from this great, not-to-be-missed opportunity, even to the point of me not taking part in any national inter-club competitions for a couple of months, well at least not until the coming championships. I could completely dedicate my time and efforts to almost full-time training and get myself into a state of super fitness; there would be no other way I would be able to reach anywhere near level terms with this incredibly talented fighter. Thinking and training like a professional would have to become priority number one totally focused and fully committed, using Danny, like he was prepared to use me. My Dad eventually agreed to give me a month and made me promise not to tell my Mum about that evening's session.

Looking back, I realise that the decisions I made throughout my early life were instrumental in shaping and moulding the events that have become so memorable to me, and this one was probably among the best.

At about this time, Colin Harrison, a keggy hander (south paw), one of our great club fighters and someone I had huge admiration for, had achieved an impressive reputation over the previous years as an amateur boxer, had turned professional and now as a full-time fighter had taken on a far more demanding training programme. Colin had undergone a dramatic change to his entire way of training, one which was more in line with how Danny would conduct his time and training sessions at our gym. I recall the whole gym had taken on a new look and had a buzz of activity, which seemed to change the way almost everyone trained. I would watch and copy Colin's and Danny's rigorous training programmes, but always included additional sit-ups, press-ups and extra bag work. I made it a personal challenge to always go that one extra mile during our twice-weekly training sessions at the gym.

I was now on a mission and, even though there were other professional fighters training at the gym most of the time, Danny's work rate was spectacular to watch. I would catch the other boxers watching him, but out of the corner of their eyes, of course. This new, no nonsense approach to our training became a sort of competition between the two of us, increasing my intensity to match and then eventually out-train him. Achieving a brutal mid-session workout of delivering 120 punches each minute during the three, three-minute rounds of heavy bag work became something of an obsession, even upping the power during the last 15 seconds of each round. I was also running before and after school on a cross country route of about seven miles, giving me a daily 14 miles workout which, I have to admit, I actually hated with as much passion as I love running today. This, together with my normal sporting school activities during the week, was beginning to take me to a higher level of fitness than I had ever achieved, and it was starting to feel good.

Additional boxing training was also taking place at home during the days when not at the gym. My Dad had acquired an old army kitbag, which he stuffed with sawdust and sand and erected in my bedroom using an old butcher's hook screwed through the ceiling into one of the timber beams. The old sash windows in the house would shake and rattle at times, probably the next two or three doors as well, in the old terraced block. Mum would shout up at me to pack it in when she couldn't stand it anymore.

When I wasn't due to go to the gym, my Dad would, on occasion, spend an hour or two with me after he got home from work, encouraging and helping me to master multiple punching sequences which were giving me a bigger variety of ammunition to use in the ring. Dad had never done any boxing himself, but he was able to teach me how to deliver a wide range of punches.

I recall one particular evening during this spell of extra training in our front room. We had been working through a sequence of punches, broken down to two to start with, then adding more punches to the sequence as I became more fluent at delivering each one. This sequence eventually becoming a wicked, five punch combination. Jab, cross, left hook to the body, doubling up to a left hook to the head and then finishing with a right cross. I practised this combination at an ever-increasing speed, Dad would shout "Faster, faster, faster!" All the time he was blocking the punches using some home-made type of focus mitts, placing them alongside where the target was. He was always good at improvising and making things.

The inevitable was bound to happen, I suppose, as he shouted "Come on then, let's go for it!" In an attempt to show him just how fast I could deliver my punches, I launched into the sequence with as much enthusiasm as I could muster. I hit my Dad with every one of the five punches except the first jab. The combination was an almost unstoppable sequence of punches once underway. The speed and the accuracy in each one of my punches, which were delivered with so much power, connected on target. My Dad slowly sank to his knees, then on to his side. He was out cold. Oh God, what a frightening sight. All I could think of was that I would cop it now and I disappeared out of the house through the kitchen, shouting to Mum, as she stood washing pots at the kitchen sink, that my Dad wanted her quickly.

It was some hours later when hunger took over and I finally plucked up enough courage to return home; I opened and gingerly poked my head round the back door. All was fine; I was greeted with a roar of laughter from both Mum and Dad, although Dad didn't look so good. He had a swollen, reddish blue-looking lump at the side of his mouth. I was forgiven but told never to tell anyone about the incident. I think now is about the right time to reveal all about the dedication and sacrifice a father would make for his son. We didn't spend any more time on one-to-one punching activities after that, though.

The second sparring session with Danny was almost a replica of our first meeting, but with a subtle difference, I was beginning to learn and understand a bit more of the finer techniques. I was occasionally being punched around the shoulder and biceps as I blocked and covered up, which slowly drained the strength from me. My first thoughts were that Danny was off target, but I realised towards the end of the third round that my arms felt like lead and were difficult to move with any speed or power. This is another big lesson to be absorbed and remembered, because over ten rounds of fighting it would certainly have a massive effect on an opponent's ability to maintain punching with any speed or power. There had also been a sense of urgency from Jacky, as the intensity of his coaching seemed to have gone up a gear over those last few weeks during our two mid-week sessions. I am sure he must have felt my impatience of wanting to get the best out of this golden opportunity of training with Danny and learning superior skills at a lightning speed.

Jacky was always a hard taskmaster where I was concerned, which I suppose would have come from his Royal Navy background. He never talked about his boxing, but I was informed that he was the middleweight Forces champion before leaving the Navy and taking on the Phoenix Boxing Club coaching job.

It's probably true to say that my fitness was still not good enough at this stage, and so to encourage speed of reaction during our training sessions at the end of the evening's workouts, I would often spend a few rounds in the ring with two, sometimes three, of the younger boxers. My hands would be tied behind my back or thumbs tucked into the back of my shorts and then the ten- and 11-year-old younger kids would attack, throwing punches at me from every direction. My job was to evade the onslaught, which would be so willingly delivered by the over-enthusiastic youngsters, an almost impossible task except when I tripped them up, taking them off their feet as a laugh just to keep them on their toes, but by the end of the round, unable to rest for a split second, I would be completely knackered. You can well imagine the enthusiasm coming from two or three young boxers after telling them that they could throw punches for all their worth without being hit back. Have a guess what amount of effort they come at you with? They would even climb over one another to get a punch in. Avoiding the keen punches was definitely not an option; this is where I learned most of my ring craft skills, not getting trapped in a corner was priority number one.

# CHAPTER 2

## Preparations for the 150-miler

"Are you bloody mental?" and "Have you got a screw loose?" , almost unanswerable printable comments among so many that were not so printable after announcing that I would be attempting to run a distance of 150 miles in one hit over a period of about 36 hours. I would be using a triple 50-mile loop of the Rowbotham Round Rotherham International foot race (RRR) as a perfect guide for the recognised distance.

The 30th anniversary of the RRR 50-mile event would be taking place on Saturday, October 20, 2012, a perfect choice because of its long-standing popularity for me to use as a great way of attracting publicity for my fund-raising targets. The RRR is a 50-mile cross country race that frequently attracts well over 350 athletes from both England and abroad each year. This event would provide me with another challenge that sort of crept up on me to start with, but mainly as a tribute to the original instigator and organiser of this race, Ralph Rowbotham, who had sadly passed away in September 2010.

Now, I don't consider or put myself in the category as being a proper runner, well not a runner in the true sense that most athletes would associate with running. It's probably true to say that I have not been blessed with a natural ability to run and was well and truly at the back of the queue when they were giving out running legs. I will never win races other than maybe a race that only 80-year-olds enter, with the possible exception of my age group category. In fact, I have never won a race, other than one or two many years ago during my school's seven-mile cross country races in which sheer bloody-mindedness and a superior fitness provided that accolade. But I do seem to have this ability to keep putting one foot in front of the other more times and for longer than most other people.

I do realise that running 150 miles at the age of 71 is not something you do every day, but this challenge has been lodged in my brain's To Do list ever since I was asked to do an encore a couple of years ago, in October 2010, by one of the Rotherham Harriers officials while posing for a photograph, having just completed a 100-mile run around the circumference of Rotherham.

This 150-mile challenge could also be used to become the vehicle for me to more easily raise sponsorship money for Blind Veterans UK and also to be able to provide funding for the specially-adapted trike that I was determined to get for the children at the Newman Special School in Rotherham.

I had been looking to find a challenge that would push the boundaries of my abilities and take me deep into my unknown capabilities, and decided that it would be a good idea to run this course three times in one continuous attempt, making it once for each ten years of the event's existence, providing me with a challenging grand total target of 150 tough miles A new longest distance for me..

There are many worldwide events in which this sort of extreme distance is attempted and there are many amazing athletes who will run this distance on a regular basis, but these events are generally on the other side of the world in some remote hot desert, and mostly these extreme distance events are taken on over a seven-day challenge.

The cost of competing in some of the world's most challenging events is also an influential factor in deciding which race to take part in, often thousands of pounds are required to enter in order to provide for the many volunteers, accommodation and, of course, flights and transfers to some of the remotest parts of the planet. But my thoughts are, why dash off to some far-flung part of the world to run 150 miles, when right here on my doorstep is exactly what I am looking for this time? The great thing about my self-inflicted challenges are that I can make my own rules, in this case run 150 miles and I will succeed, run less than 150 miles and I would fail but anything over 100 would be a PB, and if I am honest, there is also a certain amount of comfort in taking on this particular self-inflicted challenge, as this one would provide me with a safety net, knowing full well that at any time during the run I would never be much further than 25 miles away from my home. "Crafty me".

So finally having decided that I would have a go at running 150 miles, a plan of how to make it all work was the next step. The aim was to make the RRR 50-mile event and race proper, the main focus, and then wrapping one 50-mile run either side of the main event would be the most beneficial plan. The logistics of the race proper would take care of themselves with regard to the food and drink situation, having the normal recognised drink and food stations strategically placed around the 50-mile course, which would make it less of a lottery than when I completed the 100 a year ago. As long as I could get a team together to help and support me during the before and after unofficial laps, then I knew it would work.

I needed to work out the rough times it would take to complete the first 50 miles, which would enable me to work backwards to decide what time I should start the whole challenge. Twelve hours to complete the first 50 miles should be enough; I could now start to put it all together. The main race, which was due to start at 6am on Saturday morning, necessitated me getting underway with the full challenge late

Friday afternoon, running through the evening and night, giving me time to get back to the college for 5 to 5.30 am on Saturday morning. Then set off with the main race athletes at 6am and complete the RRR race again within another 12 hours or thereabouts. Have a short food break, shower, change of clothes and then set off again Saturday night to complete the last of the 50-mile legs.

Allowing for the fatigue which will inevitably come during the extended miles of running, my aim was to finish for about 10 am on Sunday.

Wow maybe I am bloody mental.

It was all beginning to sound exciting, leaving me with just over seven months to sort out the logistics of getting friends and colleagues to volunteer their time to come out to feed and water me at various staggered locations around the circumference of Rotherham. These would be oddball times throughout the Friday and Saturday night, early Saturday and Sunday mornings. The progressive training would also need to be programmed to get me anywhere near fit enough to be able to take on this huge distance.

The programme for hitting achievable times during the first and last 50 miles, together with maintaining a good pace during the middle 50 miles would be more realistically predictable once I had a better idea of how I would be able to cope with the ever-increasing miles in training.

I was already in pretty good shape, having had a good period of training and distance running in the background over the last few months. I still had logged in my mind the basics for the last successful 100k Sahara Desert race and the more recent 100-mile event and without picking up any major injuries in my preparation, I was able to stand on the start line fit and ready to perform.

It would be all about getting the training right over the coming months. Gym work also took on a gradual increased programmed effort as well over the following months, providing the confident feeling of knowing that I could rely on my boxing workouts to give me greater strength and stamina in which to put in the longer training runs. Increasing the distance needed to be carried out on a gradual basis but realistically I felt that seven months was not an awfully long time to prepare for this challenge. Mentally I was up for it. Physically I needed to get the best out of the time I had left to prepare my body to withstand the hammering that I expected would come from the huge mileage, especially the time on my feet and the pounding that these old legs would have to cope with.

The decision was now made and set in stone, I am going to run 150 miles and it was now starting to feel like my own Olympic challenge. The little imp sat on my shoulder and whispering in my ear, "You can run 150 miles", has won the argument again.

I was already committed to taking on the 100km 24-hour London to Brighton off-road challenge, organised by the Blind Veterans UK in June and I had also volunteered to assist and accompany Kerry Levins, a blind ex-serviceman, to help achieve the distance.

Kerry, a blind ex-army officer, and his training partner and long-time friend Darren Murphy had entered the event to help raise much-needed funds for the charity. I had volunteered to add my services and experience in getting him from London to Brighton, across the open South Downs countryside after leaving the Thames river path and finishing at the Blind Veterans headquarters in Ovingdean on the outskirts of Brighton. Whilst this challenge would involve just walking, it would still give me time on my feet and added experience of coping throughout the night with sleep shortage. With this event in mind, I would have a short-term goal to base my training around and which would provide me with an idea of how I was, physically.

Retirement has afforded me the luxury of being able to train sensibly for these long distances. I suppose more like I would expect professional athletes to train, using multiple runs each day in bite-sized chunks, rather than trying to achieve longer distances all in one go and risking injury. Coming home from a shorter distance run feeling good rather than knackered, dinner, feet up for an hour or so, get ready and off again for the second training session of the day. This way of training leaves me feeling comfortable and not too tired to complete the overall distance which had been planned for the day. The logistics of it all means that longer distances each day are more easily achievable as long as I can maintain the mental willingness to put the time and effort into the daily grind.

My feelings during the ultra-distance training and of course the longer distance runs can best be described as like living a long time in one day and getting even greater value out of my life.

Controlling the emotions of the ups and downs of running long distances always leaves me feeling stronger, even though I sometimes question my sanity. "What am I doing here?" and "Why am I putting myself through the pain?" seem justifiable questions and come generally at the start of most training programmes when it seems that there are never enough hours in the day. Luckily I enjoy training, which stems back many decades; even during adverse weather conditions when it becomes a physical battle which can then be treated as a mental training session. But as the years have gone by, it's become increasingly more difficult to get fully ready for any long distance event.

I get the amazing feeling of being stronger when I have completed a self-inflicted challenge that has materialised from a daydream; because it's my aim to push the years backwards and I continually need challenging targets to aim at. It's all about not putting restrictions on ambitions, if we don't push the boundaries then how can we ever experience that amazing feeling which comes from achieving?

Generally before I have completed the event I am training for, I will have another one in mind, even if they have become more and more extreme as the years have gone by. Will this 150-miler be the ultimate one for me and put me on my knees? It's certainly a bloody long way. Maybe I am trying to outrun my age if that makes any sense.

My Dad once told me that "Youth is wasted on the young." I didn't quite understand what he meant at the time he said it, but now I fully understand and wholeheartedly agree.

Once the training programme is roughly established, I can set the targets and get into my own disciplined way of training as early as possible, mostly that means running on my own and becoming totally selfish, not having to be bothered or even take an interest in anyone else's vibes, as even having to talk consumes energy and takes away concentration.

Focusing on a set pace is the best way of tuning my mind to take and maintain total control over my body, because once the mental element of running is lost, fatigue will then dictate the distance and soon the body will take control, bringing an end to the running. It's so easy to be sidetracked and lose sight of the overall target.

A vital ingredient in the armoury of all endurance runners I believe, is the ability to become great friends with yourself, many hours of solitude and would-be loneliness could be soul destroying if you couldn't become compatible and tolerant of the different mood swings which occur over long hours in isolation. You really have to like yourself and possess the ability to laugh, out loud at times, during the many thoughts and incidents that inevitably crop up during the relentless miles as they stack up.

Once the training becomes more comfortable, it will generally take 14/15 miles to become robotised, so to speak, where running becomes effortless and pace becomes automatic. When that happens, I feel that I can achieve great distances and often wonder if I had been into running many years ago, what distances I could have achieved – dreams.

I am fortunate to be blessed with strong healthy joints. Injuries are generally other people's problems other than a long-standing disc problem in my lower back and a tight hamstring from the attachment area in my butt, which lets me know it's still there from time to time and which mostly comes from doing speed work. I can usually manage these niggles by taking a daily dose of prescribed painkillers, but I have surprisingly led a pretty injury-free life over all these years, for which I am so very grateful.

By September, I had managed to run 120 miles a week for three consecutive weeks and was happy with the way I was able to recover each day prior to the tapering period over the last three weeks before the start date. This achievement was providing a comforting feeling of knowing that I should be capable of managing my target in this latest challenge, hopefully 2012 would prove to be a year to remember for all the right reasons if I could successfully manage to complete this triple 50-mile run back to back.

Days and weeks fly by as they inevitably do and all too soon it's time to put oneself on the start line. It's always my aim to be on the start line healthy, but the biggest worry I have had in these latter years is that my ageing body may become my biggest enemy during these longer distances runs. Should I really expect to be able cope with the increasingly more physical challenges and keep on a par with the mental strength that multiplies from success? What's going to crack first?

Training was well and truly over, and I am feeling great.

Friday, October 19, 2012 finally arrived and, like most mornings of any endurance running event, my mind was full of thousands of things to do and, more importantly, things that should have been done, to make the running of this event a success. I had spent hours planning with my friends and backup team who would meet me at various places around the 50-mile circumference of Rotherham.

It had been extremely important for me to get completely organised before setting off. I had planned for changes of clothes, shoes and socks and the locations for main food stations. There are a total of eight supporting friends who would be giving up their time and sleep to meet me at the pre-arranged strategic places around the course throughout Friday and Saturday nights in particular.

Sleep deprivation could possibly affect my ability to think and reason and even co-ordination might become a big problem, so it had been a good idea to put things that I would be carrying during the challenge into familiar places that I could find without having to think too much.

The team were ready with food and drinks that I had managed to get to them over the previous couple of days, which would provide me with the calories and energy that I would need over the 36 hours or so of running. I had calculated that I would need to consume a mixed variety of food during the 150 miles, including baby milk, soup, even lamb chops and baby new potatoes during the third leg. It's probable that I would need to service more than 35,000 calories over the three laps. This time I was not leaving anything to chance like the 2010 100-mile challenge when I discovered that a few dozen ants had infiltrated my container of bananas and honey that I had planted under a bush just outside Harthill, which I had to throw away at 70 miles into

40

the run, leaving me without the calories I needed until reaching the next pit stop. My friends were ready but more nervous for me than I was. Don't worry guys, we were good to go.

At 3.45pm on Friday, October 19, 2010, I left Maureen, with a good luck kiss and a see you later; I set off out of Maltby with a boot full of clothes, extra running shoes and the food and drink that I would be carrying during the next couple of days.

I was on my way to Manvers college on the outskirts of Wath-upon-Dearne; calling in at Ravenfield to pick up my beautiful 17-year-old granddaughter, Holly, who would be accompanying me for a few miles from the start of the event. She was ready and waiting, all kitted up in track suit and comfortable running gear and expressing her hopes that we would not get any rain for the first six or so miles.

We were soon well on our way to Manvers and making a phone call to my son, Gary, to confirm that he would be waiting at our arranged spot to pick up Holly.

The press photographers were waiting as we arrived at the college, together with a group of well-wishers and friends who would be running the first mile with me. I needed to spend some time having photographs taken with Holly as well and managed a few minutes with the gang before it was time to line up for the start. Good wishes were coming from my friends who would not be running with us.

Saying my goodbyes to Dominic, his daughter, Nina, and the rest of my friends who had arrived to see me off, I got underway from the start-line with a signal from my friend Brian Harney, the Rotherham Harriers official who had volunteered once again to set me off. Brian had been at the start for me a couple of years ago when I became the first athlete to complete the 100-mile challenge.

The time has arrived, "We are off" and striding out together with Holly a little after 5pm are my friends Sean Rodgers, Nick Stubley, Matt Harvey, Fiona Burkinshaw, Elly Woodhead, Fay Bird and her young daughter Niamh. We head for the waiting press photographers who had set themselves up at strategic points in the college grounds to get photographs of this one-off event.

At a steady jog we are heading out in a clockwise direction, opposite to the normal anti-clockwise direction that the race will be taking the following day, which I expect to be involved in just a little over 12 hours from now.

We are aiming for the canal towpath and the first mile where we will part company with my friends, leaving just Holly and me. I had decided to complete the first 50 miles in this opposite direction, as we head for Swinton, to give my challenge something of a different approach to the normal route of the race proper and then the remaining 100 miles following in the race direction

In no time at all, while our constant jovial banter and questions of my sanity of what I was about to take on were loudly being discussed by the lads, we reach the canal and our first mile; it gave me a strange, stirring feeling of trepidation in the pit of my stomach as we parted company. It felt like starting out on an adventure into the unknown for the first time as the stark realisation of the distance I would be travelling over the next thirty-six hours or so.

Good luck wishes were being shouted as we waved our farewells, shouting back my thanks for their support as we continued on our way heading for Old Denaby and what would be the last checkpoint with only three miles to the finish line during the final leg, hopefully sometime early on Sunday morning if my calculations proved to be correct.

It's not long before all thoughts and concerns of what I am taking on have disappeared as we stride out together along the river and then canal towpath. We are comfortably chatting and catching up about school and Elena, Holly's young Arab pony which has proved to be a great partnership in the showjumping ring and, of late, cross country events. She doesn't come back from many events without a winner's rosette, I am so proud of her dedication. Holly has that natural athletic talent which translates into a gazelle-like running action and looks effortless as she strides out alongside me. Without any training, I know she will manage the next six miles comfortably before meeting up with her Dad.

We are soon passing over the railway lines, having left the canal towpath, and heading up Ferry Boat Lane to join the main road and the short climb to the entrance at the bottom of the field in Old Denaby. This is where the last checkpoint gazebo tent will be erected for the race proper tomorrow, sometime before midday.

The entrance to the field is deep in mud and difficult to gain access to without our feet sinking deep into the mud. Trying to keep my feet as dry as possible, I manage to give Holly a hand to skirt around the muddy obstacle and make our way up the steep, grassy hill. This section is proving to be quite demanding and we are soon down to walking hands on thighs up the steep hill, sinking into the boggy as hell area halfway up. How does water hang like that halfway up a hill? It's difficult for Holly to keep her feet, because of the smooth soles of her running shoes; they are only fit for the road, really. A couple of near full-on head dives have created huge fits of laughter from us both as we make our way up the steep hill. This hill will be just as tough going down on the next two legs for me; I will pass on the news of the boggy section at the bottom of the hill to the RRR team when I meet up in the morning.

We are finally summiting the hill and passing through the gate after crossing the tarmac track at the top, before heading along the tree-lined path that leads to the broken tarmac track.

It's mostly downhill for us now as we make good time on the uneven broken tarmac track. I am expecting to be with Gary on time at about 6.45pm. He will be waiting to pick up Holly at the car park of the Earl of Strafford pub, an imposing stone building set back off the main Doncaster-Rotherham road in Hooton Roberts. This pub, which was originally the old manor house, is a great eating place.

I can see the main road ahead of us with cars streaming past as we run up the steep incline to it. This is the end of the road for Holly. Once again, I have thoroughly enjoyed our time together; it's a great feeling being able to run alongside her and for Holly to be able to share the experience of being a part of my challenge. How many Granddads ever get the opportunity to experience this amazing deep proud feeling that I am having right now? I know that she will also remember our time together again, as she did a couple of years ago when I managed to complete the 100-mile challenge, a very memorable experience for me in which we ran the first six miles or so together, from the Manvers college to Wentworth through the mud and pouring rain.

It's time to say our goodbyes with a hug, a kiss and a wave as I set off across the busy main Doncaster – Rotherham road heading for Maltby. Saying goodbye to Holly and Gary leaves me with that strange feeling again of the enormity of the miles in front of me, a feeling of trepidation and a greater sense of being on my own. I will have to get these negative thoughts out of my head and concentrate on why I am doing this personal, self-inflicted challenge.

Holly did mention later to me that after I had left them, she had felt her own fear for me, thinking that it was impossible for anyone to be able to run 150 miles in one go, but also saying that if it was possible, then her Granddad was the one who would be able to do it. Ah ah, thanks, Holly!

The light is starting to fade fast and beginning to cast a dull shadow as I head uphill into the boggy trail path through the wooded area, trying desperately not to end up on my backside in the slippery-rooted and rocky stream. This couple of hundred yards is always a boggy problem, even in the middle of summer, and tonight it's just as bad as I was expecting, normally I would be coming down the hill. My head torch is helping to light up the foot holds in the dark canopy created by the overhanging trees. I am struggling to keep my feet dry and doing the best I can to make my way up the deep muddy path, until at last the change of light gives me a sense of relief, as I leave the trees and level out on to the top ridge line of the field, searching for the path on the left which will take me diagonally down the ploughed field to Firsby Hall Farm.

It's now pitch black and the headlight is creating that tunnel-like effect as the circular beam from my head torch cuts through the night, providing me with a good clear view in front as I skirt around the small farm buildings on the gravel path. I am heading for the path towards the left side of the farm that will take me across the open fields towards the M18 motorway.

It's strange heading in the opposite direction looking out for familiar land marks that look so very different in the night, even though I have run this section of the event a good many times in training out and back, but never in this direction in the dark. I have a good sense of direction, which stands me in good stead and sees me arriving at the tunnel under the M18 motorway without any need to detour, even finding the rickety old stile at the edge of the last field. A left turn through the almost tunnel-like overhanging bushes, a sharp right after a couple of rickety stiles and then it's the climb up the right side of the uneven grassy field path to the road at Micklebring village.

The street lighting is pretty good and the tarmac makes the running more comfortable through the village for a while, until reaching the left turn down the dirt track at the farm on the busy Ravenfield to Braithwell road. This corner of the farm track is where I had stashed a Tupperware container of new potatoes under a rock on the last leg of my double RRR a couple of years ago, and is now bringing back great memories. Remembering how well I had felt at this 90-mile point was filling me with renewed, encouraging feelings for my new challenge.

The rutted and uneven path from now on proves to be challenging, causing me to slow down to a very steady careful jog until I reach the tarmac drive heading for the top of Addison Road in Maltby.

Time to ring Maureen at home to confirm my imminent arrival for a pre-arranged meal of chicken legs and baked potato. My first meal since just after three this afternoon would be waiting for me at our cottage just across from the next to last RRR checkpoint on School Road at Maltby. While deciding about running the first leg in this direction, it did occur to me that this would be a great strategic move on my part to provide a substantial feeding opportunity to fuel up, and a hot meal at that. I should last out now until meeting up with John Clarke at Harthill later on in the night.

Leaving Maureen after devouring my meal, I was underway again, heading through the lichen gate of the old St Bartholomew's Church, switching on the head torch to light up the very dark path through the graveyard, then left down on to the path which will take me over the meadow and through the Crags on to the grounds of Roche Abbey.

I am not expecting to see a soul now for the next few hours, it's dark, a bit chilly and creeping into my mind once again are thoughts about the distance of the run in front of me, but the familiar surroundings are something of a comfort and providing me with a calming and settling effect.

Well before reaching Roche Abbey I was running effortlessly, breathing comfortably, settled and ready for whatever the challenge ahead held for me. The abbey has an eerie feel about it as it usually does during these late night runs. The history of the place is the key to why my imagination switches from the running into wondering what it would have been like all those years ago when the Cistercian monks would be building and living in this magnificent abbey. What would it have been like all those years ago before King Henry VIII ordered the destruction of all these religious buildings? Even now, this is quite an impressive stone structure.

The night is calm and without any incident passing through a field full of cows, the majority of the herd are all lying along the bottom of the field near the river Beck. My lights are cutting through the dark, picking out the narrow grass path before finally dropping down the steep banking, and through the kissing gate into Stone village.

I make my way into Firbeck across the open ploughed fields, turning right on to the tarmac road down past the Black Bull pub on the corner across from the newly-refurbished village hall. I will be visiting this hall, which will be a busy checkpoint, during the race tomorrow.

Dropping down the stony bridleway path, taking great care across the dry stone ford in the dark, and up on to the pretty good, stoned-up, wide path.

I can see the silhouette of the three large shire horses in the field to my right as I pass the gap in the hedgerow where

47

the entrance to the field via the galvanised steel five-bar gate is. I have stopped here on numerous occasions while out training over the past few years to talk to the owner of these magnificent horses. One of the Clydesdale mares is a rescue animal, originally owned by gypsies I believe.

The steep hill in front of me gives me a good reason to slow down to a walk. Even this early into the overall challenge, I must be conscious of making sure that I conserve as much energy as I possibly can, which will become vital to survival towards the latter stages. After final adjustments are made, laces checked and rucksack strapped up securely to avoid any rubbing movement on my arms, shoulders and back, it's time to cross the normally busy road and head down the dark wooded path towards Langold.

With the head torch lighting up the good path in front of me, I can maintain a steady pace before entering the woods, estimating just another six to eight minutes to the lakes.

Careful running is needed for the first few hundred yards into the Langold wood, because of a long-standing problem I had encountered some years ago with this cobbled path. This is where I had tripped, stubbing my right big toe, and landed heavily on a raised stone on my right hip, putting me out of action for a while. This section of the path always leaves me with a feeling of trepidation whenever I run down this area of the route. Superstition or not, I think it's better to be safe than sorry at this stage, with about a quarter of a mile before the lake. I feel a sense of relief as I emerge from the woods on to the tarmac road, taking me into the entrance of Langold Park and up to the lake past the cleanest, most well-maintained outdoor toilet block I have ever used.

Whenever I reach this location, I feel that at any time I will be met head on by the big old fox I encountered in 2010, see my first book, Me and My Shadow, for the full low-down.

Skirting around the bottom part of the lake and turning up the slope to the grassy field just after where the derelict one-time swimming pool is situated, and running on to the twisty, winding narrow path where care and attention are needed once again, especially in this reduced light. There is faint light pollution from the surrounding area at this time of night, which actually lessens the visibility that the headlamp creates in front of me.

Safely turning left on to the tarmac road heading towards Costhorpe, and a couple of hundred yards of street lighting for a while, before crossing over the road and heading for the stile that will take me uphill and into the long, newly-ploughed field at the top of which I will make a right turn on to the wide gravel track down to Wellingwell.

The dogs are barking and making a hell of a noise from the kennels to my left, they must have picked up my scent or the noise from my feet on the gravel lane leading down towards Wellingwell House. This large white house to my right is set in its own grounds at the head of a large fishing lake; I was informed that it was a nunnery some years ago.

I seem to be on target with regard to time and looking forward to being at my next time check at Woodsetts for about 9.35pm, where this time around I won't be stopping to meet anyone but going straight through to my next full pit stop at Harthill, where I will meet my good friend John Clark. In the meantime, I will swallow the jelly-like liquid from a couple of forest fruit flavoured energy gel cartons, followed by a good mouthful of water. I must maintain the discipline of drinking and eating sufficiently to fuel my body with the calories I will be burning off, must not become complacent just because I am feeling really good right now.

The lights ahead of me over the trees on the horizon are inviting and indicating that Woodsetts is now close.

Shortly after leaving the fishing pond behind, I stumble over the rough track, like an out of control puppet with arms and legs heading in different directions, trying to stay upright. It's sensible to slow down for about a mile over the very rough, slightly elevated path which cuts across a couple of long fields before heading up the path to the main road in Woodsetts. It's been difficult to judge the lumpy terrain along these carved up paths, which has made it unsafe to run at any speed over the last 15 minutes, but I am back to comfortable running as I reach the tarmac and good street lighting on the edge of this village.

Reaching the crossroads at Woodsetts, I can see that I am on time and can confirm my watch timing by the good overhead street lighting that I am slightly ahead of my target time of 9.35pm. It's quiet in the village and without any moving traffic it is easy to cross the road to make the left turn that will take me up and out of Woodsetts.

The steady climb up the main village road heading for the golf course is well lit, even right down to the fairway, before I have to switch on the light again, fanning the beam to find the faded grass path; habit sees me looking right down the long fairway, "Fore!" daft sod, should I be expecting balls to be zooming towards me at this time of night? Habits die hard, I suppose, but provide me with a laugh and loud enough to hear for anyone who may be listening. It relieves a bit of tension, I guess, and leaves me feeling relaxed, comfortable and ready for what's in front of me as I manage to negotiate the rooted path through the avenue of bushes alongside the fairway and on to the side of the green by the transfer tunnel of the Carlton-in-Lindrick golf course.

I can hear streams of cars passing overhead as I locate and run through the tunnel underneath the very busy A57. This fairly new detour has taken a fair degree of danger out of this section of the event; where just over a couple of years ago it would have been quite a kamikaze affair dashing across the busy road in between speeding cars. I remember having to wait well over five minutes on one of the runs before a gap in the traffic opened up wide enough to get across safely.

The end of the golf course is soon reached as I head down the wide path into the valley bottom towards the canal relief stream, which had overflowed a couple of weeks previously, rendering this section of the route quite boggy. Finding a way through the thick black mud without too much hassle, it's a right turn into the woods and a climb up the steep hill on a wide, leaf-covered path through the woods. It's generally slippery through these woods at this time of year and tonight is no exception. Walking is a safe bet, which gives me time to have a good drink of water and locate the nuts and raisins that are stashed in a pocket of my rucksack – a good source of energy which will kick in later.

I was thinking that it would be a good idea if you could programme a watch or other electronic equipment to give a signal at a given space of time to remind you to eat or drink, say one bleep to eat and two bleeps to drink.

The wide path clears just over the top of the hill to a narrow but half decent soil trail , enabling me to pick up the running again down towards the farm buildings at the bottom of the hill.

After jumping up the banking to my right just before the large gate to the farm, I can just about make out the elevated faint field path as I skirt alongside the stone farm buildings and head up the narrow path towards Turner Wood. I can easily make out the dike below me to my left with the lights from my head torch, as I head for the corner of the field.

I have some great memories of this area, which usually bring a smile to my face in remembrance of some time ago while out with Adam, my eldest grandson, who was accompanying me on one of my training runs. Adam would have been about ten or 11 and was on his mountain bike. A good few miles into the run, while heading home, we were coming down this path towards the farm when he ended up running out of path, slipped down the bank side and almost went head first into the dike below. I am sure he thinks I pushed him in, but would I do such a thing to my grandson? We spent many hours together around this area, teaching him about nature and educating him about the food that he could eat.

Crossing the stile and standing by the raised track close to the railway lines, which seem to go on forever into the night towards Kiveton Park to my right and Worksop the other way, I can make out coloured lights down the track. The signal lights which slowly disappear into the night create an increase in the visual distance as I make the normal left and right looks to check that there is no danger.

The pretty little hamlet of Turner Wood, which straddles either side of the Chesterfield Canal, is my next target as I carefully make my way down the wooden-stepped steep bank on to the grass track just above the canal relief dike to my left.

It's quiet and all seems to be as it should at this time of night, but just before reaching the newly-built wooden summerhouse to my right, which is used as a cafe during the day, the peace of the night is shattered by the bright security floodlights from the old terrace cottages, lighting up the whole area like daylight across the outbuildings and even the old stone bridge as I run through the hamlet. Over the bridge and head for the gap between the hedges to my left just after the last of the old whitewashed stone cottage which I believe was once an old pub called the Gate Inn, but was nicknamed the Bug Hut many years ago.

Having reached the road in Netherthorpe, I can increase the pace at last, after having gingerly made my way across the narrow path from Turner Wood stumbling a couple of times on the bumpy, grassy path before reaching the crossroad.

Netherthorpe Airfield to my left is, as expected, quiet, but the security lights around the parked up planes provide a sighting for the faint drizzle that had started a few minutes ago and which I can clearly see through the haze of my head light in the night. It's not enough to worry about, but has the effect of taking my mind off the slight pain I had just experienced in the lower part of my back.

There is always an added risk to jolting my lower back while running through the night across country on uneven surfaces. The light from my head torch, together with the additional hand-held torch that I use from time to time, never quite picks out the severity of the drops and bumpy contours of the path, and with my style of running, heel slightly first, it's easy to come a cropper and end up giving the old back a jolt or two from time to time if I don't take care.

An energy gel and a drink of water is required after diagonally crossing the sticky, muddy field through the gap in the edge at Top Hill Farm and right on to the minor road which leads to Thorpe Salvin village. Just beyond the farm house on the right, I climb over the large laddered-type stile over the neat stone wall and on to the narrow track round the back of the house in the dip. It's worth a few minutes and the energy, I feel, to attempt to clear my shoes of the thick mud, even though it's sticking like glue.

Extra care is needed to negotiate the up and down over the broken, slippery wooden steps along the narrow path through the dark tunnel of overhanging trees.

Skirting around the house set in the valley to my right, I am now out on to the moonlit grassy field. I can just make out the silhouette of the little weather station erected a few feet inside the field to my left, with the picturesque barn-style house set in the valley below.

From the elevated position of the route, and having just passed the field entrance to the outbuildings of the house, which are all lit up by the security lighting, I can see the hedgerow in front and the gap with the kissing gate that I need to aim for and which is soon reached on the short, flat meadow grass surface. I am not looking forward to the next mile or so up the long ploughed field, which I know will need to be navigated with extreme caution through the deep, strength-sapping mud.

My head light penetrating through the black night has picked out the deep ploughed field in front of me, which looks like a sea of waves up the long field that will take me up to the piggery farm alongside the large silos which are just visible silhouetted on the horizon. Hell, at least a quarter of a mile of strength-sapping mud. My fears are justified; there are few signs of any path over the entire length of this recently-ploughed sea of mud. It's like running on water, which may sound a little dramatic, but if you have ever experienced running across a soft, wet, ankle-deep, energy-sapping muddy field for a quarter of a mile, where you will have grown six inches or more well before reaching the safety of grass, then you will completely understand what I mean. The local farmers seem to know when this race is taking place and add their own degree of difficulty to the event by deep ploughing all the footpaths on which we have to run. "Character building," they call it. There's no option, best get it over with, but must use caution as I set off with imaginary fingers crossed.

It seems to have taken me a good ten minutes to reach the safety of the hedge and at last across the minor track which leads to the smelly pig farm.

While taking time to relieve the soles of my shoes of the sticky mud, it's a good time to switch off the head lights, which had been giving me a strange sensation of running through a never ending tunnel coming across the field. I will use my hand torch for a while and settle down again before using the head torch.

One last major field to cross and another anticipated ploughed path, which tonight is proving to be fairly well padded down, making it much easier to run on than I had expected and helping me to pick up a bit of speed until reaching the gap in the hedgerow at the far end of the open field. There's a drop down from the field before crossing the minor road, up the other side and then diagonally across the three ploughed fields to where the newly-built wind turbines have been erected.

Not far now to Harthill and meeting up with John.

I am more than happy with my performance up to this time, feeling strong and trouble free without any problems and, other than that slight lower back pain I had felt a few miles back, I don't have any worries. My watch tells me that I am almost bang on time at just a couple of minutes to 11 as I reach the stile and short tarmac drive at the corner of the field beyond the woods, which leads to my descent into the village of Harthill.

It's slippery on the concrete path that will take me down to the dozen or so steps and on to the main road, which has to be carefully negotiated at a walk. A left and right on the tarmac road with the car park now in view, I can see John, who must have spotted me coming down the road, because the coffee and fruit cake are ready and waiting.

My time with John, while fuelling up on fruit cake and bread and jam sandwiches, is spent discussing the challenge in a positive way; I am just a few minutes ahead of schedule at five minutes past 11, leaving me satisfied with myself for the discipline of maintaining the pace I had set myself for getting to Harthill on schedule and endorsing the confident feeling about the overall challenge.

It's great to meet up with John and be able to discuss the event with a very knowledgeable friend who has completed the 50-mile RRR on quite a few occasions himself. Being well on time and under no pressure, I decide to have a second cup of warm coffee and top up my camelback.

The clock is ticking and it's time to say my farewells until we meet again during the last lap, which will see me at about the 130- mile mark. Oh how good does that sound!

Leaving John and waving my goodbye, I get that feeling of being very much on my own again as I head off out of the car park into the dark, making my way across the play area. My legs feel stiff and slightly muscle-bound from the inactivity of the stop I have just made, but only for a minute or two, as I skirt around the cycle tracks in the playground area and downhill to the first of the stiles that will take me down into the valley on the grassy bank side before climbing up the hill towards the hamlet of Woodall.

It's not long before my legs are back in gear and I'm feeling strong and confident that I will fulfil my ambition with this challenge.

Although the distance I still have to run is a leveller whenever I bring it to mind, it's a hell of a long way, but the thought of coming in at the finish on Sunday morning knowing that I will have achieved this incredible distance is filling me with an emotional vision of the moment. But it's time for me to get into and maintain that mental zone again and forget about the finish, I just have to concentrate on the physical aspect of putting one foot in front of the other, mile after mile, which will eventually come to an end.

The secret to running these long distances is all about managing the multitude of small thoughts and incidents that crop up during the overall run and not allowing anything to take control and turn into a major problem. A host of small problems not dealt with in time could become a massive incident that will take over later and bring an end to the challenge. This personal challenge is all about the desire to find out just how much I am capable of. I am confident enough to rely on my mental ability to take charge of any situation that may manifest itself during the event, work out the problem and then, because I have trained well, I should be able to provide the physical ammunition to deal with the situation. Achieving what I set out to do will best be dealt with by maintaining the ability to laugh if anything that I can't control goes wrong, it would be fatal to beat myself up, it will not be my fault if I have prepared everything properly.

The M1 motorway is always busy and tonight is no exception as the streams of vehicles thunder up and down this elevated stretch above me. Running north alongside the southbound carriageway on the wide grassy path after leaving the muddy field, I can get a sense of the speed that the lorries and cars are travelling at, watching the headlights whizzing towards and then past me into the night.

The grassy field beyond the tunnel under the motorway is slippery with the dew. I nearly come a cropper just before the stile which leads me down past the very imposing properties with their large ponds, manicured lawns and wide tarmac driveways, and then it's down to the main Swallownest- Wales Bar road. Right and then left on to the entry road which seems to go on forever through the Rother Valley Country Park.

The long section through the country park is completed without any significant change of pace or scenery for what seems like an eternity, but before I realise where I am, it's time to negotiate the awkward route up on to the main road

57

and then back down again under the bridge to pick up the path on the west side of the railway lines that will lead me through to Treeton. This section a few years ago only required the need to pass over the level crossings rather than the complicated switch we now have to make. The change of pace, having to think and negotiate this section, is a welcome relief and takes the boredom out of the long straight tarmac road of the park.

Treeton, my next target, is soon visible after a steady run along the lakeside path, which for the better part of the last quarter of an hour has had a mirror-like effect from the moon's reflection flitting in and out from behind the clouds, making the use of the torches for most of this section redundant. I had decided when I was planning this challenge that I would use the old route at this point and not go up to the Treeton cricket field pavilion but continue along this low level path which will bring me out at the old Orgreave- Catcliffe road and the more forgiving tarmac again.

Catcliffe village is quiet and without any traffic, enabling me to run with a sense of feeling good down the centre of the road as though it all belonged to me, before turning left into the estate. I am soon picking up the twisty narrow footpath after the houses, which leads me under the Parkway dual carriageway and the sharp left turn beyond the bridge, up the steep bank side to the stubbly grass footpath above.

I can make out the well-lit large open car sales area to my right and enjoy the downhill section on the red coloured tarmac footpath for a breather, before turning uphill on Green Lane.

It's a good time to make a stop shortly after climbing the stile into the field just past the M1 motorway underpass at Brinsworth, adjust and eat a couple of slices of malt loaf, followed by a small piece of Mars Bar and plenty of water to drink. I had been feeling a slight cramp in my right calf for the past mile or so, leaving me thinking that I was probably a little dehydrated. Must keep my wits about me and be aware should any more niggles kick in.

The restart is smooth and comfortable as I head out across the field, disturbing a couple of horses in the paddock to my left.

My head lights are soon picking up the narrow fenced-in footpath along the southbound M1 carriageway, which is leading me around the school playing fields on my right and towards the small industrial estate.

Batley's Cash & Carry warehouse on my left is past and I soon reach the main road with no traffic, which is something of a change, but at this time in the morning I suppose it's normal, as I cross over Bawtry Road without any restrictions. There's just the odd taxi travelling down towards Sheffield along this stretch of road past the Pike and Heron pub. The uneven footpath is leading me down towards the old Rotherham road as I make steady progress towards Sheffield main road and then on to the short path which takes me to the start of the canal towpath.

Without any moon now, there's a need to switch on the head light, which immediately picks up the newish white tubular bridge in the distance, leading me over to the left hand side of the canal and the muddy path that will take me shortly to my next change of terrain and pace.

I am not looking forward to the climb in front of me, which will take me up from the low level of the canal to the heights of hilltop above Kimberworth, one of the highest, if not the highest points in Rotherham

For the time being it's comfortable running along the canal, as long as I am able to avoid the deepest of the mud. I am heading south in the direction of Rotherham and enjoying the flat towpath before having to take on the tough climbs ahead of me.

A lapse of concentration and I have gone past the almost-concealed sharp left turn between the dense woodland on the bank side which leads up to the railway bridge. I make an about-turn, thinking I may be some way past the turn; but it's there almost in front of me, the track is just a couple of yards away. It's lucky for me that I haven't gone too far down the path before realising my mistake. From now on, this section of the event needs to be negotiated with care.

The old steel bridge across the mainline railway track is slippery with the dew from the night and the narrow, twisty path beyond is full of potholes and loose soil before I arrive up and out of the dark, tree-lined tunnel on to the well-lit Meadowbank Road.

Turning left on to the wide damp grassy strip heading towards Meadowhall, I can feel the dew wetting my feet and I make the decision to cross over the carriageway and run on the right side of the main road. It's far easier running on the causeway until reaching the narrow path that will take me up a steep bank on my right. The path is almost invisible and has taken some locating, but this steep climb will lead me up to the next main road above. My first attempt nearly ends in disaster as my feet slip away on the steep, slippery bank and I end up sliding back down on my backside to the causeway below. Only by grabbing handfuls of tufted grass at the sides of the narrow path and pulling as if I were holding a rope do I succeed the second time to where it levels out sufficiently for me to stand upright. This climbing is taking it out of me; my legs are on fire and my back is feeling as if I have been punched.

The climb up from the canal level to the hilltop has been quite a demanding section before coming out on to the side of the road and making a much needed pit stop.

My watch confirms that I have been making good progress since leaving John at the car park in Harthill, so bearing in mind that I will now have covered about 35 miles, I am happy enough to take a short food break. The contents from a couple of energy gels are soon consumed, together with a good drink of water from my camelback and a fistful of Jelly Babies top the break off. While the food is being digested and absorbed, it's a good time to stretch my stiff, aching back and get back to feeling good again before setting off for the last section of this demanding climb.

I wondered before getting underway again, had I made the right choice to run the first section in a clockwise direction rather than the normal anti-clockwise. Maybe it was not such a good choice after all by the way my legs were feeling right now, but it's too late to worry about that now Ray, so let's get cracking and stop whingeing.

Hilltop comes as welcome relief after passing through the narrow path of stinging nettles along the fenced in passageway between the houses, until finally leaving the last house of the estate behind and on to the highest part of this climb.

Leaving the kissing gate behind and across the edge of the grass field on the slight downhill section allows for some relaxation to my legs before the dark, steep descent on to Droppingwell Road. Having to sort of brake down this steep path is playing havoc with my lower back until leaving the narrow path and stopping as I reach Droppingwell Lane. Directly across the traffic free road, it's the very steep drop into the woods beyond and down to the stream below which requires some concentration and accurate shining of the torch in the dense woodland.

The old tree roots are sticking out like a scene from a horror movie on most of the paths in the dark woods until I finally reach the opening to the fields above the football pitches which are set out below in the valley. I would have been better sticking to the main road and going round I reckon, which is slightly further but probably safer than risking the dangerous paths through the woods and fields at this time in the morning.

Climbing up the steepish path to the Grange Golf Club entrance road is giving me a reminder that I need to consume another couple of energy gels, followed by a good drink of water, before fatigue catches up with me and forces an avoidable, unscheduled stop. Ten minutes later and the shadowy structure of Keppel's Column brings an end to the climbing and provides me with a good feeling of being in charge again without the fatigue of a few minutes ago. I am happy with myself as I steadily make my way down the boggy, uneven, coarse grassy slope to the fence below, ready to carry on and complete this first section of the challenge.

The roads and villages are now quiet and peacefully settled, providing a feeling of being totally on my own again. It's a dead cert, there's only me out here doing my thing, and now without any distraction I am able to concentrate on making sure that I am getting the best efficiency out of my running, breathing calmly and getting into that right frame of mind which takes me into a zone-like state and become sort of robotised, where distance is easily reached with less of an effort. I wonder if there are any other athletes out at this time in the night doing anything remotely like this. I have spent many hours in my garage running on my treadmill over the years, boring as hell, but the benefits' of being able to concentrate on perfecting comfortable running, not leaning forward, not crunching my shoulders up during fatigue, and getting the best out of my posture to be able to switch off and relax without thinking.

Wentworth village is my next sighting as the moon, which is now creating a shadowy light, illuminates the spire of the church and, together with the first noise from a car for more than a couple of hours, brings me back to reality. I work my way down the wide track towards the small stone junior school and the crossroads at the edge of the village. Harley to the left, Greasbrough to the right and straight on, my direction would eventually lead to Elsecar village, but the turn off to the right just after the wood yard takes me off the road again and down a wide concrete drive before finally running out on to a widish, deep, muddy path and then into the narrower path at the edge of the woods. It's downhill now through boggy sections of paths which are open to choices, either one of which is unsuitable for running at any sort of speed on the way down to Elsecar bottom.

It's about 4am, quiet, dark without any moon and a little chilly, but roughly an hour will see me at the Manvers College and the first of the 50 miles completed, sounds good to me. I have this great feeling of satisfaction that the event is well and truly achievable.

The last five or so miles have been completed on autopilot, in and out of the street lighting from the roads with recently-built houses before finally crossing the bridge by the lakes and left towards the Wath-upon-Dearne fire station. With just a mile to go to the college and the start of the race proper, my middle 50 miles, it's time to think about what food I need to collect from the car and clothes I need to change into.

Even though it's 5am, there is a lot of activity on the surrounding well-lit roads, all traffic seems to be heading towards the college with cars delivering competitors for the early morning start. Running into the complex of the college I am greeted with encouraging remarks from friends and athletes who are making their way into the main hall.

It's 5.15am and my priorities before I book into the official 50-mile race are to eat the food that I prepared before setting off last night, which I had laid out in the boot of my car to save time. Cornflakes, with a chopped up banana and plenty of sugar and milk, followed by strong sugary coffee and a change of shoes and socks will see me ready for the start at 6am with the rest of the athletes. I have also decided that I will take a wet coat with me as rain is forecast for the early part of the official race.

# CHAPTER 3

## Hanging around

A few weeks prior to my introduction to Danny, I wouldn't have given myself a cat in hell's chance of being able to stand, let alone be able to train or perform in the ring. Our meeting came a few weeks after the restart of my training and the latter end of recovering from a very serious accident. An accident which, fortunately, had not left me with any debilitating injuries, but from time to time meant I would wake up lathered with sweat as I relived, like a horror film, the experience of the whole incident.

I had, together with a group of my mates, been playing football against some large green wooden gates situated on the left about halfway down Holland Street. These gates, 12 feet wide by about nine feet high, erected in the middle of a double brick surrounding wall, were the access to Chadwick's builders' yard in which sand, cement, bricks and all the usual builders' materials were stored. We had used these gates as goals on a regular basis, usually when the yard had closed after tea time and at weekends. Often Dads would join in with the game during the summer at weekends, and the sessions sometimes lasted for hours, making them very competitive events up to when it was time for the usual boozing session at the Brown Street Working Men's Club. Afterwards, we would settle into a game of shots at the goal.

My shot at goal was deflected and over the gate sailed the only ball we possessed. The sort of unwritten law was whoever kicked the ball over fetched it back. I was helped up the ten-foot high wall on the right-hand side of the gates by my mates and, using the inside of the gate, I climbed down to the sandy floor of the yard below. I threw the easily-found ball back over into the street and, using the wooden reinforced timbers on the inside of the gates, I quickly climbed up to the menacing, closely spaced 12 inch long metal spikes which were secured to the top of the gates as a deterrent to thieves, I suppose.

I had been over these gates a good number of times over the years to recover balls. As a 13-year-old without any fear whatsoever, even sheer complacency, and almost without any consideration for danger, I launched myself high over the top to clear the menacing spikes as I had done many times in the past.

I couldn't understand for that split second why I wasn't heading downwards towards the floor, when the sudden realisation that I was caught hit me like a ton of bricks. I had felt what seemed like a light tug on my shorts, which I thought must have caught on one of the spikes and thrown me off balance. I realised then as I hung there in total disbelief that one of the spikes had passed right through the front of my right leg just above my knee and was sticking out about an inch through the back of my leg into the fold at the back of my knee. Strangely, I couldn't feel any pain at all, which made the situation feel so unreal. My first thought as I dangled there upside down, facing the gates, was "I'm in real bother now, I am gunna cop it" as I should have been home looking after my younger brothers after my dinner.

Whenever I lifted upwards and bent my leg to get a better view of the situation, the spike point nicked my leg just above my calf. Lifting my head up and back I could see my mates, who were generally panicking, shouting nonsensical comments and running about below me like headless chickens. "Bluddy 'ell, Ray, duz it 'urt? I'll fetch mi Dad," I heard one of the lads shout and he disappeared down Holland Street. The rest of my loyal mates were offering helpless words of comfort, but no matter what was said, I knew that the problem wasn't going to go away without some horrible pain.

I was just about bent double inwards in an attempt to complete a sort of inverted sit-up by using my impaled leg as a lever in my grunting attempts to reach back up the gate high enough to get a hold of the top and pull myself off the spike. No matter how hard I tried, even my athleticism proved to be unsuccessful. I was just inches short of reaching the top of the gate with my clawing fingers, but might as well have been feet off; try as I might, I couldn't quite reach anything that would give me any leverage ,as my face took the brunt of the rough wooden planks which made up the old gates. The higher I reached up with my clawing fingers, the more pressure my face took on the abrasive wood. I soon abandoned that idea when I felt the pain drastically increase from my leg.

Blood was now running freely from my torn cheeks into my hair and dripping in a crazy pattern on the concrete ramped pad below. For what seemed an eternity I hung there helpless and unable to do anything to ease the horrible pain which had now started to kick in big style.

Thoughts of having to have my leg cut off were running high on my list of worst scenarios. I couldn't figure out any other way of getting free. Maybe I could saw through the spike if I could get hold of a steel saw. Attempts by my mates to gain enough height to be able to push me up and off the spike were proving unsuccessful and were quickly abandoned, as I screamed out "Stop, stop, leave me". To be brutally honest, they were actually making matters and the pain worse.

With little else to do but stare at the sign written lettering on the bottle green gates and the floor below me for what seemed an eternity, I was desperately trying to filter and clear the mind-blowing thoughts of the alternate means of escape, amputation, which to be honest was running terrifyingly high at the top of the list of what I thought would be unavoidable to get me out of this mess.

Out of the corner of my eye, I could see movement down the street and became conscious of two of my mates' Dads, who were running up Holland Street with ladders on their shoulders. They soon arrived alongside and after a short discussion, mainly between themselves, decided that they needed to get up either side of me and, without any further comments other than "Hang on, lad, weil get thy off." "Where did they think I was going anyway?" was a thought going through my mind as they reared one ladder either side of me, resting on top of the gates between the spikes. After another short discussion of how best to get this "silly young bugger" off the spike, they made their way up the ladder to about level with my shoulders.

I could sense, even without looking, that I had attracted a large audience which had already formed into a half ring around the gates in order to get a better view. Comments like "Oh God, how's he managed to do that?" and "That looks real nasty" were not helping one bit. Neighbours were arriving from all over the place and all making suggestions of how best to get this "pitiful young lad" free. My helpers proceeded to lift my body as I gripped tightly with both my arms around their necks. They were now taking up the weight off my leg, talking to me all the time but both trying to reassure each other more than me, I think, that they were slowly winning. Instructions were coming from another of my mates' Dads, who seemed to have suddenly taken over as co-ordinator of the event.

I was now holding on for dear life with my arms around both men's neck, almost like a stranglehold, with no intention of letting go and felt a very firm hand grasp my right leg just below the point of the spike entry. The first attempt was soon aborted, they were far too low on the ladders to complete the lift, but the readjustment caused me so much more pain as they lowered me back to get a better footing on the ladder. I am sure my leg moved further down the spike as my weight settled again. My scream was not meant to startle them, only to release the severe pain I was experiencing but they both moved up the ladder with speed. "Reyt lad ah tha ready?" As they started to lift again I could feel the movement through the inside of my leg as though the spike was reluctant to let go and every inch felt like an hour in time which created excruciating pain as they gained enough height to slowly ease my impaled leg up and off that steel prison of a spike. They were working together and at the same time doing everything they could to reassure me that I was almost free and they would make it safe for me to get away from the spikes. "Tha'll be reyt in a minute, Ray."

After what seemed like hours, I was free at last, but because I was totally in their hands and unable to take control of myself, it was very difficult position to be in trying to get myself upright from the almost horizontal position I was being supported in. I felt very vulnerable, trying to place my left foot on to the top of the gate between the spikes to get some sort of balance. I was being instructed to make a complete U-turn so that I had both feet on the gate but was facing forward into the yard with my back to the street.

Because of the way they had hold of me I felt very wobbly, I was feeling dizzy anyway, out of control and vulnerable. Then, as I took a step back to put my left foot on to a rung of the ladder as I was instructed, my foot slipped off the gate. I thought that I was about to fall again and almost knocked Freddy Linton's Dad off the ladder. They held me firmly, but I felt a severely sharp pain in my left leg. The tip of another spike had punctured just under my left knee, giving me an even greater pain than anything I had experienced in my life. Near panic set in at the thought of what could have happened. For the first time, I contemplated the possibilities of an even bigger disaster if that had been my body coming down on these lethal spikes. I kept thinking, "Don't even think about that." I had to get those thoughts out of my head and concentrate on the rungs of the ladder and getting down away from the gates.

For what had seemed an eternity, I was at last standing at the bottom of the ladders, and quickly surrounded by well-wishers, all wanting to help but at the same time bombarding me with questions which I really didn't feel like answering. I was able for the first time to inspect my wounds.

The pain from just under my left knee was really killing and responsible, I felt, for giving me a feeling of being light-headed, a bit dizzy and close to passing out as everything started to spin. One of my mates was in tears, I suspect from relief that at last I was back on land and out of danger. His Dad was now firing questions at me, which seemed to be coming through a darkening tunnel and not making any sense at all, I don't recall having answered any, as my mates freely chipped in with enough comments to satisfy the growing crowd.

All I wanted was to get away from the gates to the safety of my home, but knowing full well that I would be in all sorts of trouble because my mum was singing at Brown Street Working Men's Club for the afternoon session and Dad had gone up to watch. I was supposed not to have gone out after they had left. Oh bloody hell.

I didn't normally sweat much, but right then I was wet through. How was I going to be able to hide this from my Mum and Dad? Sweat was freely running down from my forehead and stinging as it mixed with the bloodied cuts on my cheeks, which I had completely forgotten about up to that point. The closing, reddish blue hole just above my right knee was less painful, but the sight of it was frightening the hell out of me.

I could hardly put any weight on my right leg, which was now slowly becoming numb. I must have looked a proper little orphan standing there, battered and all forlorn with blood all over me; I just wanted to get home. I could well understand the concerned look from the neighbours, as freely running sweat from my head diluted the blood from my cheeks and covered the collar and front of my shirt. I must have looked as though I had been hit by a double decker bus. The flowing blood running down my left leg from the puncture had stained my socks and shoes, but strangely enough there was little or no blood coming from the holes in my right leg – weird.

I could hardly stand, let alone walk properly, and was soon lifted, with legs dangling to one side, on to the back of one of my rescuers who set off up the street to my house on Holland Place, just less than a hundred yards away.

Less than two minutes later, I was heading up our passage, being thrown about as I tried to hang on with just my arms. We barged in through the back door, which was partly opened, and I was duly plonked onto the settee in the kitchen. Back doors in those days were never closed or locked. I remember the startled look on Sarah's face at the sight of all of us crashing through the back door. Sarah and her husband, Jack, were new lodgers and staying in the front room of our house until their house in James Street was ready for them to move into.

The relentless questioning of what, where and when almost leaving me without enough time to answer any were being fired at me, but all the time my wounds were being closely inspected. My rescuers started leaving, ruffling my hair and patting me on the head like you would a dog, all hoping that I was going to be OK and leaving Sarah to get on with the treatment. We both shouted out our thanks as everyone left.

"We're gonna have to send for your Mum and Dad," was her first comment. "Oh no!" I knew I was in for it big time now. Did I really expect that I could get away without my Mum and Dad knowing? One of Sarah's first actions was to swing the kettle over the open fire, I did fancy a cuppa tea but soon realised that hot water was going to be needed to clean my wounds.

The steam from the boiling kettle was soon puffing out around the old Yorkshire black leaded range and disappearing up the chimney as my Dad came rushing through the back door. His afternoon session at Brown Street Working Men's Club had been cut short. Alan, my brother, had been sent to fetch them home.

"Now then, what's tha been up to?" came across as more of a comment than a question and followed by "Your Mum's on her way down", a comment from Dad that intimated I was in real bother by the way he said it, but at the same time provided some comforting relief.

No sooner had my Mum arrived and closely inspected my injuries, together with all the explanations of what had happened, than treatment started in earnest. Almost neat Dettol, mixed together in the bowl with the hot water which had turned a milky white colour, was soon being bathed into the main wound, as she pulled the skin apart exposing the gaping hole in my right leg. Almost immediately I felt the stinging pain followed by the excruciating agony created by the Dettol. The pain was far worse than I had felt whilst I was hanging on the gates and for the first time, I saw the concerned look on her face as the warm liquid appeared to pass through my right leg and out of the hole on the other side, drenching the newly finished home-made pegged rug beneath my feet.

The strong, distinctive smell of the Dettol filled the kitchen, making my eyes smart as it wafted up from my leg. I was experiencing a strange sensation deep inside my leg. My mind was in fearful overdrive again and giving me a feeling that the stinging warm liquid was spreading about and filling the inside of my leg before finding a way out. I could have believed anything at that stage of the treatment. Biting on a cushion that I had pulled closely to my chest was providing me with a sort of comfort; and by taking a good mouthful to bite on; I was able to subdue the full effect of the pent-up yell that was fighting to come out. I was holding back the scream inside because I knew that any complaining would go on deaf ears, as she forcefully held on to my leg to keep me from pulling away. My face, which was the least of my worries, was almost scrubbed until it bled freely again, same for the puncture under my left knee. She did ease off on the main wound though.

An old pale blue pillowcase which my Dad had found in the airing cupboard was torn into two- and three-inch wide strips and used as bandages to secure and cover the wounds on my legs. And then at last it was over, as Mum put her arms around me, giving me a reassuring hug.

There was always a comforting feeling of being safe when my Mum had completed her nursing first aid work on me and the hug of reassurance that only mothers can provide, always worked like magic. She had, of course, had more than enough practice to perfect this magic on me and my brothers over the years.

Dettol and the scrubbing brush were normally the traditional remedy in our house for any cuts, grazes or scratches that my brothers or I managed to get. The affected area would be scrubbed until it freely bled and no amount of complaining, crying, or even screaming blue murder would make a blind bit of difference.

It was only a few months ago gone since I had been running towards the Thornhill Rec, an open grassy land at the end of our street where we played for hours during the summer holidays. I had tripped, going headlong on to the newly-gritted road, completely de-skinning my chest, knees, lower arms, hands and most of the skin on my face. Limping home in that grit-peppered state, with a chest full of bits of T-shirt and legs full of bits of trousers which were implanted with the grey gravel, I knew that I was in for some hassle. I was bleeding, sore and full of pain, growing by the second as I hobbled home feeling sorry for myself, shortly to be pinned down by my Mum, who set about scrubbing me with the brush and an almost neat solution of Dettol. Blood freely ran from head to toe, but not until she was satisfied that every morsel of the ground-in dirt had been removed did she stop.

The inquest of what I had done, how it had happened and above all the fact that I was out of the house after they had gone out took all the comfort away as I realised that she had come away from the club without performing her final song, but at least the pain was at long last subsiding rather than increasing as it had been during the treatment of the last half hour.

Mum took over telling the story as she had heard it from me, before I had any chance to tell the well-rehearsed account of my last couple of hours to the visitors who were coming through the back door in streams. She was explaining the extent of my injuries to one of our neighbours, when my Dad cut her short with "Well, it's hospital for thee, then, lad". "He isn't going to be able to walk all that way," Mum said, and suggested that she went to Mrs Lynton's, who lived just around the corner in Brown Street, to borrow a pram. I think she realised right away from my response and the horrified look on my face that I was not going to be seen dead in a baby's pram. I protested for all I was worth, how would I ever be able to go out again if I was seen being pushed through the streets in a pram? Dad came to the rescue. "Go ask Frank Bailey if we can borrow his wheelbarrow." My brother Alan set off out of the door, heading for Brown Street.

A few minutes later, the amplified echo of the solid wheel of Frank's home-made wheelbarrow came rattling up our passage. This triggered off again the fearful realisation that I was about to be shipped off to Doncaster Gate Hospital and the inevitable outcome that I was dreading.

I wanted to ask the question about what I feared the outcome would be, but couldn't find the courage to upset Mum any further than she already was right now.

With a hug and a kiss on my forehead I said my goodbyes to Mum and headed out of the passage with Dad doing the first of many stints with the noisy barrow. Inquisitive neighbours and friends were making the trip down Brown Street pitifully slow, because of frequent stops to answer questions of why I was being transported in Frank's barrow. I suspect that because most of my bodyweight was across the handles, each stop would be a welcome relief for Frank and especially Dad, who was still suffering from a recent slipped disc, for whoever was pushing at the time readily swapped over whilst explanations were given. For my part, I was happy for them to take all the time in the world; I was in no rush to get to the hospital on this Sunday afternoon.

The pillows that had been placed into the trough of the barrow to support and secure my leg from rolling about were now becoming solid and giving me the most uncomfortable feeling of cramp as my legs stiffened up.

We were creating quite a spectacle as our noisy little chariot made its way over Chantry Bridge, with the prominent Grade 1 listed stone built chapel on the bridge to our left. This structure, the Chapel of Our Lady of Rotherham, one of only four of its kind in England, was built alongside the main bridge over the River Don which has provided access into Rotherham for centuries. There has been a bridge of some sort in this location since 1384, which originally would probably have been a toll. This current one was constructed in about 1483, when the chapel was added, but was partially destroyed during the reformation in 1547. The chapel itself has had many uses over the years, including being used as the town jail, a dwelling and even a shop selling tobacco before being fully restored to its original condition in 1927. This site is said to be the best preserved in England.

We turned right after leaving the bridge heading for Rotherham town centre, passing through College Square and the Red Lion pub where I had first started boxing.

The dark shadow of the high church steeple in front of us cast a chilled area around the square at this time in the afternoon as we travelled below the imposing raised site of All Saints' Church.

I could see part of the large stone Victorian Williams & Gwyn's bank building on the right as we turned left, passing my favourite shop in Rotherham, Coopers Toy Store, on the right, before taking the final surge up the very steep Doncaster Gate hill, which took a good half dozen changes over before crossing the road and finally reaching the A & E entrance to Doncaster Gate Hospital.

"You're not coming in here with that", was the first remark that greeted us, by one of the nurses, as we marched through the bottle green tiled old Victorian entrance, pointing to the wheelbarrow. "Leave it outside, I'll fetch a chair". Dad muttered something that I didn't understand and did an about turn, nearly running into Frank with my outstretched leg. I was picked up between them both and transferred on to the red plastic seat of the white tubular framed wheelchair which the nurse had brought outside to us, gesturing for us to follow. My leg had almost set straight out by then, making it difficult and extremely painful to bend. Dad reversed me through the swinging doors into the enormous oval main hall of the A and E department and up to the reception desk to register and book in. The receptionist took all my particulars, together with a short description of what had happened from my Dad. "You'll need to see the doctor. "Take a seat over there, weil will call you soon." "Take all the time you want," I was muttering to myself as Dad parked me at the end of the second row of wooden seats. I was already starting to feel jumpy and fearfully dreading the outcome.

This large communal waiting room, with its very high domed ceiling, was sort of sectioned off by the way the seating was arranged. Chairs and benches were set out facing the 20 or so different treatment rooms around the perimeter of the hall. Displayed over the top of each of the doors was a different sign. The reception desk, with its half a dozen receptionists, was situated in the centre of the hall, with a pathway from the entrance doors made by the parted chairs. I did remember where the X-ray room was, I had been in need of that service on a couple of occasions, having broken my left arm falling out of a tree and prior to that had needed an X-ray on my left ankle, which was damaged while playing football. That proved to be a sprain rather than a break, but still needed a pot (plaster cast).

I was sitting there with nothing to do but worry and trying to pronounce the words in my head and work out the meaning of some of the more Latin-sounding medical names being displayed over the doors around the room, which actually took my mind off what my vivid imagination was conjuring up. It did pass some time until I was called. Frank Bailey was heading outside for a smoke as we followed the nurse who had shouted my name. "Raymond Matthews." She shouted my name again, "Raymond Matthews," double checking in a manner that suggested I was not who I said I was. Would anyone be daft enough to volunteer to be me and go into the treatment room in my place? Don't think so, especially if they knew what I was probably in for.

The nurse took over from my Dad with the wheelchair and, at great speed, just missing the door, table, chairs and cabinets with my outstretched foot, expertly wheeled me in through the outer area and into the disinfectant-smelling treatment room with its black and white chequered tiled floor, which reminded me of being in a butcher's shop on College Road. We arrived at the same time as the doctor, who came in from one of the adjoining rooms. "Now then, young man, what have we here?" he said, while looking through the file of paperwork and at the same time indicating for the nurse to remove the home-made bandages from my legs.

I was back in that fearful dry-mouthed haze again, terrified and shaking as the doctor carried out his inspection of my wounds, all the time enquiring once again how this had happened. Manipulating my already painful leg and creating further pain seemed to be his main aim and after a few minutes it was decided that I needed to be checked out with an X-ray to make sure that I hadn't done any permanent internal damage. The sister, who had been flitting in and out of the treatment room dealing with someone in the adjoining room by the look of the blood on her apron, was asked to book me in for an X-ray.

I was wheeled out of the treatment room and into the now familiar X-ray waiting area, situated halfway up the left-hand side of the main waiting room.

We didn't have long to wait before I was wheeled through the door marked X-ray, leaving Dad waiting outside in the general waiting room. I was helped into position on the table in the centre of the room. "Right leg," more of a statement than a question was asked by the radiographer while positioning my leg over the black print frame on the rock-hard bed.

The big, light grey, steel arm of the X-ray machine, which looked to me like the long neck of an evil monster, ready to devour my leg once the operator had his back turned, was lowered menacingly into place; I was left on my own for a while as the operator disappeared behind the screen.

I heard the sort of dull bang from the machine, indicating that the first shot was done. He reappeared a second or two later and repositioned the machine. I was rolled over 180 degrees on to my side and a new plate was placed under my leg. Keeping my left leg away from the photograph frame and holding my breath, I waited in a most uncomfortable position for the monster arm to take the second shot. Another bang from the machine was followed a second or two later by the white-coated radiographer as he reappeared from behind the screen "You're done, "he said, bringing the chair to the table and helping me to get back into it. My leg was stiffening up by the minute, as he wheeled me back to the waiting room. "Wait there whilst we check the photos," the white-coated man instructed.

When he came back after a good ten minutes with the developed prints, I asked if my leg was OK but couldn't get any indication from the radiographer about what the results showed as he handed my Dad a large brown envelope.

Half an hour or so later I was wheeled back into the treatment room and after a short agonising wait where my mind went back into horrible overdrive with scary thoughts, the doctor walked back from the other treatment room and was handed the X-ray prints by the nurse who had wheeled me in. I was desperately trying to make any sense of the two X-rays as they were displayed on to an illuminated frame hung on the wall. The only thing that made any sense was the actual outline of my leg, as for what was in-between didn't make any sense at all. I was holding my breath and not really wanting to hear the expected bad news. I was trying to summon up the courage in readiness to take the bad news on the chin." Looks like good news young man", the doctor said without turning around. "Don't know how you've managed it, but it looks as though the spike has passed right through without doing much damage".

Oh God, the relief. My stomach did a flip and ended up nearly choking me at the back of my throat. I felt like you do when something really good has just happened and wanted to shout out with delight to release the tension, but couldn't have spoken to save my life as all the pent-up feelings seemed to be bursting through to the back of my throat. Does that mean my leg will get back to normal? I just wanted the doctor to confirm that I would be able to continue with my boxing and footballing, I laughed out loud with relief, turning towards my Dad to share what was probably the best news I had received, ever. My Dad, who had a big smile on his face, was just about to say something to me when the doctor commented, "We're going to keep you in for a couple of days, just to make sure." Oh no!" I was absolutely gutted and back in that black tunnel of gloom again, I didn't hear the rest of his comments as my short-lived joy turned once again to total utter despair.

Well I suppose that I will have to respect the doctor's decisions and act in a grown up manner, were my thoughts, even though my stomach was flipping inside as wheels were put in motion and plans were being made to find a bed. I knew that no amount of pleading would alter the inevitable outcome anyway; I had been admitted to Doncaster Gate Hospital.

I felt as though I was being abandoned as Dad left me to find and inform Frank of the situation. How could I satisfy the doctor that it was not necessary to keep me at the hospital? No-one was even listening to my pleading; they all seemed to disappear at the same time, leaving me stranded on my own.

All the details of which ward and visiting times and so on were given to Dad on his return with Frank, it seems that the children's ward was full and I would be spending my time in one of the adult wards. Frank, whom I had completely forgotten about, would probably have smoked himself silly outside while waiting. I had also forgotten how much he had helped in getting me to the hospital and really I should be thanking him but Dad was already going through that procedure as the nurse came to fetch me for the transfer up to the ward.

Tough as I tried to make myself look, I probably couldn't hide the real feelings inside me. For the first time ever I would be going to experience staying in strange surroundings and without the comfort of my parents. I was used to being out all day, on my own some days, but this situation was altogether different, like I was being taken away from my familiar safe environment without my consent. There were many words that would have described the way I felt right then, dejected, rejected and abandoned would adequately fit the bill.

I said my goodbyes to Dad and Frank. "Your Mum will come at visiting time", was the last comment I heard as I was being wheeled away by the nurse, as she set off almost at a trot to the far end of the waiting room, through the door to the wards, down a long corridor and eventually turning left into what looked like a room full of old men. My home for the next couple of days I thought.

I was once again booked into the hospital system at the entrance to the ward and taken past a couple of men who were sitting up in bed reading, they smiled as we passed. We stopped at the third and only empty bed on the right. "This is yours," the nurse said, turning back a corner of the brilliant white sheets. I was helped out of the wheelchair and into a chair by the side of my bed. "This is going to be a first for me," I thought, as the nurse pulled the curtains around the bed, because I normally have to share a bed with at least two of my brothers.

The temporary bandages were removed and then suddenly the horror of what was happening started to unfold when I realised there were now two of them and ganging up on me. I was being undressed and prepared for a bath." What are you doing, it's all right, I can manage by myself," I commented, feeling my face colour up. "We need to be with you with that leg of yours, make sure you don't slip and nobody gets into my clean sheets without a proper bath," said the older of the two. "I don't care, you're not undressing me," I protested, trying to sound menacingly forceful. I was so embarrassed; I was having a fit inside and felt the flush of colour rise even more in my face. This incident was bringing back memories of less than a couple of years ago when the middle-aged female assistant at Danny Williams' sports shop wanted to know, "What size Jock-strap did I want?" while being kitted out for my first fight. She was standing there with a tape measure in her hand and a big smile on her face knowing full well that I had completely misunderstood what she meant by "what size." Women!

We finally reached a compromise and, after I had been almost stripped, apart from my pants, I was given what looked and felt like an oversize nightie and dressing gown. As I slipped it on, they arrived and wheeled me down the ward to the large, white-tiled bathroom. The bath was about half filled by the time we arrived.

The embarrassment that the nurses were creating seemed to be a game they enjoyed playing. "Come on, you have nothing we haven't seen before," was one of the comments I received, trying desperately to find a good answer for it as I was asked to strip off. "I can manage," I protested, "even my Mum doesn't see me stripped, so you're definitely not". I was having a fit inside; this was a very embarrassing time for a 13-year-old boy. I think it was about that time when I realised that

I didn't like females. They start out as girls, can't fight, play football, throw a ball or even run properly; well the ones that I had met anyway, so what use were they?

It was agreed, after even more protesting, that I was to be given five minutes to bathe myself clean. The door was half closed as the two nurses left me to get on with what I had to do, but no sooner had I submerged myself into the water than one of the nurses, draped in a waterproof apron, came back and proceeded to give me a thorough cleaning. I watched where she was looking and wonder after all these years whether she was just inquisitive or was I flattering myself. After mainly concentrating on my head and face, she cleaned away all the blood from my legs and with less embarrassment than I could have imagined I would feel, she left me to dry off, get into the white cotton nightie and drape the dressing gown around me before she came back into the bath room. I do believe now that bath time for the male patients becomes a game played by all the nurses.

I was wheeled back to my bed and the sister who seemed to have a permanent smirk on her face dressed my legs and applied an ointment to my face.

I felt completely exhausted and mentally drained as the nurse inquisitively asked how I had come by my injuries, at the same time stuffing a thermometer into my mouth, why do they do that, continuing to make all the relevant checks, which were added to the paperwork and then hung the board on the bottom of my bed. She encouraged me to vividly tell my story of how, blood guts and all, I came to be hanging on a gate for what seemed to be the best part of an hour.

It was easier and more comfortable to get into bed and relax, rather than sit in the uncomfortable, straight-backed chair at the side of my bed.

It wasn't long before the quiet and inactivity of the ward lulled me off to sleep. I couldn't have been asleep for long, though, before I was being woken. I could hear my name being called from what seemed a long way away. "Raymond," over and over again, which sounded like a returning echo, "Raymond." I was being dragged back through a long tunnel, like from a deep dream, to unfamiliar surroundings, as consciousness from the surreal dream brought me back to realism and then the joyful recognition of my mother's voice. I was so pleased and relieved to see her that all the pent up emotions of the day's traumatic experiences seemed to erupt into bursts of uncontrollable sobs. No sooner had my Mum put her arms around me, than no amount of fighting the strong deep feelings I was experiencing would ease the emotional upheaval I was trying hard to control. The deep sobbing and the tears which were now streaming down my face, flooding out in an uncontrollable release, it seemed easier just to let go than to hold them in.

Eventually, when I had settled, we talked about the good news I had been given from the doctor. I was fortunate in not incurring much damage to my leg – how very lucky I was not to have done untold damage. It seems almost impossible that the spike could have passed right through my leg, missing bones, tendons, nerves and veins, it would take some time to get back to normal but hopefully I should make a full recovery.

I made myself a promise that I would never go over that gate again and could see how upset my Mum was as she told me of the possible outcome she had been thinking about while treating my leg a few hours ago. She couldn't get those thoughts out of her mind. I knew what she meant; I had had the same terrifying thoughts myself.

My Mum had been told that I was to be released from the hospital sometime the following afternoon, after the doctor had made his rounds, as long as I didn't have any complications and checked out OK.

Mum passed on all the good wishes from my mates and neighbours, who had been coming in all afternoon. It must have been a constant flow of visitors to our house by the sound of things. Clean clothes were put into the cupboard at the left-hand side of my bed in readiness for a quick getaway the next day.

Before long, and well after all the other visitors had left, we said our goodbyes and once again I felt that abandoned feeling inside as I watched my Mum walk down the ward, turning right out of the door and disappear down the corridor.

After all the other patients and I had been checked over and all recorded results logged on each wooden clipboard at the bottom of our beds, the ward settled down for the night. Strangely enough though, much as I thought I wouldn't be able to sleep, I must have dropped off almost immediately after I had got my leg into a comfortable position, even with all the snoring that was bellowing out from the bed directly across from me.

Late into the night I was awakened by the strange sound of equipment being moved around. Muffled clanging and banging noises were coming from the bed three down from mine. By partially sitting up, I could see the silhouette of activity through the fully-draped area around the bed as nurses and what looked like a doctor hurried about doing whatever they needed to. A trolley, with what looked like a large bottle of oxygen, was wheeled past the end of my bed as these almost panic-like activities continued for the best part of another hour. A nurse, on her return journey back up the ward, stopped by my bed, probably conscious of my inquisitive looks. She tucked me in and told me to go back to sleep. No point in asking what all the fuss was about as she disappeared to the end of the ward.

Just as light from the dawn came filtering into the room, two men in suits came through the doors at the end of the ward with a trolley, past my bed and into the still closed-off area where all the turmoil of an hour or so before had taken place. Ten minutes later they came back with a white sheet cover-silhouetted body lying on top of the trolley. My first thoughts were that it was my imagination and what with everything else that had happened over the past few hours, it would have been understandable. But later in the morning the draped curtains were drawn back to reveal an empty bed, it didn't take much imagination to realise that what I had just witnessed was definitely a dead body being removed from the ward.

Oh hell, I felt sick and dry-mouthed. How much more was I going to have to experience? I had never even thought about death, let alone seen a dead body. My imagination was in overdrive again and leaving me wondering about what death was.

Although I didn't know the man who had been wheeled away, I was affected by what I had just witnessed. Is it really over for him and is this all we are here for, is there more after death? What kind of life had this man had? There's a need to get as much out of life as possible from what time we have.

Breakfast was a sorry affair, with nowhere near enough food to satisfy my hunger. I hadn't had a proper meal now for what seemed like days, but the thought of going home helped to ease the hunger I still felt after the toast, boiled egg and fruit juice.

If I expected my Mum to be coming through the door as soon as the doctor had finished his inspection of my wounds, I was wrong. I was worrying about whatever my chart indicated, but the doctor nodded his head and commented that

I could go home. It was almost another two of the longest hours I can recall as I patiently waited for my Mum to arrive.

The new batches of nurses who re-dressed my legs after the doctor had removed the bandages to check for infection were telling me that I was going home just after dinner. My enquiries about how quickly I would be able to leave were bringing comments such as "Don't you like it here?" and "You won't get a better hotel." It seems that I had become a bit of a celebrity and was nicknamed Jesus, being hanged on the gate instead of a cross. I didn't like that at all.

Getting dressed to go home was one of the most joyful feelings I had ever felt, for although I had only spent a few hours on the ward, it did seem like days waiting for Mum, who arrived just after dinnertime.

I had made my mind up and was determined that I was going to walk out of the ward and not give them any excuse to keep me back. Mum had been given a parcel of bandages and cream, with instructions about what to look out for, and told should I need anything, to come back to A&E.

With Mum by my side, I set off down the centre of the ward for the door, with a determination that I would not need the old, brown, wooden crutches to be able to walk out of the ward, but was sternly instructed by one of the nurses to use the crutches to take the weight off my leg. The nurses had spent a good amount of time adjusting the old wooden crutches to fit my short legs and just about managed the task, by using the last holes.

School was given a miss for the rest of the week, allowing time for the main wound to knit together and heal. The following week it was decided that I could go back to school. Mum wrote a long letter explaining my injuries and requested that I was to be given a rest from any PE or running activities for the first week back; although by the end of the week I was almost fully involved in playground games. I was excused most activities at school which involved using my legs and became something of a celebrity when the full story of my accident was told by our teacher during one of the lessons. It was an attempt, I felt, to get less boisterous activities thrust upon me from my mates.

My time at school for the next week or so was so uneventful and boring, but my wounds were healing in super-fast time. Bandages were not really needed after that first week and it now looked as though my leg was on the mend, but not sufficiently to get back to my boxing training, according to my parents. That decision only lasted another week after continually pleading from me that I would take it easy. After another week of full-on school activities, I had soon returned to running everywhere again, once I realised that it wasn't any more painful than walking.

# Chapter 4

## The Ghost Runner

I am not an avid reader of books and feel rather guilty expecting people to read anything that I have written. I never seem to get the time to relax or sit still long enough to further educate my mind these days. But from time to time I will force myself to read a book that has come highly recommended by a friend or colleague. Such a book was lent to me by Barbara, a running club friend, who had been informed about my boxing background and more recently running. She had read Me and My Shadow, my first book, and felt that I would be interested in this particular biography.

Having just finished this enthralling book, a book that has resurrected distant memories of my time as a young boxer, it has left me with a real sense of closeness to a man I have never met in person who lived and died years ago. The book has also left me with a feeling of outrage, against the power of an association to which I once belonged.

This book, The Ghost Runner, which was recently written by Bill Jones, is a tragic story about a young boxer turned athlete, John Tarrant. John was caught up in the bygone days of bureaucratic red tape associated with amateurism, brought about by an association so full of its own importance and officialdom, at a time when class snobbery prevailed, even to the point it's probably true to say that the officials of these amateur associations felt morally superior to people who earned money for a living. It's a fair comment to make, I also believe, where professional sportsmen were thought of by these officials as being on a par with hardened criminals.

As a one-time amateur boxer myself and now distance runner, I can feel great empathy for John and his incredible story. I wonder as I write my own story would I have had the courage and mental strength to continue as he did against all odds to pursue his dreams and ambitions?

This true story is brilliantly told by Bill in an attempt to give recognition to an extremely gifted athlete and goes some way towards explaining and skilfully bringing to our attention John Tarrant's ongoing plight over the years, in an attempt at setting some of the records straight.

As a teenage amateur boxer and member of the Amateur Boxing Association (ABA), John Tarrant had accepted a onetime small donation of about £17, to help towards his expenses and boxing equipment. John was a decent boxer, but from his record not a great one, it has to be said, and eventually that realisation led him to change his sport to running, his new love.

A couple of years later, when filling in an application form to join a local running club, which would have affiliated him to the Amateur Athletics Association ( AAA), John had truthfully answered that he had received this small amount of money for expenses and equipment. The honesty of the man was to haunt him for the rest of his sporting lifetime. Unbeknown to John, he had unfortunately created for himself a professional status and was now being judged and labelled by an association that he had not actually belonged to at that time, but which was so closely linked by association. This information, which was picked up by some sharp-eyed official, had completely compromised John's amateur status. He was duly banned for life as an amateur sportsman, making it impossible for him to officially take part in any amateur running events, even at club level. No amount of pleading over John's lifetime by the public, newspapers or influential people would make the slightest bit of difference.

John's unique way of not giving in, and his only way of fighting back, was to turn up to road races all over the country and actually gatecrash the events. He would be seen slipping into the races after discarding his varying disguises. Often disgruntled race officials would chase after him to pull this numberless runner out of their events. They were never fast enough to catch him.

The AAA, formed in the late 19th century (1880) had been pursuing, and had even brought legal action against, athletes who had falsely claimed not to have taken money for gain, expenses or even gifts. Some of the unlucky ones who had been caught, I have heard tales told, were even prosecuted for fraud, tried in courts, found guilty and condemned to months of hard labour. The AAA rules, made up by so much of the basics of the ABA rules and regulations, would not be seen to deviate or change its stance on amateurism and neither would they relent on the rulings they had heavily inflicted on John Tarrant.

The Doncaster to Sheffield marathon became the inaugural long distance race for John and during that wet and dismal Sunday morning, on the start line of the race in the centre of Doncaster, stood the local mayor, who as the main dignitary in the town was called upon to officially start the race off. Shortly after firing the starting pistol and getting the race underway, it was reported in the press "that all pandemonium broke out," when this figure, loitering in the crowd, cast aside his raincoat and flat cap and quickly getting into his stride caught up with the pack, followed by the shouting, chasing officials who were trying in vain to grab John and pull him out of the event, the crowd laughed and shouted "it's the ghost runner." John Tarrant.

Over the next few years, John Tarrant became one of, if not arguably the best, long distance record breaking runner the world has ever seen. He held, and still holds, many long distance world records, I believe even today. The 40 mile distance record which he set in 1966 in a time of 4 hours 3minutes and the 100 mile in a staggering time of 12hours 31minutes 10 seconds set in 1969. John raced in this outcast manner all over the country and even travelled abroad to take part in one of the most renowned distance races on the planet at that time, the South African Comrades, where, even all those thousands of miles away, his status preceded him. He was a marked man worldwide it seems, and was not officially allowed to take part in the 56-mile endurance race across the southern tip of South Africa, from Durban to Pietermaritzburg. Such was the influence that the AAA had around the globe at that time in John's life. John did, however, gatecrash the event, but was not allowed to use the checkpoints along the route for refreshments and had to run the whole distance getting water where he could from the locals as he passed through the villages. He didn't win the race but should he have done so, John would not have received the coveted solid gold statuette on offer to all winners of this long-established race.

In 1981, the International Amateur Athletics Federation, IAAF, finally conceded that the age of amateurism was over as we had known it to be and trust funds for the athletes were finally permitted to be set up for the first time. How ironic is it that four years after the death of John Tarrant, a young, white, South African teenager, Zola Budd, running barefooted in a British vest, ran a show-piece long distance event in London reputedly for a large sum of money? How times had changed. Going further down the line of changes, in keeping with the new ideas, in 2008, Rafael Nadal, a multimillionaire tennis player, won an Olympic gold medal. This reiterates the complete U-turn by most of the amateur associations. They had finally conceded, bending to the need for change, but ironically by this time only one Olympic sport had remained truly amateur and that was boxing.

To round off the circle of time and bring us more up to date with the recent changes, a self-confessed proven drugs cheat, British athlete Dwain Chambers, was allowed by the IAAF to return to the international athletics circuit and even take part in the 2012 London Olympics.

I mention my keen interest in this amazing story mainly to provide information and to highlight some of my own similarities of the folly, as a young and totally unassuming amateur boxer like John when I accepted for all the right reasons – well, you be the judge – an even smaller amount of money for a fight. Little did I realise the enormity of my action and how close I came to being caught up in the same grip of power at that time. How influentially dominant the ABA stranglehold on amateurism was in those early days and what a very close call I had at an even earlier age than John in my boxing career.

So what could be better than to highlight this endearing story of a man, John Tarrant, the Ghost Runner, who refused against all odds to lie down and give in, but instead followed his dream under the most draconian and bureaucratic rules and regulations as set out by narrow-minded men without empathy or courage to make changes to an outdated system of operating? I do wonder if I would have had the courage to continue against all that opposition.

I sincerely wish to make it clear at this stage that it is not a suggestion or any intention of mine to put myself in the same category as John and his incredible talents as an athlete, but merely to draw attention to the naivety we both shared as young men. All of which will be uncovered as my story unfolds.

# CHAPTER 5

## Young challenger

Whenever I get the opportunity to put something back into sport I feel the sense of pure satisfaction of being able to help and steer anyone who is willing to put in the effort to achieve a goal or challenge. It's my attempt to repay my ex-coaches for all the time and effort they gave me over the years. Those qualities will apply to so many different sports today and even though the titles may have changed over the years for the training sequences, the methods and long-time psychology used to educate and train me will always bring home the desired results.

So back in time to a couple of years ago and the opportunity for me to fulfil that promise of providing help for a young athlete to experience that great feeling of achieving the seemingly impossible. Not in the boxing ring this time but in distance running, where the principle of controlling the mind to overcome what the body is demanding is almost identical. If there are no physical problems to restrict the rigorous exercise that running requires, then it really is all about the mental attitude which can be kick-started with an abundance of encouragement.

The Rowbotham Round Rotherham International off road race was once again providing the ultimate target as a challenge for a new to running young athlete. I have completed this 50-mile race myself on a number of occasions, even managing a double back to back 100 mile run in 2010, But this year the event would hold an even greater, special challenge for me by taking on the responsibility to steer a young woman to fulfil an ambition greater than anything she has ever done before and her attempt to complete the 50 mile challenge. What's even more special about this task is that this young woman, Helen, almost two years before had not laced up a pair of running shoes. Now in most cases this is not a challenge that I would normally endorse because of her young age, inexperience and of course the extreme distance of the event. But then the real determination and her hard work finally proved to me that she possessed the mental attitude and strength to succeed, which had led me to finally agree that I would help to prepare and get Helen through to the finish line.

The RRR race will always be a special event for me. There are many factors influencing this comment. The route itself around the circumference of Rotherham, the organisation of the event and the willingness of the officials, marshals and helpers, who without exception unselfishly put themselves out to make sure that all the athletes taking part in the race have a great opportunity to perform to their best without having to worry about anything other than achieving their own personal goals.

It all started almost two years before when I first met this quiet young woman, who arrived at the Cavalier pub car park in Ravenfield on the outskirts of Rotherham, South Yorkshire, which was our Saturday morning meeting point for a group of new to running, would-be athletes. I had been introduced to this training route by a long-standing friend, Jane Morley, who is one of the fittest, hardest working women I have met at the gym in Parkgate, Rotherham, where she would out-train many so-called fit boxers. We spent many rounds of training and sparring together. This growing group of young women that a great friend of mine, Phil Hague, and I had introduced to running a few weeks earlier were all coming on in leaps and bounds.

Helen arrived in her little black Mini, introduced herself as a friend of Samantha, one of the group, and asked me if she could join us on our training run which we had calculated at about nine miles. Quite a distance for a new recruit, but I was always prepared to run and walk with Helen and any new runners if necessary to start with. Generally before joining in with us, new members will have done a few miles.

As we set off, heading for Thrybergh Country Park, it wasn't long before I realised that Helen was not a runner and would be in need of time and plenty of training and encouragement to catch up in both speed and distance with the rest of the girls. If I am honest, after that first outing I didn't expect to see her again. I even remember making that comment to Phil, who agreed. But she proved us both wrong by turning up the following weeks and over the next few months continued to increase her fitness and performance levels, at the same time losing a good amount of weight. I believe she has lost more than two stone in the past couple of years. I always looked forward to our Saturday mornings, generally off road sessions with our enthusiastic group of young women, which had grown over the weeks, and now included Samantha, Jane, Justine, Joanna, Louise, Fay and Melanie, training around the footpaths and trails of Rotherham.

Slowly but surely over the next few months, Helen continued to gain fitness, having increased to our far longer training runs, and always seemed to enjoy whatever sessions we chose, always with a permanent smile on her face. It became clear to me that she had an ability to run longer distances rather than speed and was soon entering local 10k races and even the Sheffield half marathon with a two hour target to aim for; eventually over the following year it was agreed that she was ready for a steady full marathon.

Edinburgh, 2011, was chosen for her inaugural marathon and less than 18 months from our first training runs, together with Joanne, another young woman from the new members of our group, and myself, we stood waiting on the start line of their first marathon, covered in a far from elegant plastic dustbin liner to keep us warm and dry from the now drizzling weather on the outskirts of Edinburgh, with a plan in mind to get round in about five hours.

The Edinburgh marathon is a pretty fast start, being mostly downhill for the first six miles leading to Musselburgh. Now this sort of start for a marathon requires some discipline to back off and not overdo the early miles.

I could tell during the early and middle part of the marathon that they were both coping well with the distance, even better than I was in fact, Joanne was running and feeling well and happy to increase her pace after halfway and slowly pulled away from us, finishing well under our predicted time.

With fewer than five or six miles to Musselburgh on the return leg and the finish line, it was decided that Helen would increase the pace, setting off to achieve our predicted five hours. It was a great feeling for me to see her confidently pick up the pace and increase her speed at a time when most experienced athletes are struggling.

We met up at the end of the race, where I asked Helen the big question, "Could you continue and run all that distance again right now?" She had expressed a desire to take part in the 50-mile RRR, telling me that it was a dream of hers after seeing me come through to the finish of my last 100-mile run. Her answer at the time was a very hesitant yes, but the "Yes" didn't convince me that she was ready to take on her dream, but having said that, very few athletes feel great directly after running a marathon.

We continued to train and slowly but surely I could sense that Helen was becoming stronger physically and mentally. Together we completed tougher longer events and it was during the Yorkshire Three Peaks Challenge, an event that I had organised for Helen and Joanne, that I became really confident that Helen was ready to have a go and would succeed in fulfilling her ambitious 50-mile challenge.

It's a truly massive unique leap into the unknown for Helen; few athletes will ever take on 50 miles and get to find out what it's really like. She will be entering into the realms of her dreams, which I know could possibly become a nightmare before the finish line comes. It's a punishing distance for any mature, experienced athlete, let alone a young inexperienced one, and if we don't get the tactics and pacing right it could prove a costly mistake. I have seen good quality athletes take on this distance, only to be completely destroyed before the finish line comes, turning it into a death march – and never run again.

I feel a bigger sense of responsibility than at any time in my sporting life, making sure that I have made the right decision for Helen because I know that she totally trusts and is relying on my judgment. It's a feeling that I have never experienced in my life before. We have both got to be right.

Saturday, October 15, 2011, even before the crack of dawn at about 4.35am, I was on my way to pick up Helen from her home in Greasbrough, knowing that she will not have slept at all for two nights with the excitement and anticipation of the event in front of her. We need to arrive at Dearne Valley College in Wath before 5.30 to book in, collect our race numbers and prepare for the start at 6am.

I had been working on a plan to provide a pace that would be comfortable to start with, calculating and predicting times to arrive at each of the eight checkpoints, which should see us finishing the 50-mile race in about 12 hours or so, but the main aim above all else is to complete the race in one piece, knowing that any plans I had made could end up going out of the window at any time should it be necessary to safeguard her future health, which will alleviate any pressure on Helen.

The start was on time and, after the usual instructions about course changes and safety issues by Brian Harney, one of the Rotherham Harriers race officials, we got underway. Fluorescent running gear was soon glowing as the athletes' head torches lit up the paths in front of us. We also had Louise running with us, another one of the group of new runners who had decided to run what would be the longest distance she had achieved by accompanying us up to the end of the second checkpoint at Treeton.

I had wanted to get some good photo shots of what should be a dramatic start in the dark with runners casting lights from their head torches, which will light up the fluorescent strips on running gear. Positioned about 15 feet downstream of the start line, camera at the ready, I managed to get some good photos of the athletes as they came streaming past. After taking time to safely put my camera away into one of the small pockets of my rucksack, I set off to catch the girls, working my way through the groups of athletes in front of me. By the time I had reached the Wath fire station, without locating them, I had the feeling that I might have passed the two of them without realising in the dark. A few seconds after stopping to look around to check and feeling a sense of panic that I had lost them already, I heard them shout from just ahead of me. They had waited for me to catch up just before the bridge which takes the athletes across over the main road and on to the stoned-up paths by the man-made lakes of Wath.

We set off again with company all around us and soon the two of them are chatting away, as ladies do, but getting carried away at a faster pace than we need to be running. "Slow down!" I shouted to them and, after a couple of pace corrections before we reached the gravel path leading into Elsecar, we settled into a pace that would work.

We had a young athlete running alongside for the first few miles along the lakes and towpath who had travelled down from Teesside and was new to this event. He had been enquiring about one or two map references that he couldn't quite get clear in his mind. I was able to put his mind at ease after describing the relationship between the strip maps he had downloaded and the Ordnance Survey map he was using for his main navigational readings.

Reaching Elsecar, the ladies needed a predictable pit stop, not surprising with all the water they had consumed and the excitement over these past few days.

Before long we are soon into our stride again and passing Wentworth. It's time for a photo shoot with the dawn mist in the background and then back into a steady running pace which sees us coming on to our first checkpoint at Grange Golf Course.

We are just less than five minutes ahead of predicted time, as we are greeted by the cheering relay athletes, officials and spectators at the Grange checkpoint gazebo tent.

A short stop at the first checkpoint to eat and drink and then on our way towards the climb up to the hill top at Kimberworth, after clearing the woods at Droppingwell and then down on to Meadowbank Road and crossing over the railway bridge to the canal towpath below.

Helen is looking good, running strong and still smiling, Louise is looking comfortable and they are still vocal, which is making me feel settled, but there's still a long way to go as we leave the towpath and head off past the Pike and Heron pub towards Batley's Cash and Carry into the small industrial estate alongside the M1 motorway.

Treeton, our next checkpoint, is soon in sight as we head over the railway bridge to the large crowd of runners and spectators at Treeton Cricket Club, where Louise will leave us with the satisfaction of completing her own longest run to date. Well done, Lou, you can store that knowledge and feel good for the future.

Approaching the Treeton checkpoint we are greeted with well-wishers and have now been joined by Joanna, who completed the Edinburgh marathon earlier this year with us. Joanna has been one of the regular members of our Saturday morning group, having spent many long hours of training over sections of the Round Rotherham route, and will keep us company for the next 25 miles or so.

Shortly before reaching the outskirts of Rother Valley Country Park, I can see that Helen is having problems and is in desperate need to use the facilities at the park. She is experiencing severe stomach pains and needs to deal with this before moving on. We figure that the running belt, in which she is carrying water in small bottles, and other weighty items, is the cause of her problems. Or is it one of those problems that women have and she is not telling me to save embarrassment? I am hoping and praying that we have identified the problem and that it's nothing more than adjustments. It's giving me cause for concern and my initial feeling is that we may have to consider aborting this event even though she has completed a greater distance than we have managed this morning.

It's great to see the smile back on her face, thumbs up and looking good again as Helen and Joanne reach the road that will take us out of the park heading out to Harthill. But how much mentally has that incident taken out of her? These were my thoughts. Time will tell, I need to keep an eye out for the tell-tale signs that it's had any adverse effect over the coming miles; it's still a little unsettling and difficult for me to relax for a while as we continue over the hill to Woodthorpe.

We are just one minute in front of our schedule as we climb our way out of the valley and up the hill to our third checkpoint at Harthill to fuel up.

We are moving slightly faster than we need to, taking into consideration that we have had a delay of more than ten minutes at Rother Valley Park, but Helen is looking chirpy and full of beans as she makes conversation about our accurate timing with Ann, another of our group of runners, who had come out to meet, greet and cheer us on at this checkpoint.

Leaving Harthill on time and soon Helen and Joanne are full of running, we are heading out across the muddy fields towards Netherthorpe Airfield, which is now just over the halfway point. We are shortly crossing over the canal bridge into the pretty hamlet of Turner Wood and an unexpected free drink of orange, supplied by long-standing local friends of mine, Diane and Mick, whom I had introduced to Helen on one of our recce runs. Diane is telling me that she thought I was doing the double lap again.

We are well into the second half of the run now as we come down through the wooded area heading for the Carlton-in-Lindrick Golf Course and entering into the realms of the unknown for Helen. It's from now on that I need to be diligent and watch out for any signs of fatigue, physical or mental.

Woodsetts checkpoint sees us bang on target, where I have pencilled in an extra 15 minutes to change socks, shoes and any clothes that may have become uncomfortable over the last 30 miles.

We need to fuel up with soup, fruit, nuts and a hot drink. Helen is full of beans and enthusiastically chatting with Joanna; both are looking as though they have just stopped after a short training run. I am particularly pleased with how Helen is coping with the distance, although I am slightly suffering myself and have been experiencing lower back pains for the last five miles or so. I will probably have to walk for a spell or two in with the running if the painkillers don't kick in soon and ease the pain, because up to now they are not having any great effect and causing me to stoop to get any ease, not very good.

Our thanks are passed on to the marshals and helpers at the Woodsetts Scout hut before setting off across the football field to waves and cheers from friends and other athletes.

Helen and Joanna are still looking good, running together and making conversation as we head off away from the road and on to the wide path leading out to the open countryside and fields before reaching the outskirts of Carlton and Dinnington and then the woods beyond Langold lakes. It seems like no time at all before we are coming down into the village of Firbeck and the community centre which is our new checkpoint for this year's event.

For the first time we are slightly behind schedule, which is all down to the fact that I am slowing us down, having to walk for longer spells. Helen is doing brilliantly and full of running. I am now more than confident that if we maintain this sort of pace, short of any unforeseen problems, Helen will manage the distance. I am booked in as the 200th athlete, indicating that there are still more than 100 runners behind us. Brilliant!

Joanna has been great company for Helen, taking her mind off the miles we have covered, and has managed the long run from Catcliffe without any problems, but she has decided to head off on her own to Maltby, our next checkpoint, for a pre-arranged meeting with her partner. Well done, Joanna – a great achievement and looking effortless as she slowly disappears across the fields towards Maltby.

Just the two of us now, Helen, and time to dig in, these are the most demanding miles in front of us now. We are heading for Roche Abbey and time to make a call home.

Twenty minutes and we will be met at the Maltby checkpoint by my wife, Maureen, who has met me here many times in the past while doing this event. And right on time as we head up the path towards the church, the greeting and encouraging remarks from the checkpoint officials and supporters are just what is needed at this stage of the run.

We are not staying long at Maltby, there's a need to keep our legs moving. Helen has picked up her collie dog, Hope, who will come through to the finish with us; I say my farewells to Maureen and David Woodthorpe and head off for our last checkpoint at Old Denaby.

My back is becoming increasingly more painful as we step up the pace, but knowing that our time of less than twelve hours is now realistically unachievable. How ironic is it that it's actually me who is holding Helen back at this stage. It may be a good thing, but there's one sure fact over these last ten hours or so, Helen has matured as an athlete and shown great strength of character, maturity and a confidence that will enhance her life.

Over the next seven miles of more walking than running, Helen has led and maintained the pace with just the odd spell of fatigue showing as we head out from under the M18 motorway bridge across the open fields towards Firsby Hall Farm in the valley. My back is still painful but not enough to give me undue cause for concern.

The light is now fading and will soon disappear altogether for the remaining five or six miles by the time we reach Hooton Roberts.

At last the final checkpoint is in view in the valley at Old Denaby, where we receive a great welcome from the officials. I remember looking at Helen and could see the great feeling she was experiencing, knowing that we had only three miles to go.

Saying our farewells and knowing that there were still more than 100 athletes behind us, we left Ray and Jane Howarth and the gang staffing the gazebo checkpoint, feeling on a real high.

It seems no time at all before we are less than a quarter of a mile off the college grounds and the end of this mammoth challenge for Helen.

We are close to getting to the finish under 13 hours, but the only way of reaching that new target is to up the pace and run the remainder of the distance. Helen wanted to see if she could make it, my back is now making running out of the question but it's time to encourage her to go for it.

"See you at the finish" and off she went, striding out with Hope, and had soon disappeared into the wooded area before coming on to the reasonably well-lit wide cycle path that leads into the college grounds. I can well imagine how good she will have felt, seeing the lights of the college for the first time; it's always a great sight after covering 50 miles.

It is hard to describe my feeling of total relief together with a good dose of happiness that Helen had achieved her dream of completing the 50-mile Rowbotham Round Rotherham challenge and with distinction. I am so proud to have been part of her dream and so glad that I was right in the assumption that she was ready and able to take on and conquer this mammoth challenge.

A shower, pie and peas and pick up our certificates, we had already been issued with the event T-shirt and the coveted cloth badge at the registration earlier this morning.

It was time to say our thanks and goodbyes to the officials for another well run and organised event. I know it will take some time for the enormity of the achievement to sink in for Helen and my hope is that she recovers quickly from the muscle trauma she will experience over the next few days. Make no mistake, Helen will suffer, but within a week or so the pain will have been forgotten, leaving only the great memories and an enormous sense of achievement.

We said our goodbyes with a hug and a squeeze, I know that Helen feels that she couldn't have done this without me and totally trusted my belief in her ability, but she will have gained a huge amount of knowledge about herself over today's experience and will have the strength both physically and mentally now to take on her own personal challenges in the future.. It may well be the END of this dream, but it's probably just the beginning of more dreams to come for Helen. Keep on running!

# CHAPTER 6

## Fulfilling my prediction

I had managed to heal quickly and my legs were feeling pretty good within about three or four weeks of being left hanging on the gate, but even after all these years I can well remember how difficult it was getting back into full training and any sort of real fitness after only those few weeks of inactivity, but determination and full-on hard work now that my legs were functioning normally were showing enough results to be here sparring with this visiting boxer from Ireland.

The intensive hard work was paying off and soon having the desired effect. I was reaching a new level of fitness which is generally only associated with professional boxers. And now I realise, Young Men.

Youth was definitely on my side, as week after week my sparring sessions with Danny were slowly becoming much less one-sided, more enjoyable and certainly encouraging enough for me to realise that I was in fact beginning to cope better with this powerhouse of a fighter and learning how to handle and deal with his phenomenal work rate. My own speed and fitness were bringing the physical and mental rewards which were so satisfying and fuelled my eagerness to further increase the relentless work rate I had imposed on myself: a situation I now know only too well can best be achieved with less risk of self-inflicted injury when you're young and have a body capable of withstanding the huge demands that I was setting for myself.

But just when I thought I had reached the point of being able to hold my own with Danny, he would up a gear and leave me feeling I was going backwards, a bit like chasing a bus on the move, just when you're ready to grab the handle and jump on board the driver changes up a gear and moves away. Frustratingly, the master seemed to always have an extra trick up his sleeve.

I had learnt the hard way a few months ago, during that memorable evening after my 50th fight, that I must never become complacent! Nonetheless, I was becoming increasingly pleased with myself for having had the courage to make that difficult choice to continue sparring and working with Danny. I realized some time later that this was the first time I had consciously made the decision to take myself out of the comfort zone that I had cocooned around my boxing life and had for the first time ventured feet first into the unknown. I was increasingly more aware that, if I had chosen to take the easy path and continue with what was comfortable, I would never know or find out what lay beyond the edge of my capabilities. Who knows where the limits are to what can be achieved if I don't push myself beyond what can be seen?

It was just over two months since our inaugural sparring session at the gym and now I was ready for what had become the highlight of the nights' training workouts for me. We were due to take part in what had become our traditional sparring session towards the end of the evening's training session.

I nervously pranced around in the opposite corner waiting for Danny to have his gloves laced up. It seemed that the whole gym had stopped what they were doing and the sense that something was about to happen had created a quieter but tense atmosphere.

Everyone in the gym was turned facing the ring to watch what had become something of a ritual during the past few of weeks of sparring sessions. It felt like we were entertaining the club. Often parents, ex-boxers and spectators who came in to watch the boxers training and sparring, which had become increasingly more frequent and pleasing for me as the weeks passed by, settled down to watch.

Danny and I had developed a great mutual respect for one another over the past few weeks, even though I had not lost sight of the promise I had made to myself while climbing out of the ring after that first encounter, which seemed like years ago right now. I had been performing better each week as our sparring sessions had become more satisfying. I was fighting with speed and quality, even beginning to command a good amount of the rounds and managing to get on top of some of the three-minute round sessions, which had been increased to five rounds for Danny's benefit. I had a feeling that the day was coming soon when I would make it happen.

I remember feeling good about myself that Thursday evening as I anxiously awaited in anticipation of a great sparring session with Danny. I just knew that tonight was going to be what I had been training hard for and to add to the sense of occasion, for the first time during our twice weekly gladiatorial training sessions, Jacky climbed into the ring to officiate tonight's sparring session.

My plan, brought about through hours of daydreaming of this time to come of how I would command the sparring, was to work him into the ground, so to speak. I was under no illusion that I could knock him out or stop him with a punch, even in my wildest dream I knew that was out of the question. It would only come from speed, skill and fitness.

At the command from Jacky to start round one, attack was the only thing I had on my mind. I was determined to stand and work close up to him all the time. It was toe to toe and even closer. I was confident now that I was becoming increasingly faster; fast enough to block and counter, at the same time following up with combinations of punches. My attack, which became an almost non-stop barrage of pressure, was slowly giving me more control of the ring. I was determined not to allow Danny to stay in one spot at any time. He, at the same time, used his long-standing skills to grab and hold and did get through with a punch or two, but with nowhere near the frequency he had been able to inflict on me a couple of months ago. The power from his punches, which were being blocked mainly on my arms, was sending me all over the ring, making it even more important not to lose concentration and get battered.

Danny, I believe, was in fact becoming the victim of his own talent. I recall thinking about the sparring session some time later, it was as if I had been able to extract the skills from this man, which he had demonstrated against me, and use them against him. Fortunately, I was smart enough to learn, analyse and absorb the ongoing physical lessons that were freely flowing in my direction.

He had taught me by his own actions that almost every punch I delivered should set me up for the next punch to come, maintaining balance and poise, in a flowing easy manner, in which speed and power became comfortable and effortless between feet, body movement and the delivery of effective punches. I was also beginning to understand more about the principles of the professional ways of fighting, high up the list is that predictability is easily the biggest downfall in any fighter's training, but it's also very difficult to avoid as a young amateur, because most young boxers are taught to box by a system of fixed patterns and most of the sequences lead off with a jab, so it's jab and cross or jab and hook, almost every sequence taught starts with a jab. Most training methods are carried out with so much repetitiveness that predictability is trained into the average amateur boxer. I realise that it must have been so easy during those initial sparring sessions for Danny to deal with my amateurish approach. "Predictable." The need to learn how to become unpredictable had taken up a good deal of my time, practising how to come out of every sequence of punching by actually delivering a punch, leaving the counter puncher so uncertain of how best to deal with the extra punch and the aggressive fighter uncertain of when to attack. It's so unusual for an amateur boxer to deliver a right cross, for instance, without throwing a jab first.

My sparring partner and new teacher, unbeknown to himself, had provided me with another set of skills that had greatly enhanced my ability to deal with him.

I could feel him backing off and breathing more heavily than usual as we fought our way through the second round. It was now my turn to increase the pressure and take the fight to him again as we came together close to one another, trading punches in much the same way as round one. Jacky was working hard himself to keep out of our way, but was caught up by the speed of the two of us a couple of times as Danny back-pedalled for most of the round.

This super fit fighter was starting to tire as the round progressed, less able to dance out of the way of my non-stop onslaught, and becoming easier to hit. My own lungs were bursting with the effort of non-stop punching, and it's difficult to increase the work rate but I was on a mission and no amount of heavy breathing was going to slow me down.

The end of the round brought a huge sigh from Danny as "Time!" was shouted, with him ending up in his own corner trying to avoid a combination of body shots.

We had both agreed that body punching could be delivered with as much power as we each wanted to deliver. Although I didn't wear a kidney belt, I was well and truly blessed with a stomach that I felt could be hit with a double decker bus without feeling it. Our normal training sessions would end with a daily routine of 100 sit-ups at a time with a heavy medicine ball across my chest and only boredom stopped me doing more. Lying on the floor on my back, body conditioning would be carried out where Jacky would bounce the heavy medicine ball into my stomach, simulating a punch. This was never a problem, through working regularly on a speedy delivery of tension to the stomach muscles before the ball or any punch could be landed into my solar plexus.

Being able to recover fast has always played an important part in my fitness, but as I walked around the ring heaving the oxygen into my lungs, I was trying to give the impression that the last round had been nothing unusual, although for once in my life I was praying for a speedy recovery and playing down the feelings of excitement that were racing through me.

Danny was breathing heavily, I could tell, as I watched him heaving in breath, his shoulders rise and falling, as he stood facing the corner of the ring, with his head bowed between his outstretched hands on the top ropes. . Our eyes had met just before I turned away to walk towards my corner, the signs were there, and Danny is feeling the pace. This is new, he has always stood facing and looking across at me, an imposing almost intimidating presence that said "I am in charge young man".

Jacky was trying to catch my eye, and mouthed well done with a half hidden raised clenched fist in an uncharacteristic show of favouritism.

The rest of the gym members were quiet and not making any movement, they had created a degree of tension and had moved even closer to the ring, but one of the spectators, Mr Sanders, the father of Roy, one of our very good light heavyweight fighters, was sitting on one of the chairs close to the ring near my corner. He was making himself more visible to me than any of the others with his exaggerated shadow boxing moves in an attempt to encourage me I believe. I had sat with him after training on many occasions and had loved listening to him tell me about his very colourful boxing career which, like mine, had begun at around the age of ten. He had turned professional at the early age of 17, when he was considered to be one of the leading contenders for the British Cruiserweight championship and was at one time the sparring partner to the cruiserweight world champion Harry Crosby around 1931/32. I loved to listen to the vivid tales of his three-year tour of Australia, competing even in bare knuckle fighting on occasion, I believe, and earning himself a huge sum in those days of about £5,000 from his fights. He was a pioneer among British fighters. But an unfortunate accident which happened down the mine while working at Thurcroft Colliery in 1947, when he was buried by a fall, left him with a broken back which led to a two-year spell in Lodge Moor hospital in Sheffield and unable to walk properly for about three years. The accident, which he never talked about to me, did explain his slurred speech and unbalanced walk. Nonetheless, he was one of my heroes at that time at the gym.

We were both at the ready, waiting and facing one another like Roman gladiators, before time was shouted for the third round. Danny had this very serious professional look on his face and was scowling, in an attempt, I felt, at intimidating me and maybe putting me off guard. I had been taught better than that. Press home your advantage and never let your opponent off the hook is the unwritten law of successful fighters.

I set about him right from the word go with a flurry of punches, again standing close enough to be able to connect with every punch I launched. Of course, the downside to being that close, I was always susceptible to copping a good one myself, but youth and fast reactions were bringing the rewards I was after.

I was lathered with sweat from Danny as we came close to one another, our heads were locked on each other's shoulders, with his head guard rubbing against my ears, making it uncomfortable to stay in that locked state for any length of time. I had been training hard and working to master this situation over these past few weeks on staying close, even moving forward into a punch and being able to react fast enough to slip it over and past my shoulders without getting caught, knowing that there would be no other way of dominating the sessions.

It must create a very intimidating sensation for your opponent, if you're fit and with fast enough reactions to be able to stay close enough to connect with every punch you choose to deliver and fast enough to avoid any that comes your way. It must have been frustrating and strength sapping for Danny to be missing more and more as he delivered powerful punches to mid-air.

Putting myself in Danny's position, I did wonder if I would have found it difficult to accept that a 14-year-old could hold his own against me, but it was a question of getting the best out of one another and without fear of embarrassment as we became more evenly matched. I felt a great admiration for him, knowing that in this situation he would need great strength of character, certainly strong enough to ignore what anyone else could possibly be thinking or saying.

Nonetheless, I had the feeling that Danny was now trying to knock me out or at least to connect with a powerful punch or two that would stop me coming forward. But he was swinging more instead of his normally controlled punches, making it easier for me to step inside and slip any oncoming punches, creating a double impact when connecting with the multiple combinations I had been working on. I could sense the panic in him as he made more attempts to grab hold and use his superior strength to hustle me on to the ropes or into the corner of the ring.

This was beginning to feel more like a full-blown contest rather than a constructive sparring session, which was my doing I suppose, I was leaving him without an option but to fight his way out of what was coming at him. You can't expect to corner a wild animal without suffering the consequences, because I was now fighting with survival caution in mind, knowing that at any time if he was to catch me with one of those powerful punches, I could be in real bother.

Even though I was finding it easier to maintain the pressure as the minutes passed, I did realise that one mistake from me at this stage could end in a disaster, but mentally realised that I still needed to press home my advantage. I could sense that he was tiring rapidly. "Time!" was called, bringing the third round to an end. I was shattered, but doing my best not to show any signs of fatigue as I walked around the ring gulping in oxygen, a bit of professional kidology. I was learning!

The fourth round seemed to last forever, as we worked our way around one another at close range, with more combination body work taken on the arms as our heads seemed to be endlessly locked on one another's shoulders. Even though I was blocking the heavy punches, I was literally being knocked about, even taken off my feet a couple of times with the sheer power of Danny's punches.

Danny, who was now throwing fewer punches, seemed to recover as he leaned heavily and grabbed hold of me, using his professional skills to tie me up, rendering me ineffective and limiting my punching power, but in reality both of us were just wasting much needed energy.

While recovering from that hustling round, I knew that Danny had just asserted his professional superior ability on me again, without my knowing how best to deal effectively with it, but I did realise that I needed to put more effort into this coming last round, speed up and keep him at arm's length and on the move, knowing that he was tiring far more quickly than I was.

Round five started with more aggression from Danny in an attempt, I felt, to impose his professional superiority on me again, which actually made it easier for me to use counter punches and less effort for the first half of the round than would be used by taking the fight to him.

I could sense the pace was dropping towards the middle of the round; there were longer spells of inactivity from him. I could also feel his breathing becoming more and more laboured and almost taste his frustration, I had developed that extra sixth sense that I could call upon to analyse the moment as the fight was taking place. My body had also started to change shape as I muscled up more, and I was becoming stronger over the past few weeks with all this intensive training.

It was my opportunity now to up the punching rate and, more importantly, to keep on the move so he couldn't grab hold and tie me up. It was all about my fitness now and trying to maintain the pressure as Danny covered up for most of the remainder of the round.

"Time!" brought a real sense of satisfaction to a very tired but happy me. Sweat was pouring out of me for the first time ever in the ring, dripping onto the ring canvas, like a river. I did feel a sense of partial exhaustion and was glad that it was all over; leaving me wondering could I have managed another round if it had been absolutely necessary.

A moment later as I walked across the ring to Danny, I was about to put my arms around him, our normal ritual, when I felt him grab hold, beating me to it, and almost lay full weight on me. His eyes, without the normal sparkle, told me that he was spent. This tough Irishman was close to exhaustion. We hugged each other for what seemed an eternity while we both got our breath back and suddenly realized that we were being clapped by our fellow club mates and spectators.

I had finally fulfilled and satisfied my promise. Even though I don't recall feeling bullish or cocky about the outcome, I do remember feeling elated and had this wonderful glowing feeling inside which felt as though it was about to come bursting out, like winning an important contest. I was content, but above all satisfied that I had made the right decision and my plan had finally succeeded.

I was in another world for a few minutes with the realisation that I had more than earned the elation I felt. I was happy with my performance and at the same time grateful to Danny for giving me the golden opportunity to learn far more in these last ten weeks than would ever have been possible if he hadn't become part of my life. It was certainly not how I imagined I could ever have felt after that first evening just over a couple of months ago when I was on the receiving end of the biggest boxing lesson of my life. Maybe I had learnt more of a lesson than I could have realised at that time. I had certainly learnt how to control my temper and feelings, but did not realise at the time that this episode of my life which I often draw upon, would always stand the test of time. I had, without knowing how, made another great addition to my growing education. This lesson goes a long way in my mental make-up and is one that I often recall when starting out on a new challenge, confronting a difficult event or taking on a seemingly impossible task.

Determination and a willingness to put oneself on the line will make almost anything possible. Could Danny possibly know how much he had contributed to the shaping of my life and my burning joy right now? Do I need to thank him or does he feel my thoughts of immense satisfaction at this moment in time? His unselfishness towards me as the weeks had progressed with his patient teachings had left me with a feeling of great friendship that I know we both shared and will undoubtedly last a lifetime.

Jacky Pearson, the normally reserved Steelo's coach, could hardly contain himself as he slowly untied my gloves, dropping them on the bloodstained canvas floor just inside the ring. I know he felt my joy; the autopsy of the sparring session had already started as we walked over to the back of the ring. The outcome of the discussion was that, above all else, maintaining fitness was high on our priority list. It was also discussed and agreed that it was nigh-on impossible to hit your opponent if you're out of range, this would become a major part of my continued training strategy. The last five rounds had proved that to be fit enough and sharp enough to stand within firing range of your opponent, had provided me the opportunity to punch and connect as many times as my own fitness allowed..

It was agreed that training would continue using a similar programme and increasing the use of combinations of a variety of punches and continuing my fitness program. I remember Jacky did mention that it was a shame my dad wasn't there that night to have witnessed my performance. His last comment, "Can't wait for your next fight," came as a big surprise. Jacky had never shown any emotion at any time before during my time at the gym.

I had almost forgotten that I had not been involved in any amateur competitive fighting since meeting up with Danny. I was buzzing with the excitement of getting back in the ring with amateur opponents again. On my way out of the gym heading for home, Danny made another gesture of great sportsmanship with a thumb up sign and mouthed "Well done, Ray, see you tomorrow."

Danny and I would meet up on occasions and go for a run together during the week. I would set off after school from my terraced house in Holland Place, up the hill in Brown Street and College Road to the Station Hotel opposite Masbrough railway station close to Millmoor, the then Rotherham United football ground. I would generally have to wait for him just inside the entrance. Often, there would be men playing billiards in a large room to the side of the entrance hall, so if he was late coming down from his room, I didn't mind waiting while I watched them play. They would always make some sarcastic comment as we headed out of the door.

Danny would always perform some exaggerated stretching moves in the street before setting off. He was always overdressed, it seemed to me, and had confided that he had a bit of a problem and struggled to hit his fighting weight. This continual battle to keeping his weight constant meant that he needed extra jumpers, skull cap and thick joggers, would almost certainly guarantee that loads of fat burning sweat would pour from him. It did answer the question why he always seemed overdressed in the ring. I have never seen anyone lose so much sweat.

We would head off up the hill towards Fenton Park, passing the large Premier cinema house, then turn up right by the side of Robert Jenkins boiler works, skirting round the old Woodman Pub., and head out towards Greasbrough. Danny only ever wanted to run about five miles, so once we reached the area where the Ring o' Bells pub is now, we would turn off right down the path off Fenton Road on to the "old Indian warpath" to Clough Road, down to the top of Thornhill, over the railway bridge on Roger Street, right along James Street, cut across Masbrough Street and back down the hill towards the Station Hotel. His landlady was always there to greet us with a jug of home-made lemonade.

I always thought it must have been a lonely time for Danny, out here on his own and away from his family in Ireland. He never talked about them and I never asked.

Danny and I did spar a few times together over the next couple of weeks, but the sessions were never conducted in such a gladiatorial- like battle again, we made use of our time together to help each other, working as a team to perfect different punching techniques and challenges with his training in readiness for his up and coming championship fight in Ireland.

At our last training evening together, I recall there was an emotional farewell. Danny was due to leave early the following morning. As we said our goodbyes, his strong handshake and bear-like hug provided a powerful message of the friendship and respect we had for one another. We didn't have to talk; it was like saying goodbye to an old friend. He was now more like a big brother to me, even though I had only known him for just over three months.

It was almost impossible to keep in touch in those days and I never saw or heard anything about Danny again, apart from a good article I had read in one of the fight magazines which mentioned that he had won a European title the following year, together with a full page photograph, which I cut out and pinned up over my bed.

Little did I realise that the shaping and moulding of my early life would have such a massive influence on my life today. "Young Ray" is often my source of inspiration and encouragement and is a constant companion when needed in a sort of reversal of roles. Even today, I can draw upon the experiences and go back in time down memory lane whenever I need to make difficult decisions, find courage to take on greater challenges and draw enough mental strength to get me to the finish line.

Someone once said "One day when life flashes before your very eyes, make sure that you have done enough to make it worth watching."

# CHAPTER 7

## Middle 50 miles and race proper

It's now 5.30am and with a belly full of food from my car boot; it's time to collect my race number (101) and event T-shirt for this year's race from inside the hall.

The usual Rotherham Harriers officials are busy at the tables, checking entrants, providing race numbers, maps and this year's T-shirts to the queuing group of athletes who are drawn back year after year like a magnet to this great event

To the left of the partially cordoned off sports hall are a large number of competitors who will be making the later start. These sleeping athletes who are still tucked up in their sleeping bags and camp beds have been at the college overnight in readiness for the early start rather than travelling throughout the night and early morning to get here on the day of the race.

It's good to meet up with many of the regulars who take part in this event year after year; many are aware of my 150-mile challenge and make comments about my mentality but are all wishing me well and wanting to shake my hand. It's at times like this, when confronted with other people's expectations, who may think that my challenge will prove to be impossible, or that I will surely die in the attempt, that there's a need to remove these thoughts from my head and remember why I am doing this self-inflicted challenge in the first place; it's all about my own challenge and above all to satisfy my personal whim.

With less than ten minutes to the start, I am beginning to stiffen up slightly around the bottom of my back and hips and the top of my legs.

I have left my Union Jack flag and a black marker pen on a table for the runners to sign for me, making it a special memento to save for the next challenge I take part in. This flag was last used to hold aloft as I came running through the finish line in the 100km Del Sahara Desert Race and also at the end of the London to Brighton with Kerry, the blind soldier, and the mixed group of walkers a few months ago.

The growing group of athletes who are pouring out of the hall are congregating outside on the slope in readiness for the start of the 30th edition of this great ultra race. At about 5.55am, it's time for me to prepare and get ready to go again as I make my way towards the middle of the growing group of noisy athletes who are all eager to get underway.

Brian Harney, the Rotherham Harriers official starter, and my starter of just over 12 hours ago, officially got the race underway with the loud countdown, "Five, Four, Three, Two, One" and at bang on 6am, to loud cheers and shouts from the colourfully-clad early starters, we set off down the slope heading for the exit from the college.

My legs are stiff from the first 50 miles and refusing to move in an easy manner for the first half a mile or so as we all make our way on the footpath towards the fire station.

There's little need of the head torch until reaching the path beyond the bridge over the main road, providing a very familiar feeling to the start of this event as we head out past the lakes on the right.

Runners are starting to pull away already and creating small gaps in the snake-like procession of athletes up front and looking back I can see that gaps have been created by the small group who are running at my pace. Once again, it's important that I get the pace set right which suits my target and to almost ignore the rest of the runners around me. It's all about maintaining the discipline of sticking to my own pace and not getting carried away with anyone else's running speed, no matter how good I feel right now. There is still another 90-odd miles for me to go.

As I make my way with a group of about 12 athletes along the side of the canal, my spirits are high and the legs are now functioning comfortably with the pace I am travelling at, eventually reaching the turn-off after the third bridge, which will take us through to the bottom of Elsecar on a good, compacted solid, wide path.

The narrow stone path leading up from the level crossings in Elsecar brings the first stop to our small group, because of the slippery rocks, and now into single file with everyone using their head torches.

The leading group of athletes are heading slightly off course and up the left hand path into the woods, creating a bit of indecision for some of the front runners about which way to head. Once I have shouted out instructions of which path to head for, we are all back into a steady run through the muddy sections until reaching the clearing at the top of the hill.

Dawn has still not broken as we head for the main road passing the wood yard on our left and on to the well-lit streets heading up to Wentworth. Straight on through the traffic-free crossroads and past the small junior school on the left, which brings us all back together again because of the indecision of which path to take for the two leaders of the group.

There are just a couple of runners directly up front now, with a small group I can make out some way in the distance that have broken away. Behind are a small group who seem to be running at a similar pace to me as I make my way down the narrow muddy path towards the bridge over the stream at the bottom.

Dawn is ready to break and creating a dull light before reaching the outskirts of Thorpe Hesley village, making the need for the artificial lighting of my head torch unnecessary, which needs carefully putting away for later this evening, but hopefully if I am on target I won't need to use it before the last 50-mile session.

It's been drizzling for the past half hour, but not enough to warrant wet clothes other than a waterproof jacket, which also adds a degree of warmth to my body. It's good to feel comfortable after a short walk up the hill into the village and taking the time to open up another energy gel and swill it down with a good drink of water.

I can hear the first of the 7am group of faster runners who are coming up behind me as I make my way up the slippery muddy paths after locating the local health centre building to my right. These guys are moving at a pretty good pace and seem to be climbing the steep paths with little or no problem.

The sight of the large, imposing Keppel's Column can be seen through the misty morning over to my right, which always provides a feeling of being close to the first checkpoint.

I am being passed by a steady stream of runners now as I make good progress myself along the tree-lined narrow path of the ridge line above Scholes. Steadily down the four stone steps and turning right into the village on the tarmac at last and a chance to clear the mud from my shoes.

I am more than happy with the performance and pace that I have been able to steadily maintain up to this distance of the challenge, not quite half way but at least 60 miles without any problems, although is it a little premature to be thinking that I am well on target for my pre-arranged meetings tonight. I have got to maintain the positive attitude, though.

Climbing the boggy field heading towards the top of the hill and Keppel's Column is somewhat of a drag through the tall gorse grass and waterlogged ground, until reaching a sign indicating that a cameraman would be waiting to take photographs of the athletes as they negotiated running along a temporary bridge of wooden pallets which were set into the mud to avoid the worst of the boggy area. All the athletes in front seem to display a surge of energy in readiness for an action shot from the waiting camera man." Best foot forward and all that"

No matter how hard I try, my photograph tells the truth, it looks as though I have been running for at least 60 miles, tired and bedraggled, ha, ha. Well I can't find a comb, and that's my excuse.

Keppel's column is soon passed and, as we reach the main road through the small housing estate, I am surrounded by a large group of athletes who have caught up and we make our way together down Wortley Road. This road runs out of any footpath adjacent to the woods on the left, leaving no option but to use the road edge as we descend the hill. Hell, it's like a free-for-all, almost like playing chicken with the startled-looking unsuspecting car driver, as hordes of runners on both sides of the road completely take over, slowing the drivers down to a crawl until the bulk of the runners have turned right on to the entrance of Grange Golf Course.

The first checkpoint, looking as inviting as ever, is in sight at the bottom of the hill and surrounded with a large group of spectators waiting around the gazebo tent. There are also athletes waiting for the relay runners to come for the first leg and, of course, the officials, who have provided a table, full of food, cordial drinks and water. Most of this group are friends and local running club athletes who are aware of my challenge, all waiting for answers to their questions for longer than I intended to stay, but all are genuinely interested and inquisitive about how I am coping with the mileage. I seemed to have been there for ages, but in reality no more than four minutes before getting underway again, having topped up the camelback and enjoyed a couple of bread and jam sandwiches and a large piece of fruit cake.

I need to maintain the discipline of hitting times throughout this middle 50-mile leg of the event and set off to waves and good luck messages, heading out with a new group of runners. We run up the wet grassy hill around the back of the junior football pitches before dropping into the woods, down to the stream on the narrow slippery path and finally up the steep, black as coal path to Droppingwell Road. We are all moving together like a winding snake.

Average speed is King in ultra running. My theory is to start off steadily and then, when everything feels great, slow down. Well, for me at the moment I need to slow down to a walk as we make our way up the steep path on the far side of the road. There's a steady stream of runners heading up the tree-lined path to the turn off leading on to the field and Hilltop on the far end of the grassy path.

Passing through the houses on either side, we reach the footpath sign and head down the narrow, nettle-filled path, which is full of partially-submerged rocks under the grass and needs some concentration to avoid tripping and causing damage, but with that thought in mind a steady stream of runners come past making it look so easy and among this fast moving group comes a friendly "Hi, Ray" as I pull to one side to allow them through. It's Kevin Doyle, from one of our local running clubs, Kimberworth Striders. Kevin is positioned towards the middle of this group, but not far behind the lead runners and looking good as he pulls away and disappears over the track heading down towards the first of the roads, which leads down to Meadowhall shopping complex. That young man is going to win this event before long.

Meadowbank Road is the next target, as I catch up with a small group of mainly women runners from Kimberworth Striders on the tricky narrow path. They are experiencing problems on the sharp descent on to the main road. It's the reversal of last night, when it took me a couple of attempts to climb this steep bank side. My easy descent seems to have encouraged the ladies to go for it rather than pussyfooting about and risk sliding from top to bottom. They are soon following me, running towards our next turn-off just after the old Rother Boiler Company and TDE, the demolition company yard.

I can see in the distance a runner has passed the almost-concealed entrance to the footpath and shout out instructions to save him heading any further down the road towards Rotherham. Just before we reach the half hidden path, the runner who had turned back was waiting to thank me for providing him with the directions. It's not a problem mate, I know what it feels like to miss a turn and add more miles to the run than necessary. The overgrown trees could do with a good trimming; many unsuspecting athletes will miss this path before the day is out.

The narrow path leading down to the steel railway bridge is in need of a good sorting out, it's crumbling, full of potholes and the stone foundations to the path dangerously fall away under the steel mesh fencing to leave the unsuspecting athlete with a big chance of damage to feet or legs. I later found out that I was in fact unfortunately right and more than one of today's runners has picked up injuries at this section of the event, needing hospital treatment.

The old steel bridge over the railway lines is as slippery this morning as it was last night and makes me cautiously slow as I cross over the warped chequer plate floor panels and down the steel steps that have had the pattern worn off over the years with constant foot traffic. The graffiti-covered steel safety panelled sides are bright and vivid with newly-painted images from would-be Banksy artists. Not my cup of tea, then neither are the abstract or expressionism paintings of Pablo Picasso, but mark my words, Banksy's work will soon be selling for hundreds of thousands of pounds.

I mentally give myself a pat on the back for making it safely as I reach the bottom, turning right on to solid ground and the safety of the canal towpath.

Steady running gives me a chance to stretch out my legs, while following a stream of athletes who are all trying to avoid the deepest of the black muddy pools, as we head for the old Rotherham-Sheffield road.

A small group of athletes in the distance are catching up, among them I recognise the voice of Richard Hawcroft, Richard makes comments as he comes alongside about how well I am looking and stays with me for a couple of minutes to discuss my finishing time. Both he and his wife Adele will accompany me over the last three miles to the finish line in the morning. We make our tentative arrangements before he comfortably pulls away, and disappearing over the white tubular steel bridge and on to the other side of the canal.

Bawtry Road is as busy with traffic as it always is on any Saturday morning and there's a need to be cautious about crossing over to the right hand side before it's time to leave the main carriageway just after the junior school on my right and head up to the small industrial estate with Batley's Cash and Carry.

I have just turned right off Bawtry Road on to the estate road and am about to take the slight inclined road when I feel the most excruciating pain at the top of my right hamstring, stopping me dead in my tracks. Whilst looking around for the sniper who must surely be hidden in the hedge across the road, It felt as though I had just been shot and I wouldn't have been surprised to have seen blood gushing down my leg. The language I screamed out in my head didn't make the slightest bit of difference to the pain. So what's gone wrong from running comfortably a second ago without any signs of fatigue or pain, to a complete full stop and now generating great fears of not being able to move? This is not what I would have planned in a million years! God, this challenge is going to be tough enough without adding this sort of problem to it.

A couple of minutes of vigorously rubbing the area around the top of my leg with as much effort as the pain would allow and a couple of strong pain killers have provided little or no amount of comfort. I am fighting the horrifying thought of having to pull out.

Short of not being able to move at all, I was determined to get back into making some sort of forward motion, even if it meant walking for a while if that was possible.

It took a good minute of summoning up the courage to make a start at walking, the horrible feeling that it wouldn't be possible to make my legs move was making me sweat with fear. What would Phin Robinson, my physiotherapist advise I wonder?

The athletes who are passing me now are enquiring if I am OK, but knowing that there was nothing anyone could do; my answer was "Yes, I am just having a minute mate."" Lying sod" I am close to tears.

I am in deep pain, feeling tired, suddenly fatigued, mentally drained and sorry for myself; surely this is not the end. This is one of those classic moments with genuine reasons to give in rather than summon more effort than you feel you can muster at the time, and makes me think about one of my sayings of "being only as strong as the weakest moment."

Running was out of the question now as the pain kicked in severely at the first attempt. Walking was just bearable and the only way of making any progress. No option, I have to get under way with walking until the pain eases, hopefully before I lose too much time and put the challenge out of reach.

There are a number of regular RRR participants heading down the service road toward DHL, the parcel delivery company, and shouting their good wishes to me, lifting my spirits a good deal and making me determined to get as much speed as I possibly can muster.

Hopefully the painkillers will start to work soon and make it more comfortable and allow me to put even greater effort into keeping this challenge alive.

I will have to concentrate more than ever now and get my head in gear as a group of runners are looking for a clear path alongside the M1 motorway, bringing me out of my deep thoughts, it's easy for me to pull in to one side letting them through the narrow, tree-lined path, especially as one of the group is my good friend and Maltby Running Club mate, Phil Hague, who will be one of the group coming out to meet me on Sunday morning to run the last three mile with me from Old Denaby. We have a few moments' conversation and I make enquiries as to where the young runner was who he was guiding around the course. Phil commented that he had been holding Nils back; and commenting that Nils was too fast for him and had let him go off on his own. I later read in the Rotherham Advertiser that this young runner, Nils Hofmann, who was relatively new to running, and who had lost more than ten stone in weight over a short period of time, did in fact finish this race as the first Rotherham Harrier runner. Well done, young man, obviously a name to watch out for in the future. "See you in the morning," shouted Phil as he set off to catch the group of runners who were now well ahead and climbing over the stile leading into the field approaching Brinsworth Road. "Hope you're right, mate," I thought.

I am determined to complete this challenge no matter what and set off running under the motorway bridge heading for Green Lane, but didn't make the length of the bridge before having to stop again. The pain is too much to bear with the running and I decide to take another couple of Paracetamols with a piece of fruit cake before heading down the road at a brisk walk, which is proving reasonably pain free progress, but knowing full well that I am slowing down and won't make the times for my predicted checkpoint stops tonight at this rate.

My friends Louise and Joanna, who have come out from Treeton to meet me, have spotted me coming across the grassy field just beyond Sheffield Airport; they are shouting and waving to attract my attention. It's easy to spot the colourfully-clad girls coming towards me and it helps to take my mind off the problem with the hamstring. They are pleased that I am still making headway, having come out to accompany me to the next checkpoint, make a quick about turn just in front of me. After their greetings, we set off back towards Catcliffe. Luckily, they are both in front and unable to see my screwed up face as I make a feeble attempt at running across the tufted grassy field, but as we negotiate the steep steps down under the Sheffield Parkway carriageway bridge, it's back to walking, it's impossible to run anyway until we reach the houses and tarmac road which leads up to the site of the famous Orgreave Battle.

The notorious confrontation during the UK miners' strike between the police and the picketing National Union of Mineworkers, NUM, which took place on the June 18, 1984, at the British Steel Coking Plant at Orgreave, is as famous around these parts as any major battle throughout the years. The striking miners had organised a mass picket of the coking plant with the intention of blocking any transport movement in or out of the plant. MI5 had infiltrated the plans and deployed up to 8,000 police officers who were represented from over ten counties. The NUM striking miners were represented from across the country by up to 6,000 pickets. During the well-documented police baton charges, there were a large number of injuries on both sides, 51 miners and 72 police. The police made 93 arrests, which included the outspoken president Arthur Scargill.

I am just under half an hour behind time as the Treeton checkpoint comes into view over the railway bridge, but the pain is no worse than it has been for the last 20 minutes, which is reasonably encouraging as I reach the checkpoint table staffed by David Hayward, one of the Rotherham Harriers officials and a good friend of mine who has been stationed here for a good many of the RRR events, including during my last successful 100- mile run. As soon as he spots me, David responds with a cheer, then jumps up out of his chair and literally picks me off my feet with joy at seeing me make it this far, he is making a real fuss.

If the runners and spectators were not aware of my challenge beforehand, they certainly are now. There are also a good few runners and spectators from Maltby Running Club, together with many team members waiting for relay team athletes to come in, Ozy, Karen, Jim, Bob, and Barbara pass on their good luck messages. Sarah is waiting to set off on this next leg as one of our ladies' relay team.

I need to fuel up with water and bananas after drinking coffee at this busy checkpoint, it's a long way to the next one and with the slow speed and extra time of just being able to walk, I will need loads of food and drink.

Shouting my farewells to everyone, I set off after only a few minutes at the checkpoint, hoping to be able to pull back a bit of time that has been lost over the last few miles with having to walk. I feel stiff and sore around the lower part of my back, which kicks in big style almost before reaching the path above the car park; I am praying that once I get into my stride again it will ease off and hopefully soon.

Running again trying to get a feel for the injury along the tree-lined path above the car park, there's the familiar voice of Adele Morris asking me how I am as she easily catches up and runs alongside me for a few yards up to the green tubular pedestrian barriers, which restrict us down to single file. We share a few seconds before she heads off, leaving me just before the large stone boulders. By the time I have rounded and gone through the gap by the large stone blocks that lead on to the narrow path down to the lake, Adele is almost down on the lower path ready to cross the narrow steel bridge. Adele will be there to run the last three miles with me into the finish tomorrow morning, what a great group of friends I have.

This section of the RRR is one of the longest and generally requires plenty of concentration before reaching Harthill. The stiffness is loosening off at last as I reach the bottom of the path which takes my down to the level paths of Treeton Dyke and over the small steel bridge on to the wide muddy path between the trees.

Adele has disappeared, leaving me once again on my own, giving me time to reflect and analyse the situation. I have just managed a short distance of running but wishing I hadn't a few minutes later when the pain hits me again like an electric shock. It's a proper pain in the arse, as they say, and true as far as I am concerned. Oh God, I wish it would go away. It's beginning to feel more like a game of controlling the pain than anything else and leaves me wondering how much longer it could be before I am not able to deal with it.

The relay runners are coming past more frequently now, easy to spot by the speed they come whizzing through in an attempt to catch the runner in front.

It's a great team building event running for your club and trying to manage a personal best (PB) to reduce the lead of the competition, unless you're in the lead and winning, which is a position that I have never been in, but nonetheless the challenge of the event takes the best part of the day up and generally involves at least eight members per team. It's a great event for bringing athletes of all abilities and from all walks of life together. Most of these runners will know and will have raced against one another during the year at some event or other, often two or three times a month over distances from five through ten miles to half and even full marathons.

Walking for the best part of three hours has provided a small degree of comfort as I leave Rother Valley Country Park behind me. I don't seem to recall much of the time spent between the Dyke at Treeton and entrance to the park behind me which delivers me onto the A57. The last section has been so monotonous through the park and has provided trance-like hallucinations, where I had almost convinced myself that this was the last part of the challenge, oh dear does running make you lose all sense of reason. The upside to this is that for the last seven miles or so I had managed to blank out the pain.

I am thinking about running again but have decided to hold off until leaving Harthill, about seventy three miles for me, and my next checkpoint, which will soon be reached. Sure enough, before much longer I can see Harthill in the distance as I leave Woodall village behind, passing the horses to my left, ducking under and stepping over makeshift stiles on my way down the narrow midfield path towards the valley over this recently-ploughed field.

A distinctive path has been created by the hordes of athletes who have already passed through, making it a lot easier than last night's tough, heavy muddy uphill trek.

I am now almost an hour and half behind schedule and getting worse by the mile as Harthill checkpoint is reached. Have I calculated and built in enough time to be able to make up some of the lost time? I don't want to even think about it at this point. I need a positive attitude, otherwise there will be a big struggle when it comes to keeping going as my body starts to rebel and it will, I have no doubt, sooner or later, I feel.

"Must maintain the fuel intake and control the discipline," is my thoughts right now. It's of paramount importance to keeping going, let alone complete the whole distance, and I set about filling myself with bread and jam sandwiches, fruit cake, coffee and a couple of banana segments. I have just topped up my water bladder and added a few drops of electrolyte to keep the salt levels up, which should control any cramping.

Brian Harney has just arrived at the centre and will take a couple of injured athletes back to the college. One of the male runners has sensibly pulled out of the race because of a very swollen ankle; he's finding it difficult to stand, never mind walk or run, and looking in real pain. "At least I can move forward," I am thinking, and set off with more optimism than I came in with.

It's frustrating, but I am slowly coming to terms with only being able to walk, it's vitally important to maintain the enthusiasm to keeping going right now. I am feeling better than I could expect to feel with the pain that only comes after I have been running for a short distance, but it's imperative that I get the best speed I can out of my legs now and maintain it for as long as is necessary.

I have set off out of Harthill with a new frame of mind. If I can keep going, then at the worst I will probably have to rearrange the meet times for my support group, but there's plenty of time to make that decision if I have to.

The new wind turbines overlooking Harthill are in full swing, taking advantage of the wind coming over the hills. The thump, thump, thump of the propellers can be heard for miles, I expect, but other than the odd farm and, of course, Harthill village, it's probably not as big a problem as the local residents first feared, but then I don't have to live near them.

It's an effort, as I try running for a while but find it easier for a longer period than for some time, although I decide against any prolonged distance for the time being, settling for caution at this stage. I must slowly ease myself into the running and hopefully coax whatever the problem is into playing ball.

I am slowly catching a group of walkers who are just visible ahead of me on the horizon as the three large storage silos come into view. These guys are providing a target for me to catch and have created a bit of competition for me.

Squeezing through the opening in the hedgerow by the side of the pig farm, I can see that the earlier runners have padded down a pretty distinctive path down the long field which proved troublesome in the opposite direction during the night only a few hours ago.

My thoughts are drifting forward towards the latter part of tonight and how much easier it should be on my last leg if the rain holds off. God, I will need as much help from the terrain as I can get by the way things have panned out up to now.

The group are much less in front than I was expecting and as they reach the edge of the field, I am only 20 feet away.

It feels good to have had a sort of competition to work against, albeit with myself, but it's doing the trick and taking my mind off the fatigue which has starting to make itself felt.

The long field has been a drag, more solid underfoot, but the sticky mud has a strength-sapping, tiring effect over such a long distance. Back off and get some energy food inside while taking a sort of on the move but slowing down break. Mars Bars, Jelly Babies and a good mouthful of electrolyte water will soon kick in and provide the energy boost that I feel is much needed.

Before reaching Top Hill Farm, I have caught up with my new companions, who are aware that I am that "silly old bugger" who is attempting a ridiculous challenge. My fame has preceded me and is the topic of conversation for the next mile or so.

While getting my head into gear around what I know is achievable but what these guys feel is an impossible task for me, it's like renewing the faith in my own capabilities again. There's nothing like telling a pigheaded old sod like me that some task may be impossible for providing the booster that I need at this stage. Seventy-five miles has been accomplished and roughly marks the halfway point in the challenge as we cross the airfield at Netherthorpe. I am on my way home.

My energy and mental state are in gear again, it's time to say my goodbyes to my new sceptical friends, wishing that I could run away from them but lengthening my stride has the same satisfactory feeling and is creating an increasing gap between us as we head out over the fields leading into one of my favourite picturesque villages, Turner Wood.

I am looking forward to meeting my friends who have lived in this small hamlet for a good number of years. They are waiting on the far side of the canal over the small stone bridge and as the contours of the bridge allow, our heads become visible, I can hear the cheers from Diane and Mick and as they become more visible. I can feel the joy that good friends feel when you meet after a long period of not seeing one another.

I have spent many hours of training on the Chesterfield Canal over the years, running up and down through this beautiful hamlet; I had spent a fair amount of time with Roy, the old man and father of this lovely couple who have been providing free drinks for the athletes as a sort of unofficial drink station for a good few years. It's good to catch up with news and Diane mentioning seeing me on their cameras when I had run through during the night, after triggering off and activating the flood lights.

Memories of an extraordinary event usually come to mind whenever I reach this Hamlet. I had made friends with Roy the old man, who must be close to 80, and has this laid back approach to life that very few people have. He had invited me to come and have a look into an old greenhouse one afternoon while running up from Worksop on a training run. The old greenhouse was empty except for a pigeon, which was busy feeding on corn and walking about on the trodden-down soil floor. Roy had spotted this bird, which had been floating down the canal seemingly dead when he spotted some twitching movement, at first he thought it was possibly the fish nibbling at it. He scooped the bird out of the water, realising it was still alive but barely, he massaged the pigeon and wrapped it up in some old rags, leaving it in the greenhouse overnight where it was warm. Next morning, not really thinking that the bird would be alive, he went into the greenhouse to find that the pigeon was moving about. After a few days of feeding and watering the bird appeared to be making a remarkable recovery.

One afternoon after the bird had been fed; the pigeon did the most incredible thing. It flew, but in a circle, like following a Ferris wheel with a diameter of about four feet.

Round and round it would fly but it couldn't fly in a straight line. We christened the pigeon Loopy and joked about him having giving the bird the kiss of life. We reckon that the poor thing was brain damaged from the time in the water. I called in a couple of times over the next few months to see how Loopy was, but about two months later it seems that a fox had got into the greenhouse and poor Loopy had become part of the food chain. Incredible, unusual memories …

It's time for me to get under way again, but before leaving we discussed the Newman School and the special trike that I was hoping to raise money for. How ironic is it that Diane had lived just opposite the school in Whiston, on the outskirts of Rotherham, and had worked close to the school?

Before setting off, Diane stuffed a ten pound note into a pocket in the camel back, making it even more important that I manage to complete the challenge. Before finally getting underway I promised not to trigger the security system off on my last leg in about 12 hours or so. "No chance."

It's good to get running again, leaving my friends and the sceptical group who had caught up. I can feel tightness in my legs; the muscles have expanded and are trying to pop out. But it's just stiffness and soon eases as I walk across the railway lines, checking up and down the line and climb the stile, turning right along the narrow path alongside the relief dyke below.

The climb up to the woods above the edge of the golf course is not as demanding as I feared, providing me with the feeling of satisfaction that the food and drink intake has been adequate and is providing the energy that has kept me going so far.

Carlton-in-Lindrick Golf Course level ground provides a good reason to pick up a bit of speed and I decide that it's time to experiment with a run walk programme I had been thinking about until I reach Woodsetts Scout hut, the next checkpoint. I set off at a steady jog, hoping and praying that my hamstring will stand up to any prolonged running. But before reaching the underpass tunnel, I am in agony again and have to slow down to a walk. This is so frustrating, my fitness levels are fine, I am not particularly tired, I feel strong and full of energy, if only my hamstring was functioning as it should, it would be great.

---Renewing the mental positive attitude is priority number one right now and getting shot of this feeling of frustration that has had the upper hand for the last few hours. There's only nominal pain from the hamstring just under my right buttock when I am walking at a decent pace, but at least I am making progress, even though it's not as fast as I want to be travelling. Maybe this injustice may turn out to be a blessing in disguise and will leave me with enough reserves in the tank to make this challenge less traumatic than I expect before it's over. Time will tell, but I know that sooner or later I will have to make the decision of coming to terms with not making the predicted times for our meetings later tonight and in the early hours of Sunday morning. I reckon that I will be just over two hours behind schedule by the time I reach Woodsetts, which is my next checkpoint.

I have been using a small group of walkers as a target to catch since reaching the eastern side of the golf course and by the time we reach the road and the stiff hill climb away from the fairway, I have caught them up. It's less of a problem than I had anticipated maintaining the pace and passing the strung-out group before heading down the village to the crossroads.

Shortly after leaving the old church, I make the right turn down the drive towards our checkpoint at the local scout hut and the waiting marshals.

Less than 20 yards from the Scout hut, I am greeted by Mick and Sue Harvey, who are there to meet their son, Matt, one of the earlier athletes, and who had run the first mile with me at the start of my challenge. I manage to cadge a couple of Paracetamols from Sue just to top up my own stock in case.

The reception at this fourth checkpoint is, as usual, great, but with added enthusiasm this year from the knowledgeable officials, lady helpers and unexpectedly my good friend John Clarke is there to greet me as well. They are aware of what I am up to and make comments about my challenge and give compliments about me having reached Woodsetts. John is in fact waiting to accompany Paul Williams for a couple of checkpoints. Paul is my accountant and one of the group whom I put through their paces every week at our keep-fit class and is also a friend of John's. I have pencilled in an extended stay time for this stop to change socks, shoes, and shirt which will be in my carrier bag that has been brought over from the college. Provisions are made for anyone who wanted to use this service, by placing their bag of fresh clothes and shoes in the centre of the room at the college for transporting to this checkpoint.

It's always been my intentions to spend some time here and fuel up with soup, fruit cake and hot coffee, which would help with the energy release after this mid checkpoint. The atmosphere in the Scout hut is perfect for charging the mental larder and provides me with the supercharged boost I need. There's nothing like food, an almost complete change of clothes and footwear to round off that good feeling. But it's time to make my exit and after passing on my thanks for their excellent help once again I wave my farewells.

The sun is shining as I head out across the football pitch with about 20 miles to go for this middle 50, knowing that I will have a target of two walkers who had set off about five minutes ago to aim for.

This is all I need, with the sun on my back and the energised feeling from the feast of food in my stomach, which will soon start to kick in and generate the energy needed to get me to the next checkpoint.

I have decided that it's time to give running another try. The wide track behind the last house on the left in Woodsetts is relatively dry and flat, much better for running on than last night. So with fingers mentally crossed, it's time to break out into a steady jog and then shortly into a full blown run. I am half anticipating the pain will resurrect itself before putting much distance behind me.

Quarter of an hour on, still running, I am slowly catching the guys who had set off before me out of the Scout hut. There's just a hint of pain again but not quite as sharp as before and I decide just to run the next two or three hundred yards until catching the walkers, probably a wise decision at this stage of the challenge. Pulling up just before reaching the two Long Distance Walkers Association (LDWA) members, I am feeling pretty happy with that last mile and at last a bit of decent running, I felt fairly comfortable for most of it,
After about half a mile of walking with my two new companions, putting the world to rights, it's time to get underway again as we spot a lone walker about quarter of a mile away in the distance, which once again provides another target for me to catch before we reach the lakes at Langold.

How good is that, the last couple of miles of running have been easier than it has been over the past six or more hours and is providing me with optimistic thoughts of being able to making some time up rather than progressively losing the pace for a change?

I am soon passing a strung-out group of walkers just in time for me to correct the wrong directions that the leading member of the group has just taken, saving them all from going wrong in the woods at the back of Langold Lakes. This area is a bit of a warren with paths leading off in different directions and has been the cause for many runners over the years to have taken the wrong route, adding miles to the distance of this race.

Wow, I am still running and feeling strong rounding the lake on the tarmac road, passing the cafe across from the play area and down alongside the junior football pitch to my left before the short climb up to the park exit. Through the gates and locating the entrance to the woods with the RRR sign attached to the post, I make a right through the narrow steel pedestrian barriers and in to the darkness of the tree-lined path through the woods, with the slivers of sunlight filtering through on to the path in front of me.

Suddenly, my thoughts are with figuring out what food I may need for the next couple of miles after realising that I haven't eaten anything since leaving Woodsetts. It's a potential problem if I don't keep the energy levels on song and I give myself a severe mental telling off in the hope that I don't forget as the miles pass. A couple of energy gels and water should get into the system quickly and top me up. I must not let many miles go by without putting something back; it's so important, never mind important it's positively vital to the success of this challenge.

Safely out of the woods and a steady run across the grass path alongside the open fields. I have caught and passed a lone walker just before reaching the horses in the paddock to my right. The two horses, mother and daughter, if my memory serves me well, are showing only a mild interest in my activities as they stand munching on the short grass close by the fence.

I have left the lone walker behind, after exchanging a few words. A good gap has been created by the time I enter the small woods at the edge of the fencing

. Running on the recently-laid wide stone track to the main Dinnington road through the woods is comfortable and pain free for the first time in more than six hours.

By the time I have run down the long grit track leading into Firbeck, my watch reveals that I have pulled back about 15 minutes of the lost time and I decide that, with Maltby being only about four miles away, I will only stay at the Firbeck checkpoint long enough to book in and have a good drink.

Although I am now running for longer spells and feeling much better as the miles go by, I am conscious that this is not the time to become complacent and consider fitting some forced walking into the miles rather than trying to pull back too much of the lost time, too soon. I have got to use some sense and hopefully, as long as the hamstring problem doesn't fully resurrect itself, then I should be able to get back on target for my meetings tonight.

By walking up the hills, running the down hills and flats, the miles are now passing in a much more economical manner, leaving me feeling on top of the world again and, even though it's a big ask, I am becoming increasingly more optimistic and confident that my new plans will produce the goods as long as my legs hold out.

Twenty minutes to Maltby at this pace as I make my way past the old Roche Abbey ruins and through the kissing gate heading for the lower wood path, with the high limestone rock cliffs to my right.

After crossing Gypsy Lane, the River is visible below to my left as the muddy tree-lined path rises via a very steep, slippery path to the higher path under the arched brick railway bridge.

It's time to ring Maureen and let her know my estimated time of arrival at the Maltby checkpoint, which this year is set up just opposite our cottage on Church Lane.

This is my very familiar training area as I make my way towards Maltby, passing the Crags on my right.

Time is flying by in a sort of trance with the familiarity of the area until I reach the open field known locally as the meadow, which has aquired a quite distinctive trodden down path across the grass to the kissing gate at the far side of the field.

The old St Bartholomew's Church spire is visible from the new steel kissing gate and in less than a couple of minutes I am passing through the church lichen gate and being greeted by Maureen. We walk over to the table which has been set up outside the church hall and staffed by David Woodthorpe again, who is excited that I have made it this far, passing on his congratulations and telling me that I am looking good.

Once again, it's my intention to book in, have a quick drink after refilling my camel back and get away before my legs start to seize up. I will eat the remainder of my stored food before reaching the next and last checkpoint at Old Denaby. It's time to make my way up Church Lane after a minute with Maureen.

Travelling through Maltby soon passes and much before I realise after a good spell of running across open fields and down a fairly narrow raised path, the main Braithwell road appears up ahead. A few years ago, the route would have been left at the T-junction and head towards Ravenfield, keeping as close as possible to the grass verge, which does contain a fair risk of getting hit by fast moving cars, but by taking a right and then sharp left on the country lane which is now the new route into Micklebring, it does provide a greater degree of safety at this time in the afternoon and is especially beneficial in the evening for the slower athletes after dark.

It's time to ring through to Vonnie, a new friend of mine who has travelled up from Cobham in Surrey, the south side of London, to be there on the finish line tomorrow morning. I must let her know that I am behind schedule and will be at least an hour late before reaching the college. Vonnie had planned to travel up during the day and had booked into a hotel close to Dearne Valley College for Saturday night so that she could be there to greet me in the morning at the finish. We had also talked about her accompanying me for the first of the 12- mile sections on the last 50-mile leg. We had first met while taking part in the 100km London to Brighton 24-hour challenge a couple of months ago, when she, together with a small group of inexperienced athletes, needed my help and motivation to get them through the long night to the finish.

I am running well now and free of pain, do I attempt to pull as much time back as possible or continue with the run walk strategy which is working for me? After about a mile of considering my options, I make the decision to continue as I am and make sure that I arrive back at the Dearne Valley College checkpoint feeling as good as possible, and ready to take on the last 50 miles without feeling handicapped.

The disciplines of making correct decisions while running long distances often come into question during the relentless long miles when fatigue and sleep deprivation get a hold and cloud normal rational thoughts, and right now is exactly what I mean, it's just taken the best part of a mile to reach a fairly simple decision. But after more than six hours of almost mental depression, not knowing whether the hamstring will seize up totally and refuse to let me go on any further, I am now experiencing an almost opposite effect of being on a high, which is providing that feeling of invincibility; it probably needs a more disciplined period of control now to make sure that I don't make any rash decisions that might be detrimental to the later miles.

Micklebring village is now in the distance behind me as I head under the M18 motorway tunnel and shouting the usual echoing "Oggy, oggy, oggy" without the reply of "Oy, oy, oy" from any absent group of athletes, but it does add a bit of fun for me to the very serious moment anyway. Oh no, am I cracking up?

There is a small group ahead of me just passing out of sight through the bushes on the outskirts of the second open field as I emerge from the tunnel, can't see how many there are but they are providing me with my next target to aim for. After climbing over the rickety old stile off the dirt track heading south, I can get back into a steady run across the reasonably flat field before back into walking up the hill, ankle deep in mud, to the hedgerow and across the path that leads to Ravenfield on the horizon.

By the time I have reached the Firsby Hall Farm buildings in the valley bellow, I can hear the voices of the athletes ahead of me. Rounding the last building, the group who are now just ahead are hesitant about which direction to take and are about to go past the diagonal field path in the now fading light. Two have gone past but the remaining three have heard my raised voice providing instructions to take a left on the very narrow faint path which takes us all diagonally across the field and up to the ridge line on the horizon. I have decided to stay behind the group up the hill on the narrow path and make use of the steady walking by eating malt loaf sandwiches and fruit cake and consuming a good amount of electrolyte water to make sure the salt levels are maintained before reaching the high-level tree lined path on the horizon.

The watery path down to Hooton Roberts from the ridge above the farm is proving to be just as difficult as I had expected and frustratingly slow. It's probably a good thing

147

being held up by the new group, because it's now fairly dark through the boggy, tree-lined path and proving risky trying to hurry down this avenue of slippery, tree-rooted muddy river. It is much harder coming down, than in the opposite direction last night. Instead of taking any undue risks with the terrain, I make an extra effort to continue down the avenue in a slow, safe manner. There are one or two shouts of "Oh, shit!" and other words that indicate the ankle-deep mud has claimed another victim, until at last we are clear and able to shake and scrape the mud off our shoes on the wide grassy path below.

There's a constant stream of traffic coming up and down Doncaster Road as we wait to cross in safety. My thoughts have drifted back to last night, when I had said goodbye to Holly and Gary after the first six miles or so, God that seems like weeks away, but was in fact only about 24 hours ago.

After crossing the road, with head light activated in the fading light, I am on the move again and running pretty comfortably down the decent tarmac track. Soon after making a right turn, the track climbs up between the fields on a less than perfect broken tarmac drive; I reach the large tubular steel barrier across the ten-foot wide farm track. Rather than "limbo" under the barrier, I decide to climb the bank to my left and walk around the gate post; I am impressed by the much more sensible thinking, ha ha. I had given the group behind me directions to get to this point, hoping to save them going straight on at the right turn and adding miles to their own challenge.

I can see the lights coming from the valley below at the checkpoint tent on the outskirts of Old Denaby and remembering the problems that Holly and I were confronted with late yesterday afternoon climbing this boggy steep hill in front of me, I decide to take a cautious approach with the descent and avoid risk of slipping in the bog.

Torches from the guys below are casting a beam of light up the grassy field in front, illuminating the glow strips on my clothes and picking me out in the dark. Don't know how, but they have recognised me in the dark and shouts of "Come on!" and "Well done, Ray!" are coming from my friends at the gazebo tent at the bottom of the field. The cheering group, Ray and Jane Howarth, Ken Chapman, Teresa Elliot and Val Rivers, who are waiting at the bottom of the field, have made a sort of bridge on the mud, out of planks and old boards, making it far easier to walk through the gate, than when I struggled earlier with Holly on the makeshift boards.

I am being excitedly congratulated, hugged, slapped on the back and made to feel like a celebrity. They are making me feel as welcome as it's possible to feel, which provides a great lift. Food of every description is on offer on the well-lit table and a "Here, lad, take the weight of thy feet", from Ray, thrusting a white plastic chair at me. "Sorry, guys, daren't sit down, won't be able to get going again if I do." A couple of pieces of fruit cake and a white plastic cup of dilute orange refreshes my mouth and taste buds.

It's time to get under way again before my legs stiffen up. We have a group hug and good luck wishes from the gang for the last 50, before I leave, heading off down the road towards Old Denaby. "I'll ring through and let them know you're on your way," shouted one of my friends just before I disappeared round the bend by the entrance to the Manor Farm pub which is set back in its own grounds on the left.

Just three miles left to complete the second leg and my 100 miles. What a great feeling, it's easy to increase the pace as I make it down Ferry Boat Lane to the level crossings, over the railway lines and on to the towpath by the side of the weir. The towpath is providing a good flat surface to run on until reaching the concrete fish structure which marks the point to turn off the canal and on to the narrow river path which will take me to the railway underpass.

I must phone Vonnie to let them know how close I am to the college, she and her husband, Andrew, are already at the college waiting for me coming in. It looks as though I will be just under an hour and half behind time by the time I get there.

For the past mile or so, I have been trying to sort out in my mind how best to make up the time that has been lost while walking for the six hours earlier in the day. My thoughts are that if I don't have a shower or change my clothes or spend too long at the college resting, I will have a chance of reaching Helen, my first food stop on the last 50 miles at Droppingwell, pretty close to the estimated 11pm

Just one other problem to sort out; taking Vonnie with me could prove to be troublesome, especially through the tricky boggy sections in the dark, and at the pace in which I will have to be running over the first 12-ish miles. Should we experience a problem with slipping and the possibility of picking up an injury in these remote areas, then my challenge would greatly suffer or could be over. I must make her aware of my concern. I have to be bloody-minded about this problem and hope she totally understands my dilemma. I just daren't take the risk with the little or no time tolerance that I have in front of me now.

The college lights are providing a target on the horizon like a homing beacon as I leave the large playing field, just beyond the canal, and head for the cycle path which will take me into the event controlled area alongside the synthetic pitches to my left. The taped, cordoned-off area guides me freely away from any moving vehicles up the slope to finish and the end of the RRR 50-mile race. One hundred miles completed, 50 miles to go!

Vonnie and Andrew are in the entrance to the college hall and pass on their congratulations and enquire about how I am feeling now after 100 miles. Must keep on the move and, while steering them into the hall after a photo session in the doorway, I make her aware of my concerns about the first 12 miles. I could tell that she totally understood my concern, which alleviated my feelings of letting her down; I know how she was looking forward to spending those first few miles with me. It would have been great to have company at the start of the last 50, but I will need to pull out all stops to get back on target.

June Harney and her daughter, Jacky, together with Pat Rowbotham, are behind the makeshift counter as usual, preparing the food for the finishing athletes. Hot pie and peas are on the menu and soon a large portion with hot coffee is placed on the table in front of me. I had just about collapsed into a white plastic chair while attempting to lower myself down gracefully. Probably going to regret this.

Jacky is enquiring about how I am feeling, hovering over me, and no sooner had I finished the first pie, than she was ready to bring a second meat pie with peas and mint sauce. I am getting the VIP treatment from my friends, making this stop a very memorable time for me among so many others that will last a lifetime, however long I live.

There are many comments of good wishes from the finishing and resting finished athletes who are recuperating and getting ready for home.

There's also a good few signatures and good luck messages written on my Union Jack flag, which I am now stuffing into a pocket of my small rucksack, must remember to get it out for the run-in at the finish.

A fresh bladder of water with a couple of drops of electrolyte, new small sealable plastic bags of nuts and dried fruit, together with segments of Mars Bars and Jelly Babies, make up the rucksack in readiness for the last 50 miles.

Bloody hell, I can hardly stand up, let alone move.

# CHAPTER 8

## Fairground episode

Not long after Danny had left for Ireland, our local traditional fair arrived in Rotherham on its annual visit and the fairground people took up their usual position on the large waste ground opposite the central railway station on the fringe of the town centre.

For many years throughout my childhood and on into my teens, there would be a funfair held every November in the car park and waste land where the new police station and law courts are now built. The fair was known to everyone far and wide as The Stattis (Statutes) Fair. Like most other remnants of my youth in and around old Rotherham, this too is now gone and disappeared – it closed in 1978, but the history of fairs in Rotherham is pretty well documented; it is recorded that in the year 9 John (1207AD) a fair was granted at Rotherham to last for two days on the Vigil and Feast of St Edmund, November 15 and 16, which usually went to the nearest Friday of these dates. Fairs were, I reckon, a very different kettle of fish in the old days to the more modern funfair of the 1950s. Fairs were places then, where chapmen, colporteurs, journeymen, merchants and entertainers turned up to sell their wares. These could well be items that might not have been available in the town at any other time of the year, like books, inks, spices, pins and needles, ribbons, laces and fine cloth. In the boring world of the agricultural lifestyle around Rotherham at that time, the fairs were probably a great highlight of the year for many of the local workmen and women and, as recorded in journals, there was much boozing and rowdy, manly, boisterous bad behaviour. This was probably where the first boxing booths and bare knuckle fights originated.

Rotherham seems to have been a leading steel manufacturing town going back to the 16th century and has provided thousands of jobs year on year in steel manufacture and later mining throughout its early existence and following on more up to date became one of the leading industrial locations in the country. When the need for iron castings and steel smelting became of great revolutionary importance, Rotherham became an ideal location.

The Walker family became one of the leading names in iron and steel and were responsible for putting Rotherham on the map as one of the major sites for industries producing the famous Walker cannons from between the 1770s and the end of the Napoleonic Wars. Samuel and Aaron Walker had relocated from Grenoside, Sheffield, on September 29, 1740, when they leased a large section of land along the east side of the River Don at Holmes at a cost of about £8 per annum. Shortly afterwards, a large foundry was erected, in which all kinds of different metal casting were produced. The Marquis of Rockingham had obtained a large contract for the foundry to produce and supply cannons for the American War of Independence. The Walkers used water wheel power, which was fed from the river and waterways alongside their factories for turning and boring. By the 1780s, three-fifths of all metals cast at the Walker foundries were supplied to the government. HMS Victory was fitted out with 104 cannons, of which 28, 32- pounders, the same number of the 18- pounders and 23 of the 12- pounders were produced at the Walker factory in Rotherham and were mounted on the three decks. The logo of W&Co. is cast on the left trunnion, making it easily identifiable.

We – my brother Alan and some of my schoolmates – had met up shortly after dinner around the fairground and were attracted to a noisy commotion coming from the far side of the ground. Intrigued to find out what all the commotion was about, we worked our way around the fairground, following in the direction of the loud noise. We soon found ourselves standing in this growing crowd outside the fairly large, newly-erected tent as we watched the proceedings taking place up on the four- foot high wide stage.

As we reached the tent, I could see a variety of about eight different-sized men, who were all standing in different defiant boxing poses. Some of the boxers were just standing in a typical Lord Lonsdale-style pose, with others dancing about the stage in a show of intimidation and almost growling at the crowd in front of them. Some with colourful dressing gowns, others showing pumped-up flexed muscles in just vests and long shorts, but all were waiting for volunteers to come along and take up the challenge to fight them for a fee, the price tag varied in value from the heavyweight down to the lightweight.

Above the platform on which these boxers were standing was a colourful handwritten banner which gave the owner's name and the fact that this was a boxing booth, stating that all fights would be carried out to the Marquess of Queensberry Rules inset into a sign-written Lonsdale belt insignia which almost covered the length of the wooden sign attached to the tent.

I had heard about this distant long-standing ruling and from memory this code of boxing was generally accepted many years ago to provide a sportsmanlike set of rules for the noble art of boxing. It also provided the basic set of rules upon which modern boxing is based today. Further investigation reveals that they were named with this title because John Douglas, the 9th Marquess of Queensberry, had publicly endorsed this code of fair play. Although in reality the rules were not written up by the Marquess but were in fact put together and set out by a sportsman of some repute, John Graham Chambers, who was a distinguished wrester, rower and walker. The Queensberry Rules actually mentioned boxing gloves for the first time and were used to provide rules for both professional and amateur boxing matches, which went some way in separating the new gentlemanly style boxing, from the gruesome bare knuckle fighting of yesteryear with the less popular American Fair Play Rules, but they were mostly intended for amateur matches.

Generally these long-standing rules are:

To be a fair stand-up boxing match in a 24-foot ring or as near that size as practicable (12ft by 12ft) and no wrestling or hugging (clinching) allowed.

The rounds are to be of three minutes' duration, with one minute's rest time between rounds.

If either man falls through weakness or otherwise, he must get up unassisted, ten seconds to be allowed for him to do so, the other man meanwhile to return to his corner, and when the fallen man is on his legs the round is to be resumed and continued until the three minutes have expired.

If one man fails to come to the scratch in the ten seconds allowed, it shall be in the power of the referee to give his award in favour of the other man.

A man hanging on the ropes in a helpless state, with his toes off the ground, shall be considered down.

No seconds or any other person to be allowed in the ring during the rounds.

Should the contest be stopped by any unavoidable interference, the referee to name the time and place as soon as possible for finishing the contest; so that the match must be won and lost, unless the backers of both men agree to draw the stakes.

The gloves are to be fair-sized boxing gloves of the best quality and new. Should a glove burst or come off, it must be replaced to the referee's satisfaction.

A man on one knee is considered down and if struck whilst in this state, is entitled to the stakes.

"And this one I love." That no shoes or boots with spikes or springs be allowed.

The contests in all other respects are to be governed by the revised London Prize Ring Rules.

John Chambers was also a catalyst in the formation of the British Amateur Athletics, having founded the Amateur Athletics Club in 1866, and was present at the formation of the Amateur Athletics Association (AAA) in 1880. Chambers also rowed twice in the Boat Race for Cambridge in 1862 and 1863, losing both times, and coached six Light Blues crews in 1865-66, again defeats, and 1871-74 when Cambridge did put together four straight victories, including the first on the new sliding seats in 1873.

We took up our position towards the front of the growing crowd, but with a gap of about four feet or so from the stage front, which seemed like a sort of no go area, creating a sort of fear barrier with wild animals waiting to pounce. I felt that most of the quickly growing audience wouldn't dare stand any closer in case the foreboding gladiators standing around the stage would be able to reach out and grab hold of them like a predator taking hold of its victim, ha ha, that would have been so funny.

Each one of the posing fairground fighters was waiting to be announced and one by one the promoter with a loud bellowing voice introduced the entire group of fighters making them seem impregnable. All the fighters lining up from the heaviest to the lighter weight had colourful names like Battler Bill, Buster James, Destroyer Dan or Powerhouse Sam. You get the idea!

I do recall that we were all skint, as we stood there mesmerised by all the hype taking place around us, we had spent what bit of money we had come to the fair with, on the Waltzer, Helter Skelter and Bumper Cars. We had gathered here to watch this free theatre-like event taking place in front of us before heading off for home. So with not a penny left between the gang of us on this late Saturday afternoon, it would probably be about 3pm. Proper skint and as always hungry, we watched what was taking place for more than the best part of half an hour as all the fighters, one by one, were being matched up with local colliers and steelworkers, leaving only the last couple of fighters to be matched up with takers from the growing crowd.

It had been dawning on me over the last ten minutes or so, that if I were to take on the flyweight for the one pound ten shillings which was being offered to fight him, we would all be able to stay at the fair for some time with lots of money to spend. My thoughts turned to reality as the flyweight was being announced for the third time without any takers. I can well understand that there were no volunteers, because this man looked as though he had been hit by a bus, a proper bruiser. The bent nose and huge cauliflower ears were a dead giveaway that he would be easy to hit and would probably be a fighter who led with his nose rather than a boxer who would be able to control and dictate a fight. It was difficult to see just how tall he was, but from where I was standing I estimated that he would be about as tall as or not much taller than me.

With butterflies in my stomach and a feeling of sheer excitement in my body, I raised my hand high and shouted "I'll fight him!" This statement was greeted with a huge roar of laughter from the crowd. I was being totally ignored by the man on the stage, who seemed to be looking anywhere but in my direction. He continued to ask for takers for the last of his fighters, making me more determined to press home my enthusiasm to take on their last fighter. After waiting another minute or so I raised my hand again and shouted "I'll have him!" But this time he couldn't ignore me, as the chants from the crowd of "Let him have a go!" were being shouted with gusto. "How old are you son?" I was asked by the man with the loud bellowing voice, as he came closer to the edge of the stage. "Sixteen!" I shouted back. "Where do you work then?" I was asked. "Steelo's!" I shouted back with as much authority as I could summon up. Eleven thousand people worked at Steelo's, (Steel, Peech and Tozer) during this time and I figured that no-one would question that statement. At this point, the crowd really got at the back of me; even pushing me forward shouting "Let him have a go!" Leaving him without much choice, I felt, but to accept my offer to fight his one remaining fighter.

Alan asked me for a second time if I knew what I was doing, but without any real conviction. The thought of being able to stay at the fair with money in our pocket, I felt, was a big influence on his eventual encouragement of my challenge.

I was suddenly invited up to the stage, with a "Come on then," as he finally relented and agreed to let me take up my challenge. "Go on then, Ray, mek 'im havit", was the enthusiastic type of comment from my mates as I started to make my way to where I was being directed. Climbing an old handmade set of steps without any handrail, I made my way up to the right-hand side of the stage and was ushered over to stand next to my opponent, who was about the same size as Danny in height but less heavy.

As I walked over to stand to the side of my opponent he made an attempt to show his status as a hard man over me by growling like a wild animal. I felt a kind of excitement, knowing with a certain amount of trepidation that I was getting the chance of earning a few bob for us doing something that I loved.

I could see the ring inside the tent for the first time through the curtains at the back of the stage, which were flapping about in the breeze. The man with the loud voice announced all the volunteers' names to the crowd, all of whom were now roaring and cheering with gusto as each of the new challengers' names was shouted out.

We were then taken down to the back of the tent, past the slightly smaller than normal ring. I noticed that there were no seats, making it standing room only for the crowd.

We were steered through the back of the tent to a changing area, where almost immediately the first of the fighters was being gloved up ready to start the show. I could see through a gap in the drawn curtains that the crowd were gathering around the ring all trying to gain a good vantage position, I could just about make out most of the elevated ring.

"You are on third bout," I was told by a really scruffy-looking gypsy man. I had never seen a man with earrings before, except in pirate films.

My opponent was almost laid out in an easy chair in the sectioned-off area to the left of the fighters' portion of the tent, smoking a cigarette and looking as though he hadn't a care in the world.

After another few minutes of winding up the large crowd by the compère of the booth, to come inside for a bob (shilling) and support their local lads, "They are all going to need it!" he shouted out, to loud boos and jeers from the ever-growing crowd, and the booth filled up in record time.

My opponent was giving me really dirty looks from where he was sitting in the sectioned-off changing area, maybe disgusted that he was about to enter into the ring with a young boy. I was not going to be intimidated by this disfigured, I suspected ex-professional boxer. My analysis of him was that he had probably been a punch-bag for others to practise on by the look of his damaged face. I had no fear of him; maybe if it had been the boxer who had done the damage to him, then I would have to worry a bit. I felt confident that all the training I had been through with Danny would be more than I would need to be able to deal with this battered fairground fighter.

While giving my name to the compère, I had insisted that my mates and brother should be allowed into the tent for the show along with the droves of spectators who had paid to watch the eight or nine bouts of fighting, but I couldn't see them anywhere in the fast-filling booth.

The stories I had been told about gypsy people were leaving me without any trust at all with these fairground guys whilst looking for Alan and my mates who I couldn't see inside the tent. I found a way out of the back of our section of the tent through a flap. I knew it! My brothers and mates were standing to the side of the stairs on the outside of the tent and I shouted for them to come round to the back. We all entered through the back flap and through the changing room into the ringed area where they had the best view of the ring at the far side, within touching distance of the apron and close to the ropes. I felt a certain degree of comfort that my brother and mates were, well, just there, not that they could do anything if things went wrong, but they helped to alleviate the uncomfortable feelings that were creeping in.

The first fight of the afternoon due on was, I guessed about middleweight, and through the flap in our dressing area I could just about make out what was going on. I dragged a rickety old chair that my jacket was on to the flap of the inner tent, giving me a great viewpoint to see the entire proceedings as the two fighters came together into the centre of the ring to be announced to the crowd. "Our" fighter, with sleeves rolled up and trousers tucked into his socks, really did look the part, well muscled up and showing loads of confidence as he stood in the centre of the ring glaring at the fairground fighter and looking as though he would tear him apart. His mates and the crowd were all cheering and shouting abuse at his opponent as though they were out on the street. This should be good.

Round one was announced by a loud bell as the two fighters came towards one another in the centre of the ring. It

160

was evident that right from the start the challenger hadn't a clue about ring craft or boxing skills. With arms swinging like a windmill in a storm and wild attempts to knock out the fairground fighter as fast as possible, it looked as though this one would end up being a short fight.

The challenger's breathing soon became laboured and a major problem as his more skilful opponent took over and completely dominated the proceedings, picking him off with ease. Blood was oozing from a busted nose, covering the front of his shirt and rolled-up sleeves.

Our man was on the canvas twice from exerted swings that didn't connect and then again from a punch that did! The crowd was going wild at each attempt to connect with massive swings from the challenger! Definitely round one to the fairground fighter as the clunky bell sounded.

Oh dear, round two was much the same and didn't last more than a minute after another fruitless attempt by our man to knock the fairground fighter into another world with wild swings, the wind from which I could feel from where I was standing. Our man slowly sank to his knees, unable to get his breath from all the exertion he had put into the powerful swings. He just couldn't get up and was counted out.

The crowd was going wild, as the baddy triumphed over the goody (our guy). What an atmosphere. I had never heard this sort of mob-like noise before and as the strutting winner's hand was lifted up in a defiant triumphant pose, loud boos and jeers that had been increasingly created over the two rounds boomed out from the partisan crowd.

A quick departure from the ring by the fairground fighter was probably the best to save him getting mobbed; our man was much slower at exiting the ring.

Blood was all over the place as he held his head back and pinched his nose in an attempt to stem the flow. He was handed a small coloured piece of cloth which looked like an old piece of blanket by one of the fairground workers as he came through into the back of the tent. Our guy headed quickly for the outside flap to get some fresh air and, pulling out a pack of Woodbines, managed to light the cigarette with his shaking hands and take in deep drags, puffing out billows of smoke with a great sigh. Fresh air …

The unfamiliar smell from the animals that I suspect had been paraded through Rotherham town centre earlier on during the week to announce their arrival, wafted through the flap. Damp straw, camel and other exotic animal dung, don't make for a nose-clearing smell, well not for us town dwellers anyway.

The gloves had been put on to our second fighter by the dark-haired gypsy; our shirt-sleeved man who I guess would be about 30 years old had turned white-faced. Probably the sight of all that blood was giving our much heavier fighter second thoughts about entering the ring. I could see the fear in his eyes as he was being directed towards the flap and then as though he was being swallowed up, he climbed the steps into the ring to the cheering encouragement from his mates. This one-sided crowd would have helped to revive his courage I expect, but he still looked very nervous and a little white around the gills.

The two fighters were soon caught up in the razzmatazz of the announcement as their names were being bellowed out from the compère in an extended verbal manner and then cheers from the crowd drowned out the announcement as the two men were brought together in the middle of the ring to be told, I expect, the rules of the fight.

Round one and almost half a minute went by without anyone laying a glove on one another as the fighters cautiously moved around one another like caged animals. The crowd wanted none of this inactivity, as instructions were being shouted out for our man to attack. Well, maybe not quite as subtle as that, but "Cum on, get bloody stuck in!" or words to that effect are certainly some of the more printable instructions. All of a sudden they came together in a flurry of punches, but not really making contact. The announcer, who was now performing as referee, stopped the fight and gave some instructions to the two of them. I can only think that they were being told to throw punches at least. Once again, our man was breathing heavily at the end of the first round as he stood in his corner for the usual one minute. I do believe that our challengers, while all were fit-looking men and probably strong manual workers, were far from fit enough to perform for three three-minute rounds against opponents who were more used to fighting.

It was time for me to think about the strategy for my own bout. From what I could see, none of the fairground fighters was very fit, which should make it really easy for me to quickly control the fight without having to get involved in any inside mauling from my stronger-looking opponent. He wouldn't be expecting me to know how to box, so speed should wear him down and keeping him on the move with hard body punching would probably be the most effective way of keeping out of trouble, with my aim to shorten the fight to less than the three three-minute rounds that were planned. That's the basic plan I had in my mind, but I would always be ready to change tactics to suit the situation if it became necessary.

I had been paying attention to the two fighters in the ring and wondering if they were ever going to make a fight of it, when out of the corner of my eye I caught a glimpse of my opponent as he came swaggering over to me through the other flap, which was used as the dressing area for the fairground fighters. He tapped me on the shoulder and proceeded to tell me how he would take it easy on me for two rounds. He spoke deeply and in an intimidating manner, standing close and making himself taller than his normal height in an attempt to hover over me. His breath smelled of the cigarettes he had been smoking and, as I held my breath trying not to inhale any of his stale breath, he continued "We'll put on a show for the crowd and then you take the count and go down during the middle of the third round, I'll tell you when."

I was gobsmacked to say the least. I couldn't believe I had heard him right. This only happens in gangster films doesn't it? I was absolutely fuming and really taken aback. I was at a loss for words, not knowing how best to answer and deal with this thug's remarks. He must have taken my momentary silence as an agreement to the request and had turned away from where I was standing to have his gloves put on and laced up by the waiting gypsy mate.

I felt rooted to the spot, shocked and almost sick with the situation I had been put into. My mind was now in overdrive. How best do I deal with this situation? My very first thoughts are running wild in my head. I have a feeling of being vulnerable and in a different world to the one which I was used to. People have disappeared in gangster films for disobeying the baddy.

It's a no brainer; no-one was going to talk to me like that. I was well and truly fired up and having great difficulty restraining myself from running over to him and starting the fight there and then. Control was what I needed right then, as I walked slowly over, staring him fully in the eyes and delivering in the deepest voice I could muster "No chance mate, that's not going to happen." I walked slowly away, but keeping an eye on him all the time, and almost tripped over as I bumped into the last fighters as they walked through the flap into the changing area. I can best deal with this in the ring I thought, among the large crowd who would offer some sort of protection for me against this bullying situation.

The other gypsy had signalled me to remove the gloves from our second challenger who was sweating heavily and looked a little bruised around his forehead and eyes.

While putting the eight-ounce gloves on my fists, I wondered if there were any favouring problems with the gloves my opponent had on. It did seem strange to me that the fairground fighters had kept to a set and not allowed their opponents to have any choice, which was bringing back memories of the missing horsehair padding from the first set of gloves I had ever worn at the Red Lion Pub, leaving little padding to the knuckle part of the glove. I felt that they were probably capable of anything, which made me more determined to not let this fight dawdle on.

"Have I bitten off more than I can chew?" I thought, trying to control this sickening, lumpy feeling in my stomach. I have never had such a strong desire of wanting to hurt anyone and with as much venom as I feel right now.

I walked up the steps and climbed through the ropes to be greeted with the biggest cheers of the night from my brother, mates and the whole Rotherham crowd. My scar-faced opponent was already in the ring and deep in conversation with the booth owner, announcer, outside promoter and now referee. What a stark contrast in dress he was to the usually immaculately turned out officials I was used to. Our referee was dressed in boots, heavy dark green corduroy trousers, brown hacking jacket and cravat round his neck, topping it all off with a tilted-to-one-side brown trilby. I suspect my opponent was probably passing on my remarks about not playing ball with their arrangements.

The floor of the ring was made up of a mixture of odd-sized boards, the contours of which were visible through the heavily bloodstained light grey canvas. It felt quite bouncy towards the middle, which I had encountered while walking across to my corner. There was only one set of steps to get into and out of the ring, which meant that I had to walk fully across the canvas to my corner. Luckily I was wearing Woolworths pumps on my feet, a T-shirt and, apart from my trousers, I was far better kitted out than the heavy clothes and footwear that the previous two challengers had on.

This antiquated set-up was bringing back memories of a few years ago when I first started boxing at the Red Lion boxing club, but this time without the friendliness.

Before the proceedings began the ref walked over and almost spat out "Hope you know what you're doing, young man," turning away before I could get out my reply. But standing in the ring, "my world," I was slowly beginning to feel calm and in charge of my emotions again, soaking in the atmosphere of the local Rotherham crowd and ready to take on whatever I was going to be confronted with.

The ref had started making the announcement to the noisy crowd, I was introduced first but as Roy not Ray Matthews.

My group was shouting their encouragements, "Take him out, Ray" and "Give him one for me!" but while all the shouts of encouragement were coming, I never took my eyes off my much older opponent, during or even after the announcement and instructions from the ref, as I backed into my corner, all the time willing the time for the start of the fight to come quickly. I had blanked out the sound from the noisy crowd which was something that I had learnt to do with concentration as I focused on my opponent in front of me.

I didn't hear the bell sound off for the first round, but my natural instincts took over as my opponent made a move towards me. "This is it; let's go," I remember thinking. I was in my calm, familiar, controlled zone.

He came out of his corner in a rush to attack me and ended up going back just as fast. The shock on his face was worth a fortune to me as I counter-punched his swinging right Haymaker, which was meant to knock me out. The swing nearly took him off his feet as I sidestepped, making him miss by a mile; it looked almost comical from my position in the ring and then I hit him hard with a combination of three punches before he realised what had happened – it was easy. Wow, was it easy. I am not proud to say that I enjoyed toying with this man like a cat with a mouse for the remainder of the round.

Intimidating him was a guilty pleasure that I felt justified in doing. Every time he made a move to punch, which was pitifully slow and telegraphed, I beat him to it with one or more of mine sending him backwards, the partisan crowd raised the roof with almighty cheers. I could see the frustration in his face as he tried to corner and then make a grab for me in an attempt to tie me up, but my opponent was nowhere near fast enough. My speed and ring craft were far superior and more than he could cope with. Before much longer he was also having real problems with his breathing, as he stood almost bent double in an attempt to get air into his lungs at the end of the first round.

I could feel the presence of Danny as though he was there, encouraging and watching over me while stood in my corner at the end of the round.

I searched for my brother and mates and could see the joy in their faces.

Analysing the round in my mind and formulating my plan for the next round, I felt that it was evident that this man could take a hard punch to his face, which was something that I had realised early on in the round when he didn't go down or move much from one of the best right-handers I had ever delivered. If I wanted to get this one over and done with quickly, then my plan would need to be changed slightly and the new task would be to hammer him around his body for the coming round and take the air out of him as soon as possible. Avoiding him grabbing hold of me was also high on the priority list.

I recall Danny once telling me "Don't hang around, get it over with as quickly as you can, you don't get paid any extra money for working overtime in this game."

This small ring was something of a bonus for me; I could stand in the centre and be in range almost without having to move, making it impossible for him to move out of range of my punches. He didn't have a great deal of ring craft either and was finding it difficult to use the ropes to any advantage. "There's nowhere for you to hide mate," I was thinking.

The one minute rest between the rounds was extended, I guess, by at least a further half minute to help my opponent regain his breath. Even the noisy crowd was voicing its disapproval at the lengthy extension. Eventually the bell sounded for the restart.

Round two started out very differently for my opponent, he almost didn't move, just stood up from his stool, but stayed in his corner and waited for me to come to him.

It was so easy to fake a punch to his face and then connect with good solid punches to the body. "This is it, spot on, it's working." Almost right from the start of the second round I was able to connect with a combination of some heavy hooks to his body.

Surprisingly, he sank down on to his knees inside the first half minute of the round, clinging on to the middle rope. His shorts were touching the floor, making the image in front of me look very comical. He looked as though he had no legs in that kneeling position, his feet must be dangling outside the ring, making me want to laugh.

A very slow count of eight from the ref and he was back on his feet trying to grab hold as I came in again.

He was novice-like in covering and guarding against any more body hooks, dropping his elbows low in an attempt to soften the impact but leaving himself almost totally without any defence to the rest of him.

A big target had been presented and was now available for me to hit him around his face as he almost led with his forehead. I was at this stage only getting a token retaliation from him as he did his best to grab a hold and smother my punches or concentrated fully on attempting to block the relentless attacking combinations of punches.

Within another half a minute of pummelling his face and to save him any more punishment to his head, he switched his defences upwards and back to his head, leaving me with an opening for a cracking double left and right hook to the body again. The last right body hook wasn't really necessary; he was well on his way down to the canvas again before it connected. I almost hit him on the floor, having great difficulty diverting the last punch once it was on its way. I knew, no matter how long this count lasted, he wasn't going to get up for a while.

This time the crowd, in a chant-like manner, took up the count and in a more accurate ten seconds this time, they counted him out.

I had felt and heard the air leave his body with the second hook and the look of desperation on his face had provided me with a sort of satisfaction that justice had been delivered. "I have never felt like that ever again."

I was right in my assumption of his capabilities; he could take some punishment to his face, that was more than evident by the damage you could see, but he was not fit enough to absorb body shots.

I didn't acknowledge him as the decision was announced to the boisterous partisan crowd and would have felt less hostility towards both the referee and my wimp of an opponent if he had had the guts to come over and shake my hand or made some friendly gesture. My brother and mates were jumping about and shouting their approval of my resounding win.

"Where do I get my money from?" was the first question I asked as I took off the gloves to hand them over to the gypsy man who had been mostly involved with the challengers. "The first fighters will get paid in the interval. There's gonna be a break after this next fight," he said. "You won't be getting anything," I thought I heard him say, as he disappeared through the flap and out into the booth area.

What more could these ruthless thugs come up with? I found the second of our fighters was still outside puffing hard on a cigarette. "How'd tha go on, young 'un?" he asked. I realised that he hadn't moved from where he was standing and had probably smoked a full packet of Woodbines. "OK," I said. "Have you got paid out yet?" I asked him. "No, not yet, but I'm going to see him after this bout to get it. Why?" he asked, turning to face me, with smoke billowing from his mouth, nearly choking me in the process. "I have just been told they aren't gunna pay me". "They'd bloody well better; else they'll be in bother. Cum wi' me then, weal go see 'im together. Tha'll get thy money, lad, don't worry thysen." Although I felt somewhat better for the support from this new friend, I still had reservations about the outcome of getting paid.

A plan was hatching slowly in my mind, a bit confrontational, but I was sure it would work if necessary. My thoughts were that if they refused to pay, I would threaten to stand up in the ring or booth and shout out to everyone about not getting paid. My determination to get paid the money they owed me after all the hassle they had given me was making me shake with the anticipation of the possible confrontation that I felt would be coming. This was a totally new situation for me; I was not used to answering older people back or being disrespectful to my elders, which was making it difficult to even run the scenario through my mind. But the very thought of what they had hatched up was helping me to reach my decision on at least confronting, them, should it be necessary.

The end of the next bout and once again a resounding win for the fairground fighter brought the first half of the show to an end. It seems that our man had thrown the towel in, so to speak and needed help to get down from the ring to the dressing area. Once again, blood was spattered all over his shirt and trousers. He was helped into the chair I had been standing on.

Shortly after announcing that the interval would last for 15 minutes, the boss man came into the dressing area and proceeded to pay out the challengers. "What's this about young-un not getting paid then?" shouted out my new best mate. "Well, he's not getting same as your lot, he's only a lad." "Tha should be payin' him double for what he's just done. Get him paid, else theil be trouble mate," he said, putting his hand on my shoulder.

"Here," he said, as two red ten bob notes were almost thrown at me. "Ah tha alreyt with that?" my new-found friend asked. "Ye, that's alreyt," I said, just wanting to get out as fast as I could, "Reyt, then, if tha're 'appy."

"Where you learnt how to fight like that?" the boss man asked. I got the horrible feeling that I was being sidetracked so he could grab the money out of my hand. "At a gym," stuffing the ten bob notes into my pocket. "Fancy a job fighting with us for the rest of the week? Come down, stand in the crowd and take on our man, 7.30 tonight and then Monday night." The thought of earning all that money and not having to really work hard for it was giving me goose-bumps. "OK, I'll have a think about it," but deep down knowing I wouldn't be there. I didn't feel comfortable anywhere near this gangster. "Don't forget, then, see you before 7.30," he shouted as I turned and walked through the flap into the smoke-filled booth, signalling to Alan and my mates to go to the exit of the tent. Lifting the flap and leaving the crowd, I had no intentions of watching the rest of the show.

It looked as though the booth was on fire as the trapped cigarette smoke billowed out in a cloud-like plume from inside. I walked out to find the sky now very dark, the loud music from all the different rides and arcades merging into one noise, I was excited and bursting to tell all.

We stayed at the fair until almost 10 pm, having been on the Waltzer more times than I can remember. Alan had been sick midway through one of the deep spins; hot dogs were blamed, but not enough of an excuse to deny us any more rides. I went home the hero of the day, with some money in my pocket for the first time in my life.

The following Monday night, as I walked through the gym doors, I was confronted by Jacky, who had been waiting for me to arrive at the gym. He marched over towards me, grabbing hold of my jacket, and half dragged me down past the ring into the changing rooms, without saying a word to me. I was dragged passing a few bewildered, open-mouthed parents and spectators who were sitting on the chairs close to the changing rooms. What the hell was going on, I was thinking, but decided not to say a word as my feet almost didn't touch the floor before we entered the room.

He launched into me before I could ask what was wrong. I was given the biggest rollicking I had ever experienced in

172

my life. What the hell was I thinking about, fighting for money? At first I couldn't understand what the hell he was going on about and then it dawned on me about the fairground fight. "You bloody silly young bugger, half of Rotherham knows about your fight at the fairground. Do you realise that you have just put your boxing career in jeopardy? Your amateur fighting days could be well and truly over if word gets back to the ABA, you could well have ruined your amateur status." I was asked to explain the full story of what had happened.

I couldn't understand what all the fuss was about and certainly didn't believe that I had broken any of the rules of amateur boxing.

My explanation of the events of the afternoon was not enough to pacify Jacky and the severity of what I had done still didn't fill me with any sense of wrongdoing. My thoughts were that if I had accepted money for fighting in an amateur boxing ring, tournament or an amateur contest then I would probably be guilty, even though, if truth be known, I didn't fully understand about the rules of the ABA, or what all the fuss was about anyway. I had taken on the fight to be able to stay at the fair with my mates and brother, not just for me. I had spent time sparring with a professional without breaking the rules and couldn't see what the real difference was.

After a lengthy discussion about the rules and regulations of amateur boxing, it was agreed that I should lie low for a while, keep my mouth shut and not take part in any club tournaments for the time being. Maybe things would settle, hopefully the isolation we experienced up north at that time would work in my favour.

It was openly discussed and most people agreed that the boxing clubs from north of Watford, during my boxing career, were the poor relations of the ABA, especially in and around Yorkshire. Even though we had a good handful of British

Champions at the gym, not one of us had ever been selected to represent our country.

By the time I had gone over the fight and fully described the episode about the money, Jacky had mellowed slightly, even cracked a smile. It seems that the exaggerated rumours that were going around the town, and which had reached Jacky's ears, had been blown way out of all proportion, but it did make for a far bigger and better story than what had actually happened.

Too late to do any training by the time we had further discussed the gravity of my actions at the fair, so I left the gym for home, where I copped it again from my Dad as I entered the back door. This time my Dad had a smile on his face as he described to me the version from one of his workmates, who had been in the crowd during my episode at the fair. I never mentioned about the money problem, thinking that would add to the worrying my Mum had been going through. I made a promise for the second time that day to both Mum and Dad that I would never do anything like that again. "You are sending me to an early grave," was Mum's comment, which made me realise that she had been having bad thoughts about what could have gone wrong with my actions at the fair.

How close had I come to ruining my boxing career for thirty bob, how easy would it be to have been kicked out of the ABA and the end of my boxing? Even ignorance of the rules would not be accepted as an excuse for taking money.

Luck would be on my side in this instance. The ABA never did find out about my episode in the fairground booth, as far as I am aware. "Not like John Tarrant, the Ghost Runner."

# CHAPTER 9

## Venice Marathon

I have been asked many times, "Which is the best marathon that you have ever done?" Well, apart from the obvious London Marathon, which I believe is by far the best organised and spectator attended event in the world, and ranks as most people's best remembered, this is followed closely by New York. Both are brilliant for the logistics of the organisation of the huge number of athletes. My first marathon was in fact the London Marathon, which spoiled me for almost all the other big City Marathons, but the most unusual and therefore the one that stands out in my memory more than any other in the world has got to be the Venice Marathon.

So why do the Venice Marathon in the first place? Good question. Firstly, it's a marathon that was on my to-do list. It's run at a time of year when there is still a chance of catching some sun and provides an opportunity to have another holiday for Maureen and me. Secondly, I suppose part of the answer lies in my interest in the culture and history of this small but influential island which rises from the Venetian Lagoon, and which is partially protected from the open seas by the islands of Lido and Palestrina. I am reliably informed that Venice is slowly sinking, making this marathon a special one to do, before time runs out.

Venice is steeped in history and is closely associated with the exploits of Marco Polo, who was one of the most outstanding influences around the 13th century. Venice has always held an historical interest for me. The city is made up of a series of "Campi" – the typical Venetian squares – creating 118 little islands. These islands are interlinked by 354 bridges over the narrow canals. Almost every church, house and building is unique and is generally of great architectural interest.

Venice is literally built up from trees driven into the substructure, mud, which supports almost every building, somewhat like the modern structures of today, where to provide stability, it's necessary for the buildings to be supported on piles driven deep into the ground.

Travelling around Venice is wholly by foot or boat of some description, with of course the famous gondola being the traditional means of getting around and always on hand. The typical black gondola dates back centuries and is one of the main tourist attractions. More recently, the water buses have been brought into use and make frequent stops around the Venetian districts, almost like our local buses.

The holiday started with a water-bus transfer direct from the Marco Polo Airport to a landing stage close to our hotel in Arsenale. The small basic hotel we were staying at offers very little in entertainment and, other than a clean, bright room, was chosen because of its close proximity to the finish line of the marathon.

The 26th Venice Marathon, held on Sunday, October 23, 2011, started for me with a 5am rise and a breakfast which had been specially arranged to cater for the nine Italian athletes who were booked in the hotel to take part in the marathon, but the early breakfast was lacking in anything substantial which would convert to energy for the race.

Leaving the warmth of our hotel, we boarded the water bus that would take us up the Grand Canal to Piazzale Roma, the main water bus terminal. The water bus made frequent stops to pick up athletes along the way. By the time we reached the end of the line, the little flat-bottomed boat was packed with runners. Venice is a very cold place at this time of year if the wind is coming from the wrong direction, as I found out, and the journey up the Grand Canal was a lengthy cold affair with the wind and occasionally the spray from the sea, which would come pouring into the river buses' open doors, causing the athletes to huddle together for the majority of the half-hour journey.

Leaving the water bus at Piazzale Roma, I followed a stream of athletes who seemed to know where our next target was situated as we walked a few hundred yards underneath some warehouses to the land bus station and the waiting buses that would take us up to the start area some 20 miles inland in Italy. Queuing for these buses along with hundreds of athletes from around the globe reminded me of a sort of mini New York marathon and the queue of thousands of runners, all boarding the little yellow school buses in the city centre to be taken and dumped on Staten Island prior to the start of the race.

We were packed on to the reasonably comfortable buses like sardines in an attempt to avoid a longer wait than necessary and many of the athletes were asleep by the time we finally arrived at the starting area some two hours later.

After leaving the bus, I managed to get settled into a large open tented area to prepare for the race and take advantage of free warm drinks. By this time, the light was starting to filter over the walled area of a massive old house, which looked as if it had been converted into a museum on the outskirts of a village. It was time to get into our running gear and stack away the warm clothes we had travelled up in into our kit bags.

The sun was by then skimming the top of the large wall in front of me and it looked as if we were in for some decent weather, hopefully at least better than the day before, which had been rainy with swirling bitter winds, making the canals look more like the middle of the Atlantic Ocean than the normal calmer waters surrounding Venice.

9am and time to leave the warmth of the benched changing tent and walking at last towards the starting area among the growing group of athletes, where I managed to hand in my baggage at the waiting articulated lorries that would take our spare clothes to the finish. I was able to find my numbered baggage transport without any problem and didn't have long to wait before my bag had been safely deposited inside the container.

It's now just after ten past 9am and time to make my way down to my start area. I continued walking towards my penned area on the now closed-off road, together with a French runner who had struck up a conversation with me when he recognised the Union Jack on the back of my running vest. I had told him about the friendship we had formed when my local running club had offered to host a group of runners from Saint-Quentin in France and what a great experience we had had on a return trip hosted by them a year later. The Saint-Quentin runners had become great friends, we contact one another quite frequently, "Wouldn't it be better if everyone in the world spoke English?" only kidding, that's the great part of these foreign races, the challenge and great fun involved in making yourself understood. Even though it seems that everyone does speak English anyway.

My predicted timed pen area, number five, was towards the back of the line of starters. I said farewell to my French colleague who was entering into the second waiting area and obviously a good runner at a less than three hour predicted pen. I must have walked for a good five minutes before reaching and entering my own designated start pen. The race was due to start at 9.29. What a strange time!

It wasn't long before a friendly, familiar voice asked me if I was from Maltby near Rotherham. Definitely a north eastern accent as he introduced himself, "Hi Ray I'm Ian." We soon struck up a conversation and discussed how we were always meeting Brits no matter where we entered races. There seemed to be someone from England no matter what start line you stood on and the Union Jack on the back of my running vest always gave my nationality away, providing a good starter for any conversation. Our predicted times were about the same and for that reason we were both in the same pen. I had also been talking to another British runner in the very familiar blue running vest of the 100 marathon club. I would have a couple of running mates alongside for a while. The 100 marathon runner lived fairly close to me; we had met during the Two Bridges ultra race in Scotland I believe, or some other long distance race, but definitely in the UK.

I heard the bang for the start of the race, but like most of these events and long after the race has started, the runners towards the back don't even move for a good few minutes, but eventually we are on the move and walking towards the start line then at last it's into a trot, back to walking and then just before reaching the start line some nine minutes later we were up to our running pace, activating my watch as I cross over the line on the road beneath the large billowing, blow-up structure. We were soon into steady running and setting up the pace that would hopefully take me through to the finish at my predicted time.

The warm sun has just risen above the trees, casting a silhouetted reflection of bright running gear along the river to our right which will be with us for a good 15 miles according to the race map. It's now time to concentrate on my own efforts and not get caught up in any other athlete's pace; my plan is to finish just inside five hours and maintaining my own steady pace is the key to achieving my goal.

Mile after mile there is the winding snake of colourfully-clad athletes all keeping up the relentless pounding on the tarmac road in front of me and the mental timing clock is working, clipping target times at each mile and kilometre board as we head for the finish. I could still see my 100 marathon club mate who had slowly moved ahead of me, but Ian, the Geordie guy, had disappeared; we had probably parted company at one of the drinks stations.

I am on my own now as the half marathon sign is reached, looking at my watch reveals that I am bang on target at two hours twenty-five minutes and feeling pretty good anticipating that I will shortly be reaching Parco San Galliano and expecting that the five kilometre long bridge leading into Venice is not too far away and my next target at about 32 kilometres, after running through a large park complex where the Expo for the event had been held for a couple of days previously and where we had collected our race numbers, T-shirts and goody bags.

Heading across this never-ending bridge, which is the link between the mainland of Italy and Venice, it is a soul destroying straight long road, with a middle that never seems to come.

My pace has dropped and I need to dig in, but I am running out of energy and time is disappearing fast at this late stage. I am unable to maintain the pace and come to terms with the fact that a week ago I had been involved in a 50-mile trail race and no amount of pushing was going to see me achieve my target now.

It's decided: enjoy the rest of the run into Venice and get as close as is reasonably comfortable to the five hours. In the last five kilometres, the runners have to take into account 13 bridges as we head into Venice. These bridges would normally represent a course equal to any full obstacle race, but the organisers have erected wooden ramps for the runners to cross over, they are certainly easier to negotiate but very bouncy and strange to run over at this stage into the race with fatigued legs.

The link from the mainland into Venice has been made by a sort of newly-erected Bailey Bridge, which crosses over the Grand Canal and takes runners into and around the packed-out- with-spectators St Mark's Square.

Thank God we don't have to run over the entire 354 bridges which there are in Venice.

New to this year's race is the introduction of the Italian School of Rescue Dogs, who are strategically placed on the route alongside the canal banks as we enter the Venetian canals. These dogs are ready to dive into action should any wobbly-legged athlete end up in the canal. As far as I am aware these dogs, which to be honest all looked bored to death as I passed them, were not needed. Contrary to popular belief and comments suggesting that I can run on water, well, I didn't feel like putting that theory to the test, not even to entertain the dogs.

Counting off the bridges now with the finish line almost in sight, the crowds are large and very noisy, even shouting and at times screaming to get more speed from the weary athletes as we run around a cordoned-off St Mark's Square. Three bridges to go, two bridges to go and then coming over the last bridge, the finish area is in full view with only about 200 yards to the finish line.

I can hear a familiar voice shouting and recognise Maureen, who has spotted me running down the last make-shift bridge. She has her camera ready taking photographs as I come past her and on to the finish line, with a very loud We

Will Rock You bellowing out from the sound system and the DJ enthusiastically encouraging the weary athletes to sprint through the last few yards.

It's over as I stop my watch at 5.09.27, just outside what I wanted but I am delighted and more than happy with my performance.

The usual process of handing in the race chip, having a medal placed around my neck and then moving down the avenue of the tented area, picking up a goody bag full of food and water, and then funnelling out to pick up my luggage bag which had been placed on the baggage vehicle at the start, all in all takes up about ten minutes.

It's another one over and one that will last in my memory. It's time to locate Maureen and make our way back to our hotel for a well-earned shower, a change of clothes and out for a meal at one of the many restaurants along the Grand Canal Boulevard. We sit for a while with a coffee watching the last of the runners coming in; I will treat myself to a well-deserved pint later. And, believe me, I did, together with a burger special at the Hard Rock Cafe overlooking the gondola pick up area in a sort of bowl alongside a landing deck.

While waiting for our flight back to England, we met up with Ian, my Geordie running mate from the marathon, and his wife, who were sitting in the airport departure lounge waiting for a flight back to Newcastle, and with loads of time to spare we struck up a conversation about, of all things, running. Ha, ha.

Ian Hopper, it turns out, is a dedicated Investor in People and a very interesting my sort of guy who is passionate about providing outdoor activities for adults and children alike. He was originally a geography teacher at a high school, then head of geography and is now running his own family business, Pinpoint Adventure. Ian, who had originally lived in a small mining village north of Newcastle, has spent most of his life in an idyllic small hamlet in the North Pennines surrounded by amazing countryside which provides a wonderful mix of fells, woods, paths and the old Haltwhistle to Alston railway line, brilliant walking and running territory. What more could anyone ask for?

I can feel the passion and enthusiasm bursting out as Ian, who is one of a small number of UK-based qualified International Mountain Leaders, describes his experiences taking school groups on to mountains all over the UK, even including visiting such places as the Alps and trekking in faraway lands such as Tanzania and Ecuador.

His easy manner and passionate enthusiasm for a wide diversity of outdoor activities including Forest Schools and bush craft, underground cave exploration and even snow shoeing in the winter, while working alongside and in partnership with the National Trust, surely mean that Ian and Pinpoint Adventure will always be in big demand throughout the coming years.

There can surely be nothing better in life than being able to pass on and teach the values of discipline, respect, commitment and instilling passion using outdoor activities to willing and open-minded kids, at the same time working in some truly awesome locations. How can you beat taking a group of adults or youngsters through one of the old lead mines in the Alston area, investigating the geology and engineering remains and being able to empathise with the 19th century working conditions? Or building shelters and sleeping rough on a bush craft weekend in fantastic woodland in the Upper Allen Valley? Or leading a group snowshoeing, north of Hadrian's Wall, in deep snow with dramatic scenery all around? Or, maybe best of all, watching primary school children grind wheat, make bread dough, start their own fire using traditional methods and then bake their own bread?

Spending time with children, I believe, is more important than spending money on them. What a fantastic way of life and what a great way of providing a living.

Ian, as I am sure he realises, is in a position of immense trust; I am confident that his influence and teachings will shape and mould young minds. Academic education is one thing but the education in life skills for open-minded children is equally important and will bring out their individual characters by providing the knowledge and disciplines that will always be a reference they can draw upon and use to take each person through life. As with my early coaches, Ian will always be a source of inspiration when most needed, even though he may never know when or in what circumstances.

We have kept in touch since Venice and it was great to meet up with Ian a few months ago in June 2013 for a meal at the King's Arms pub in the village of Shap on the outskirts of the Lake District, Cumbria, during our 192-mile Coast to Coast run. The famous Alfred Wainwright route, which travels across country from St Bees on the west coast of England just above Liverpool to Robin Hood's Bay on the east coast, passes through some of the most beautiful scenery England has to offer.

We shared a good evening meal together and were able to introduce Vonnie, my companion for this long distance challenge. We put the world to rights for the best part of an hour, but because of business commitments, Ian had to leave before too long, with us both promising each other that we would have a get-together on a walking or running event in the near future.

# CHAPTER 10

## Blind Veterans 100km London to Brighton 24 hour challenge

Sometime during January, after discussing the event with the organisers at the Brighton HQ and suggesting offering my services to one of the blind ex-service men or women who were taking on this challenge, the organisers of the event suggested that there would be a member of the Blind Veterans who could probably benefit from my help and they would make enquiries to him about getting in touch.

Kerry Levins, a blind ex-army officer, made contact with me a few days later and, after a short conversation about his training and training partner, he suggested that we could become a team and said that he would be happy for me to help and accompany them. Darren, his sighted training partner, was doing a great job by the sounds of what they were up to with the mileage they had been getting in on their training sessions. My thoughts were that I could help to take some of the pressure off Darren and make the challenge less stressful for them both, if they didn't have to be worrying about the navigational side of the event.

Just the thought of what I had agreed wholeheartedly to do brings goose-pimples to the back of my neck, the realism kicks in from time to time and gets more frequent as time draws ever closer to the mammoth task of being partially responsible for the welfare of another person for an estimated time of between 20 and 24 hours. I would be entering into the realms of either stupidity or madness, because I really didn't know what I was about to take on or what the experience would be like. This thought brings me down to earth with a thump. Just walking blindfolded around a familiar place within my home never mind the daunting task of being partly responsible for the safe passage of a blind athlete over the 100km distance, full of every obstacle that nature can provide, is more than I can get my head around at this stage. Maybe once I have met the ex-serviceman and his sighted guide and the image I had formed in my mind has materialised then I would be able to settle into the challenge in front of us.

I was due to be interviewed by Rony Robinson during his BBC Radio Sheffield show, on the morning before the event. The show had been transferred to the Ponds Forge swimming complex for the day. I discovered during our live telephone link that Kerry Levins, the only blind participant in this year's 100km challenge, was undergoing treatment on his physiotherapist's table as we talked about the challenge on air. From what was coming out of our conversation, I felt that our challenge would probably turn out to be an eventful one before the event had reached its conclusion.

Leaving Rony and the Radio Sheffield Shoreham Street car park in Sheffield, I headed out to Doncaster to board the 16.45 train to King's Cross, London, with some new friends whom I had met at a Blind Veterans UK fund-raising evening near Doncaster. We were all travelling down for the event on the same train and staying overnight in the same hotel close to the start. I had many a worrying thought on my way down to London about the injuries which Kerry was being treated for, which he had received post his eyesight problems. I learned later that Kerry had smashed into a Rolls Royce while riding his bike, the car belonged to Lord Carrington, oh, bloody hell. If you're going to crash into a car do it right and pick on a Rolls, but not just any Rolls, pick one that belongs to a lord. Kerry doesn't do things by half, it seems.

I was unsure about the protocol so to speak, with regard to Pedro, his guide dog. It seems that, while the Labrador is a very adorable animal where petting and making a fuss would be so natural, when he has the harness attached, he is working and this is not a good time to distract the dog.

On Saturday, June 9, the morning of the event, we travelled to the events centre by sharing a taxi from the hotel we had stayed the night in and met Kerry and Darren for the first time. Kerry was easy to spot, Pedro his dog was a good giveaway. I introduced myself and, right from the start as Kerry introduced Darren Murphy, his training partner and guide, we hit it off and confirmed ourselves as a team to the event organisers and made them aware that we wouldn't need any help from the official guides. There was plenty of time in front of us to get to know one another better.

The course had been described as being extremely difficult by the officials, because the weather had been stormy leading up to the start that day.

We set off at 10.20 towards the River Thames towpath and encountered our first obstacle within the first three miles. A large fallen tree, which had blown over during the storm, was blocking our way. Pedro had to be lifted over and some of the branches removed from the tree to allow Kerry to get under the main branches.

I was slowly coming to realise the way in which Kerry reacted to Pedro's moves and was politely scolded when I had distracted his attention by walking alongside Pedro, more or less sandwiching him between the both of us, which restricts his movements and gives less room for the dog to steer Kerry. Pedro would have undergone his training from being a pup to work on the left side of his handler and with me becoming an obstacle he would find it difficult to steer Kerry away from any other obstacle. On one occasion, a loose dog came running and barking at Pedro, Kerry's verbal response to the owner was venomous and it's easy to see why, because the dog is Kerry's eyes and will have had precious time spent training him to the standards required to be of great help to his blind owner.

Kerry's sighted guide and training partner Darren is a friendly and very likeable guy, easy to get on with and making the three of us a very compatible team. The banter between the two ex-schoolmates created an easy atmosphere. Kerry had attended Sandhurst, the military officer training college. Darren was probably the rebel of the pair. I think that the chalk and cheese difference between them works well. Kerry being the blunt, no nonsense, ex-army officer used to issuing orders and probably getting his own way, while Darren is the estate agent with the patter of a car salesman who has his own way of dealing with and defusing Kerry's demands.

The bulk of the challengers were well ahead of us coming into our first checkpoint, but some were experiencing problems with setting off far too fast and suffering from blisters already.

The event organisers had provided a number of guides to assist the athletes who had expressed a need for help to navigate throughout the challenge; I get the feeling that these groups, mainly women, were, it seems, new to this sort of distance and by the time we reached the second checkpoint, we had passed many of these athletes.

Reaching Oak Park Cafe at checkpoint three, arrangements had been made to drop off Pedro, who was showing signs of tiredness in the heat of the afternoon. We fuelled up with food and drink and set off for our next checkpoint and immediately Darren took over, with an uninterrupted dialogue of descriptive guidance of the terrain in front of us for Kerry.

Darren, with an unselfish almost telepathic performance in which hours of training had brought them together, was providing Kerry with step by step instructions of where to put his feet for the coming terrain, uncannily avoiding obstacles, Darren had the ability to filter and react to the instructions almost as they were being relayed. It was awesome to watch the pair of them work together. I felt slightly useless at this point, but knowing my time would come during the night, when navigation and an extra pair of eyes to pick out the dangers would be greatly needed.

By the next checkpoint four, Godstone Village Hall, and now mid-afternoon, we were informed that a large group of athletes, together with some of the event guides, had pulled out of the event, mostly showing signs of problems with blistered feet. We were joined by a couple of young women during the next few miles who were in need of company and encouragement.

Kerry is starting to struggle with his hamstring over the next miles as we head out towards late evening and our fifth checkpoint, where we were met by his physiotherapist who had travelled for quite some time to get to the Felbridge Village Hall and was waiting as we arrived around 12.30am. Work started in earnest to get Kerry back into a state of being able to carry on and at the same time the BVUK nurse who deserved a medal for all her efforts, was well and truly occupied sorting out blistered feet. My help did ease the queues slightly while I was waiting for Kerry.

Off we went at last, leaving the warmth of the hall, and heading out to the sixth and next drinks station; this leg soon became a very demanding section as almost immediately we encountered severe ground conditions, ankle-deep mud and great problems for Kerry as we were unable to predict the troublesome, submerged rocks. New swear words were being shouted out as Kerry on a few occasions came sailing past headlong into the mud.

Upon reaching our next checkpoint at Sharpthorpe Lions Club, a distance of 67 km, an emotional Kerry called it a day, unable to carry on.

I was thinking that if Darren was feeling like pulling out with his mate then I would get underway and make some time up with running, I was feeling comfortable at this stage and would have been quite happy to get under way on my own, but Kerry's wishes were that his training partner, Darren, and I carry on and make it through to the finish. Darren was happy to continue after a call had been made for Kerry's wife to pick him up; the time was now about 3.30am.

Setting off and wishing Kerry well, I soon realised that our group had increased to about eight as we made our way through the night towards Gatwick Airport before turning east and on to the South Downs. I was beginning to feel more and more responsible for our party of inexperienced mixed ability athletes, taking on the lead and having to stop from time to time to regroup as one by one they showed signs of fatigue and pain from damaged feet. All were experiencing pain from blisters. I was now on a mission to get our newly-formed group through to the finish line.

Dawn provided a spectacular scene as the sun broke through the mist alongside a large lake just before Scaynes Hill Millennium Centre, checkpoint seven, and bringing a welcome relief from the dark and searching for the chemical light sticks during the night with our little scouting group, who had performed well as a group, making it easier than map reading and orienteering in the pitch black of the night.

Severe blisters were causing more and more problems with the majority of our group and the pace suffered, but I was more than determined to see them conquer the pain, especially after I had been informed that Vonnie, one of the young women, had only three weeks before been admitted to hospital to have an emergency operation to have her appendix removed – but the pain from her pulling stitches was not going to stop her.

Sheer determination and a bit of encouragement from me was showing results as we continued to make steady progress, although I felt that a bit of reverse psychology would be beneficial during this period. My thoughts were that I would not answer their questions about what I had done and what my capabilities were, so I either played these down or didn't answer, changing the subject when necessary. I wanted them to feel that if this doddering old man could keep going, then they wouldn't stop either. We had picked up a couple of young men just before dawn, but I wasn't surprised to see them withdraw from the challenge at the penultimate checkpoint, at Plumpton College.

The rain was lashing down like stair rods now as we continued up and over the steep range of hills on our way towards Brighton.

With just less than half a mile to the finish, I heard a cry from one of the young ladies, Jo, who had come to a full stop, declaring that she felt as though her right foot had just exploded. I helped her to sit down on the roadside and carefully removed her shoe and sock, which revealed that her blister plasters had become attached to her sock and they were pulling the blisters and causing much of the pain. One of the blisters had exploded and, together with the blood weeping through her sock, it looked a proper mess. The relief on her face as I peeled her sock off her blistered foot was brilliant; discarding her sock, she slowly fed her right foot into her shoe and stood up with relief on her face.

We set off again on our last climb, regrouping just five feet from the finish line. Linking arms and spreading out my Union Jack above us, we all ran through the finish line together as a team of determined athletes in a time of about 30 hours.

I would like to pay my tribute to Kerry and his sheer determination to have reached the 67km point under extremely difficult conditions and really against all odds. The unselfish and mentally draining ongoing dialogue of instructions to Kerry for the best part of the challenge delivered by Darren, and then to continue with the rest of the determined group of men and women to the finish, deserves the highest accolade. To Jo, Vonnie, Bernadette, Jane and Rory, we became members of a team of mixed abilities, with a passion to complete the challenge at any cost. "You didn't give in," but worked together as a group to make dreams come true.

If I had to choose a team to take on a difficult task, or challenge, I am confident that I could now rely on this small group to conquer their fears and see it through to the end. They have all learned something special about themselves that will last a lifetime. We have kept in touch and often contact one another.

My request for the group to express their feelings, and thoughts during the challenge has been passed on to me and is documented at the end of the book.

# CHAPTER 11

## The Liverpool episode

About a month after Danny had left for home in Ireland, we, the Phoenix Boxing Club, were invited to compete at a boxing tournament in Liverpool; our club had never competed there or been invited before. I don't actually recall the venue, but I do remember that it was one of the largest halls and the biggest crowds I had ever seen.

The decision had been made to stay overnight to save the long journey home through the early hours of the morning, because of the distance we would have to travel and the time the event would finish. The team had been booked into a rather grand hotel close to the centre of the city.

Liverpool seemed to be about as far away as could be without going to another country, which created a good amount of excitement in the gym for those of us who had been matched up with opponents.

Jacky and I were scrutinising my Liverpudlian opponent's impressive CV. He held the Northern Counties Schoolboy title at my new fighting weight of about seven and a half stone. He had had fewer fights than me, at 38, but had won quite a few lately on technical knockouts (TKO). It was pointed out that I would possibly have to fight him, if I was successful in winning the coming Yorkshire Schoolboy Championships, which progresses through to the Northern

Counties. Sooner or later our paths would have to cross. He must be good, to have got so many wins inside the distance in his impressive career.

In those early days of matching up fighters, boxing club managers had to almost totally rely on the opposition clubs providing true and accurate descriptions of their club fighters whom they were trying to match up, this was the only way to enable them to put an event together. I suspect that the truth was not always accurately forthcoming, leading to many a mismatch.

This was going to be a tough opponent I was thinking, as his details were being read out to me, fuelling my determination to maintain my training programme, with the knowledge that three rounds rather than the five I was fit enough to maintain would be much easier to manage. Even though I was confident, I wasn't going to be complacent about this one either, but I was looking forward to testing out my new skills.

I was enjoying school more at this time in my life, probably my most productive, at a time when I felt able to take on almost anything that was put in front of me, but with regard to my education, probably channelling my energies in the wrong direction to what my parents wanted or expected of me. It did seem to me that I would inevitably take up a sport of some description for making my living; I also felt that my teachers believed the same. I represented and captained the school at all the team and individual competitive sports. I loved football and cricket, throwing myself wholeheartedly into physical education, and of course boxing was my life, but the academic side of my education was carried out with just enough enthusiasm to get me through.

On the Saturday morning of our trip to Liverpool, our normal big modern shining coach was ready and waiting outside the gym at Ickles as I got off the number 69 bus from

Rotherham. Jacky was waiting with Jack Cox, our club manager, today was one of the rare occasions when he was coming with us. Probably the free weekend trip, I heard one of the senior fighters comment.

My name was ticked off the list as I settled down on a nearside seat towards the back of the luxurious bus, spreading out with as much room as I wanted.

The bus was now about half full, but fully loaded with the fighters and officials, together with a couple of regular spectators who gave their time to help wherever they were needed, I expect they would be called "roadies" today, about 20 of us in total.

We set off for what would be the longest coach journey I had ever taken during my time at the gym, stopping off for a break after about three hours of travelling at a large transport cafe somewhere in the middle of nowhere for tea and a bacon butty, which the club paid for. I don't recall ever having to pay for anything that involved the Steel, Peech and Tozer boxing club. We were a very privileged team of fighters, who were fully subsidised by the Social Services Department of Steel Peech and Tozer, representing the more than 11,000-strong workforce of the company. As a club, we wanted for nothing and had nothing but the best, but we were expected to maintain the club's high standards that we were credited with on the amateur boxing circuit, a far cry from my first boxing club in All Saints' Square in Rotherham town centre.

I can well remember the way and how my boxing first got started. I often vividly recall frequently arriving home from school with a black eye, bloodied nose and usually torn clothes, sometimes all three; and all because I didn't know the meaning of diplomacy or have the sense to back away from any argument no matter how many of them it involved or the size of the opposition. I just couldn't back away; I suppose that's how I was made, I would then cop it again from my mother when I arrived home and generally as I walked through the back door after school. Most of my problems centred on my full head of bright ginger hair, which I hated with a passion. World War Three would erupt any time I was called Ginger by any of my schoolmates. They would either have to back down verbally and apologise or defend themselves with their fists. It was like triggering a bomb off inside of me, even though my Mum, who had red hair herself, had tried to convince me that we were special people. I was the only one of my brothers except Peter with as much ginger hair.

I had decided after having to take on the Murphy twins one day while coming home from school that it was time to do something about it; realising that I needed to either learn to keep my violent temper under control, my mouth shut or find a better way to take care of myself. It might be easier to learn how to fight properly and look after myself, rather than using enough brains to talk my way out of arguments. I needed to find a boxing club; that's exactly what I needed to do.

Having made some enquiries I found out that the Red Lion pub, which was situated just off the centre of Rotherham's All Saints' Square, had a boxing club at that time and decided that I would go down and give it a go.

Without saying a word to anyone, not even my Mum or Dad, it would have been a Tuesday or a Thursday evening when for the first time, this ginger-haired, short-trousered, terrified 11-year-old lad opened the tap room door and ventured into the Red Lion pub.

It seemed that everyone inside the packed out pub had stopped what they were doing and silence fell as I walked through the door. It was unheard of in those days to see kids or even women enter a pub on their own. It felt as if all eyes were upon me as the entire crowd turned to look me up and down as I walked inside the smoke-filled tap room for the first time. I remember gulping, my legs buckling, and the back of my throat seemed to close. The landlord, who had spotted me from behind the bar, pointed to a door in the corner of the tap room that led to a flight of stairs. How did he know where I wanted to go, I wondered? Later I figured it out, I wasn't there for a pint was I? I am just glad he hadn't asked me what I wanted, because I would not have been able to have got a word out. I then had to walk across the full length of the bar again, with all the eyes of the smiling drinkers following me.

The 13 steps to the dark green door above were steep and not very well lit. I remember reaching about halfway up the stairs, my legs had turned to jelly and I really did feel like turning round and leaving. I somehow plucked up enough courage to continue to the top of the stairs and knock on the door. I could hear the sound of boxing activities inside, but no-one answered my knock. I really did feel like turning and running down the stairs and out of the building.

The hardest thing I have ever done in my life was to knock on that door again for the second time.

The door did open this time and a broad-shouldered, middle-aged man with a well-worn face, bent nose and a cauliflower ear towered above me. "Na then, young man, what can we do for thee?" he bellowed out at me. I will never forget these first words of greeting from this man, Benny Kemp; who would change my life forever. "I wanna learn how ta box," I said, looking past him into the room full of what looked to me like very experienced and professional men and boys. They were all going about their own training, skipping, sparring and shadow boxing and one big, strapping lad was knocking hell out of a big heavy punch bag in the back corner of the room. "Reyt," he said, "tha had best kum in then so we can have a look at thy."

I followed this man over to the middle of the room; well I don't think I had any option to be honest, he sort of had his arm around my shoulders in a reassuring way, but I really think he was making sure I didn't make a bolt for it and disappear through the door never to be seen again.

A ring was set up at floor level towards the right hand side of the room with bare, light brown hairy hemp rope sticking through the mainly taped-up three roped arena. It was probably spattered dried blood marks that covered the canvas floor and what looked like old pillow cases in each of the four corners which made up the ring.

"Reyt lad, let's see what tha made on then," he said and then shouted one of the lads over who had been skipping with a group towards the back of the gym.

"This lad will feyt thy, so let's see how tha goes on wi' him and then weil let thy have a go wi' a boxer," he said to me as he started to put on and then lace up a pair of at least 25-year-old battered dark brown leather boxing gloves. The insides have bust open over the years and the horsehair is coming out as I struggle to get my fists into a comfortable position inside the gloves.

I don't know what I had expected to happen on my first visit to a boxing gym; maybe sit and watch for a bit, that would make sense wouldn't it?, then possibly a bit of bag punching. But what was about to happen and the speed of what was happening was like a tornado that had a hold and was spinning me out of control, Flippin' 'eck, I had only just walked into the room and now I am ready to fight, he hadn't even asked my name. I was at this stage of affairs in a complete daze as Benny put his arm around me again and with a gentle push we both walk over to the ring.

Now what could be difficult about getting into a ring? I looked at the gaps between the ropes and couldn't make my mind up whether I should roll in to the ring between the floor and the bottom rope, go between the middle two or vault over the top. I decided between the top and middle rope was for me. My legs, I soon found out, are nowhere near long enough for this stupid choice. I nearly ended up with a high pitched voice for the next month as I trapped myself between the legs and the middle rope. Bloody great start.

Finally I was through into the inside of this "arena" and I stood facing my opponent, who seemed to have grown two feet since getting into this ring that now suddenly felt as though it were a cage and closing in fast with nowhere to go.

"Time!" was shouted long before I was ready; I think probably about three months too early at this stage.

I don't remember very much about the first 30 seconds or so, because I was in another world, there certainly weren't any preliminary niceties or sparring around, but I must have done what I was supposed to have done, because what I do remember is that I was suddenly being stopped, I was able to punch this lad with a sort of ease that I had dreamt about and was well and truly dominating this fight. "Stop, stop," I heard as the coach, Benny, jumped into the ring to grab hold and peel me off him.

"Reyt," he said, as he grabbed a hold of my shoulders and firmly steered me into the far corner of the ring. "We now know tha can feyt," he said, looking into my eyes, and then he turned signalling over this lanky lad who had been watching from the side with the rest of the room full of boxers. They had all stopped their own activities and were now watching what had been going on.

"Let's see how tha gets on wi' this lad". He's gunna box thy," said Benny. One of the other men was gloving up my next sparring partner; Benny was offering me advice on how best to deal with my next boxing challenge, but to be honest I really don't remember a single word he said.

This time facing me was an opponent who gave me the impression of being in complete charge of his ability to deal with whatever came. He was also much taller than me, but skinnier and completely different to my last fighting opponent. Just the way he stood in front of me and the air of authority coming from him gave me a sinking feeling. I knew this lanky kid was going to be a different kettle of fish, a much more demanding few minutes and it was probably going to hurt; A LOT.

Time was called and with hands held high like a professional boxer presenting me with no target at all, Cloggy Clarke, as I would get to know him, came swiftly towards me, in and out, just hitting me where and when he wanted. He moved out of range with ease any time I went in to strike a blow.

Within a minute of chasing him around the ring and swinging my arms about like a raving lunatic with all the determination to knock him out, I was completely knackered and gasping for breath. I was quickly running out of energy and hardly able to deliver any worthwhile punch. I didn't know whether I was coming or going. All I could do was defend myself as his punches kept on coming at me from all directions. How many arms does he have? I did have the satisfaction, though, of landing one good right hander on him that stopped him coming forward, but only for a second or two. I think he was probably tiring himself out with all the punching he was giving me.

One round was more than enough for me with Cloggy and as time was called, thankfully my first education in the art of boxing had come to an end. There's more to this boxing lark than I first thought.

We sort of shook hand in the centre of the ring. I think Cloggy, who had this kind of smiling smirk on his face, had enjoyed himself, as he turned away to have his gloves removed. He had avenged his mate and had given me a pasting at the same time. I thought to myself "Cocky bugger, I am going to get my own back on you, mate, sooner or later."

"Well done, young 'un" Benny said" as he steered me to the same corner of the ring, unlaced and took off the old gloves, asking me to pack the horsehair back inside.

"Reyt, then," he said, patting me on my head, "ah think we can mek sumatt on thy, if tha still wants to be a boxer."

"Wow, I'm gonna be a boxer!"

I have come to realise over time, that those first few weeks at the Red Lion Boxing Club were to have one of the biggest impacts on the rest of my life as Benny set about teaching me not only how to box but also about ME. Our time together was spent not only on one to one tuition in boxing but he also taught me about the values in my life and how sport, and in particular boxing, would provide me with all the rules and values I would need for the rest of my life: respect, discipline, determination, commitment and, high on the list, passion. All these life-skills were discussed during our half hour of one on one privileged coaching sessions over the next couple of months. We would agree about the meaning of each one and how important it was for me to fully understand before moving on to the next.

What did I want out of my life and how important was it for me to achieve what I wanted was an early question Benny had asked me one evening. I was told to go away, think about it and give him the answer at a later date. I always thought that he already knew the answer to that one anyway.

We finally arrived at our hotel in Liverpool. Rooms had been allocated; I was sharing with one of the senior fighters and, of course, didn't get the choice of which bed I wanted. I was gobsmacked by the grandeur of the room, which was certainly far more luxurious than I could ever have imagined and couldn't care less, to be honest, which bed I was given. Even the bathroom was larger than any room in our house. It was also the first time that I had ever seen a fixed white bath with taps which delivered hot water without having to boil the kettle up first.

Bath night for us at home was a traditional weekly ritual, started with taking down the tin bath from a hook on the outside toilet wall in the back yard, carried into the kitchen and placed just far enough from the coal fire so as not to burn our naked bodies, which varied between summer and winter. The bath would be filled with warm water from the kettle above the fire in the old black-leaded Yorkshire range.

I felt like royalty in this four star accommodation and couldn't wait to try out the bath and the enormous bed later that night.

Just after our snack of a meal later in the afternoon, in the restaurant part of the building, we were summoned with instructions to get ready and meet down in the foyer in half an hour.

The whole team had congregated in the reception area on time, all prepared and dressed in smart light grey slacks, black blazers with the red and gold Phoenix emblem on our breast pockets and ready to board the coach, which had been brought around from the large car park to the front entrance of the hotel. We did create a stir in the hotel as all heads turned without exception to watch the team file out through the revolving doors and board the coach, which was ready to set off for the tournament.

Looking around the coach as we got back on the road after leaving the comfort of our hotel, my team mates all seemed to have different ways of dealing with the nerves and excitement of representing a club with a great reputation.

They were, without exception, all quiet, some were nail biting, but most of them were deep in thought and dealing with their own inner fears I expect. I was no exception on this occasion, wondering about my opponent and his pretty good record. It was impossible to pre-empt how I would tackle this one, eventually reaching, I suppose, only one conclusion, to wait and see what way would be best.

By now, we had perfected the timing of our arrivals at these tournaments and this evening was no exception. Full visual impact was generated almost like a fanfare being sounded as we filed, almost marching with military precision, through the venue doors and into the reception area of the event where we were met by the promoter and his entourage of helpers. No-one could miss our entrance, heads turned and, almost comically, mouths opened as we walked all the way across the hall to our changing room.

I can well understand the impact we were making and vividly recall being part of the opposing Red Lion team some years ago when I first got sight of the "Steelo's" boxing club entrance at my first fight and how intimidating the professional-looking team of boxers were. It's a small thing, but nonetheless provides an edge of psychological dominance with which to start the fight.

The usual formalities of changing room allocations, doctor's checks and listings of when I was fighting on the programme were soon dealt with. Sixth fight on for me and the last before the interval, which meant that I would have plenty of time to get ready. I would probably manage to watch our first couple of fighters perform.

I hadn't met or had any sighting of my opponent yet, which was quite unusual; normally we would be brought together and introduced during the doctor's inspections or, most importantly, at the weigh-in. I mentioned my thoughts to Jacky, who informed me that he had actually been at his weigh-in and that my opponent's manager had mentioned to him that his boxer's superstitions were not to have sight of his opponent before getting into the ring. "Weird." I find this so very strange, wondering what makes anyone superstitious anyway, especially in boxing. It's certainly not a problem for me and leaves me wondering what else he might be superstitious about that I can upset before we meet in the ring; surely it's a big disadvantage that can be detrimental to any sportsman?

The hall was filling up with noisy spectators, all searching for seats that would give the best vantage points for what promised to be a cracking tournament, if the larger than normal glossy programme, which had been printed in full colour, was anything to go by. The tournament was full of national talent; from junior weights that were not actually recognised to super heavyweight.. From junior potential champions to senior English and Scottish full champions. Almost every fighter had a title of some description on the end of his name and, as I remember, there was even a National Coal Board Champion. Our team names were printed on the right hand side of the pages, and it highlighted the fact that the Phoenix Boxing Club would be taking on fighters from more than five different northern clubs altogether, including six bouts from the local Liverpool club. So it was us against the rest, no pressure there then.

This was going to be one hell of a competition and I intended watching as many fights as I could.

Jack Cox had pinned up the programme close to a serving hatch on the middle wall and then disappeared. The programme, which provided the sequence of events and when we were listed for fighting, gave us all an idea of working out the timing of getting ready and when to start warming up so that we would be ready and on time for our individual fights.

Jacky was well into the motivational team talk whilst the first two of our young fighters were getting ready for the opening fights of the event, when Jack Cox burst into the room, announcing that the first bout was set for a few minutes, cutting the pep talk short.

The first of our junior fighters were soon heading out with Jacky, and closely followed by Jimmie who would be assisting him in the blue corner for tonight's tournament.

I couldn't see the ring clearly from our changing room, but moving further into the hall alongside the back wall provided me with a much better vantage point as long as the crowd kept on their seats.

There was a tension among the lads that was greater than ever I could remember. No-one wanted to talk and I was glad to get out of the gloomy atmosphere of the changing room, time to start my preparation would come soon enough. Everyone else stayed inside the changing room until it was time for their fight.

A great start to the night, as I watched our first junior boxer outclass his opponent from the local club over three rounds to make it a resounding points win. He had a big grin on his face and was looking over the moon as he came past me clutching his wooden biscuit barrel prize and disappeared into our dressing room.

It wasn't long before our second fighter was on his way into the ring. Our team were out of the dressing room first and into the ring, followed by the local boxer. It would become like a production line from now on, and the only way to be able to stage a large event like this one, I suppose.

I always felt proud to be a part of this great team of fighters and tonight was even more pleasing. We were here representing Yorkshire against the north of England and

Scotland. The MC did make a point of letting the spectators know that we were here all the way from Sheffield, Yorkshire, after announcing our names. Only one thing not quite correct was that our club's location is Rotherham, but Sheffield was near enough I suppose.

The next three rounds were soon over, with a more even match between the second fighters, resulting in a slightly biased points win decision for the home team. I followed the Steelo's contingent back into the dressing room to prepare for my bout.

It's now when the adrenalin starts to kick in; I have been here in this situation on many occasions, but tonight feels a little different. The normal butterflies make their even deeper presence felt inside me. It's like a feeling of being scared, but I am never scared; excited I always feel, but this strange feeling is making me sweat while I am getting into my boxing kit. It's probably because this is my first competitive fight for more than four months and suddenly feels even scarier than my first fight more than three years ago in the Red Lion pub square.

By the time the next two fights are over I am settled into the right frame of mind and feeling ready to perform, excited but without the fear of a few minutes ago.

"It's time to go," mouthed Jacky from the door leading out into the hall.

I have always loved the long walk to the ring, using the build-up to get my mind into gear in preparation for the fight. Tonight is no exception as we make our way out of the dressing room between the larger than normal seated crowd, along the wall side and then the right turn down the left hand side of the central avenue of chairs on our way to the ring in the middle of the room. Close up now I can see the whole of the ring, which looks full size and brightly lit from the large cluster of lights suspended from the ceiling above.

It's a powerful feeling, knowing that all eyes are focused on me, most of the crowd will be hoping I lose I suspect and will be trying to work out what my capabilities are just by looking at me, even before they see me in action. I have just loved upsetting local crowds over the last couple of years. Jacky followed me as we climbed the five steps into the ring and "our blue corner." He didn't come into the full-sized ring, but stood on the large apron outside the ropes.

My opponent hadn't arrived yet, but from the loud, excited cheering from the local crowd I could tell he was on his way. He was definitely a favourite with the crowd as they chanted his name, "Sammy, Sammy, Sammy," and judging from his record he had given these fans something to cheer about over the last couple of years or so. "I have every intention of upsetting them all tonight," I thought, as we waited for him to climb into the ring

Jacky was trying to talk over all the cheering noise in an attempt to undermine the impact he must have thought I was experiencing. There was no need, I was settled, in charge again and was ready for anything that my opponent could throw at me. The intense training with Danny over those last couple of months had given me an even greater sense of inner strength and confidence.

The first impression I got of my opponent as he climbed through the ropes into the ring was that he was slightly shorter, but stockier than me. Strangely, not once did he look over in my direction while he was being stripped of his bright red and black silk dressing gown, which revealed his brilliant red silk shorts and a white vest which was covered in an array of championship badges. We were never allowed to sew any of our badges on to our vests. Club rules, they make perfect target to aim at. Many of our guys had their championship badges stitched onto their shorts.

"You're going to have to look at me some time, mate," I was thinking, while Jacky was softly issuing instructions in his usual calm manner, keeping my attention and making me look at him, offering the water bottle for a mouth wash before it would be time for my gum shield.

The start of any of my fights has been exciting, but tonight I felt that I would be taking on this huge intimidating boisterous crowd as well as my opponent by the noise they were making. I will have to shut it out, I was thinking, as we were being summoned into the centre of the ring by the smartly turned out referee.

As I turned to face the ref, who was now standing between us, I could see my opponent's face for the first time. He didn't make eye contact or look at me at all during the normal referee's instructions as we stood what would normally be face to face, but my opponent's head was bowed with chin almost on his chest, revealing the short cropped dark hair on top of his head. I couldn't score any points in this encounter. He was definitely shorter than me, but much more heavily built.

As we turned to walk back to our corners for the start of the fight, I knew I was going to be successful tonight, but I wasn't going to get cocky or complacent with this one, as I had during my 50th fight some five months ago, which was still burning in my mind and lying heavy in my heart.

We had travelled to Leicester on a freezing cold evening a few months ago. I was billed to fight somewhere in the middle of the evening. The usual ritual of doctor's inspection, warming up and getting ready was all taken care of without anything unusual happening but I was, of course, pretty excited and conscious that this very significant 50th fight would be a special occasion for me being still unbeaten leading into this fight.

The memory of that episode flashed quickly through my mind again as I recalled the fight. The first round got under way and right from the start I was surprised at the inexperience of my opponent; I had been used to fighting the best in the country and was anticipating another talented opponent, but he was far from my expectations, looking awkward, slow and clumsy, not what I had come to expect over the last dozen or so fights. It's not a very good match. "This lad should never be in the ring fighting me, he isn't ready. I'll play about with him and then knock him out in the last round," I thought, as I set about playing with him and not really laying a glove on him throughout that first round.

I got a real telling off from Jacky as I sat down on the stool at the end of the first round. "What the hell are you playing at? Come on, let's get on with it."

Round two panned out pretty much the same and went according to "my" plans of knocking him out in the last round. Jacky went absolutely berserk at the end of the second round. He really did blow his top, coming out with a mouthful of real abuse as I stood in my corner waiting for the last round and for the first time ever Jacky, fired a deserved venomous mouthful of bad language at me.

The bell rang for the third round. I set about carrying out my plans and almost met him coming off his stool. I could see the amazement in his eyes as I hailed punch after punch in a non-stop barrage searching for his chin; he covered up and backed away. This was becoming the most frustrating round I had ever fought. I chased him round the ring, throwing punches like a madman, trying to land the one that would fulfil my plan of knocking him out. He ducked and dived for the next two minutes and somehow avoided any full-on contact from me. The referee stopped the fight a couple of times to wipe my opponent's gloves after his back pedalling at speed had caused him to topple over and go down, each time wasting precious seconds that I couldn't use to get at him.

The bell sounded to bring the last round, and the fight, to an end, which was far too soon for me. The fight was over. I was numb inside and realised that I had just made the biggest mistake of my life. Maybe I had done enough to have won the fight, I thought, as I was walking back to my corner, but knowing full well that that was not the case. The look on Jacky's face told me all I needed to know. He was speechless as he unlaced and then took off my gloves.

Less than a minute later, the referee brought us both to the centre of the ring and raised my opponent's hand instead of mine for the first time ever. I had to force myself to shake his hand, knowing full well that I had given him this fight on a plate. I was mad at myself, not at him.

I wanted the ground to open up and swallow me, as I went through all the self-imposed, pent-up emotions. I knew full well that I could blame no-one but myself for having violated the spirit of what I had been taught over the last couple of years.

The self-inflicted punishment that I would put myself through would not be enough to mend the wrong I had done. It would take a long time for me to feel good again, if ever.

Jacky steered me to one side after we had left the ring and calmly but sternly told me to take a couple of weeks off, to think about what I had just done, and then come back to the gym and apologise to the whole team and himself for the attitude and poor sportsmanship I had just shown . I more than deserved that comment and felt so ashamed of myself. How could I have been so arrogant, so disrespectful, so self-centred, and full of my own importance, so big-headed, so up my own backside, I could go on? I realised then that this moment had been coming for some time. I had become something of a celebrity over the last few months. Press coverage and comments that took me from being just an amateur boxer to a great prospect for the future. But these are just excuses for the real reason, I had lost sight of the most precious lessons I had been taught during my time with Benny Kemp, my first coach, and in turn Jacky – Respect.

I went through all the emotions of remorse, sorrow and humility over the next couple of weeks as I tried to blank out and come to terms with what I had allowed to happen to me. Looking back on the couple of weeks after my disastrous 50th fight, they were the unhappiest days of my life; I went to bed almost every night close to, or in, tears. I just wanted to die.

Entering through the gym doors for the first time after the Leicester event was quite traumatic for me. I nearly didn't make it, knowing full well what was waiting for me; I nearly turned back a couple of times on the way down to the gym.

Jacky spotted me as I opened and walked in through the big brown gym doors. It seemed the whole gym had anticipated what was about to happen as he came over to me, taking the kit bag out of my hands and dropping it on the floor by the ring. "Quiet!" he shouted out, after getting through the ropes into the ring, sending the two boys who were sparring out.

The room seemed to be closing in on me as I was invited to join him in the ring. Jacky outlined the chain of events during my farcical fight of two weeks previously and invited me to comment, to the now quiet, inactive group of boxers and spectators, disappearing out of the ring before I had said a word, leaving me feeling oh so vulnerable and totally exposed. I had worked on the speech that I should make while I had been travelling down to the gym on the bus, but couldn't remember a single word as I stood there feeling small and so insignificant, with all the eyes of my team mates and everyone else inside the hall looking right through me. It felt as though I was naked and fully exposed.

"I am so sorry for letting you all down," I started. "I am so sorry for letting the club down and not doing my best." I was stuttering, stammering and gasping for breath as I humbled myself in front of my team mates for what seemed an eternity. In the end, I just stood feeling vulnerable and had run out of voice; no sound would come out as I tried to bring my humiliating speech to an end. My heart was pounding in my ears as I repented, pouring all the heartfelt feelings out, unable to say another word and finding it impossible to stop the tears from streaming down my face. Jacky appeared at the side of the ring, foot on the middle rope, and held up the top one for me to come out of the ring. He never took his eyes off me as he steered me, one arm around my shoulders, towards the dressing room. Once the room was cleared, he said "That took some guts, I am proud of you," giving me a tight squeeze. "You will never forget this lesson but put it aside now, we are going from here on to better things," he said. I could feel the tears flowing, but this time with relief and the realisation that I was in some way forgiven; I was still a part of the Phoenix Boxing Club. I had envisaged being kicked out of the team after letting them down so badly. "Swill your face and get yourself home. See you Thursday," he said, giving me that all-knowing wink I was so used to.

The hardest thing I have ever done in my life and the biggest lessons I have ever learnt in my life I believe all happened before I had reached the age of 14 and both to do with boxing.

I am determined to put the ghost of that encounter to rest with my performance tonight.

The bell sounded for the first of the three two-minute rounds and before I could make any progress into the centre of the ring, my opponent came almost running towards me with arms swinging like a windmill in an intimidating aggressive style that would put most opponents off their stride. A very severe sidestep from me saw him pass like a train out of control. Wow, so this is how he has won so many bouts, he certainly is an aggressive fighter.

He turned immediately and launched himself into an almost replica attack, but this time I sidestepped and caught him with a cracking left hook, almost lifting him off his feet.

I had the feeling that if I stood in his path and blocked his punches, I would be bowled over like being mown down by a raging bull.

The partisan crowd were screaming as he launched himself full on again with swinging attempts at catching me.

His punches were far from the standard boxing style and would probably end up as slaps rather than effectively punching with the knuckles, but they would be difficult to block without causing damage to the blocking arm.

Well before the end of the first round, though, he was running out of steam fast and breathing more heavily by the second. It was now easy for me to get him under control and score heavily with frequent combinations. I did notice that the hostile crowd had gone quiet, giving me the added satisfaction of being in control of them as well.

The bell sounded in mid-stream of one of my full on combinations. "Definitely my round," I thought on the way back to my corner and the smiling Jacky.

Jacky, calm, but with quiet excitement in his voice, was instructing me to keep calm, keep him on the move, let him run out of steam, then up the pace and get it over with.

I was on track, the fight was going well and I felt in control, but knowing that I just had to make sure of not being caught as I sidestepped the swinging attacks.

Looking across into his corner I could see the frantic instructions he was getting from both the corner men.

"Seconds out, Round two!" shouted out from the timekeeper, the same time as the bell sounded. I was already on my feet and ready for him. Just as predicted, he came rushing across with arms swinging like a windmill again. This dominant style would be so intimidating for most opponents and was probably why he had won many of his fights with TKOs. But this time, instead of sidestepping, I ducked under his right swing and hit him as he came running forward with a cracking right hook, which spun him round. The perfect target for a left hook to the body opened up before he was able to present any guard, quickly followed by a sharp right cross and a hard left hook to his body, which stopped him in his tracks as he slowly sank onto his knees in my corner facing Jacky.

I was pleased with the way I had been able to deal with the very aggressive style of my opponent as I stood watching the proceedings being carried out by the referee, waiting for the count to end and being ready so that I could take full advantage of the situation.

That initial cracking right hook had landed with the increased power which had been created by his forward speed, but the delivery was not quite accurate enough to have caused too much damage. Eyes are the give-away when you have connected with the right punch, in the right spot, eyes are glazed and don't focus. Sometimes fitness will enable them to continue, but a referee who has enough experience will know when to step in and bring an end to the fight.

He made it on to his feet by the count of seven, but by the time the referee had talked to him for what seemed an excessive amount of time and wiped his gloves clear of the resin from the canvas, my advantage had been lost.

I could see that he had fully recovered, but was not so keen to come at me in the aggressive manner which he seemed to enjoy.

It's time to take advantage of the situation, put him under pressure and get back into dominating the fight again. He couldn't produce a straight punch, only swing, which made it easy for me to stand close on to him and slip any attempt from him over my shoulders and round my back. I was moving forward now and managing to push him around the ring. With about half a minute to go, I backed him into a corner and with nowhere for him to go, I set about hitting him with all the power I could manage. He ducked low in an attempt to cover up, but there are always gaps and targets to aim at.

He suddenly jumped out but upwards at the same time in an attempt to get out of the corner, catching me with his head just over my left eye as I hovered over him. Stars were flashing everywhere, making it difficult to pinpoint where he was. I moved to one side, wondering how bad it was and realising that the swelling was growing by the second.

If the referee had seen that happen he wasn't letting on, leaving me feeling that if the swelling got any worse, the fight could be stopped.

The bell sounded loud and clear, ending the round and putting an end to my train of thought. I almost ran across the ring to my corner before the referee could see the extent of the damage.

My two corner men were ready, waiting in position, and as I reached the safety of my corner, Jacky almost lifted me off my feet and plonked me down on the stool. No sooner had he inspected my eye, than treatment started with the miniature iron which he had in his right hand. I could feel the urgency of trying to control the swelling, as Jacky worked the iron in a slow circular motion but pushing upwards towards my forehead at the end of each circle to reduce the swelling around my eye. Looking into his unchanging face, I couldn't get the answers I was after, but did I really want to know how bad it was? It turned out, I was later informed, that a small piece of bone over my eyebrow had broken off. Jacky worked on the slowly-swelling lump for the rest of the one-minute interval, smoothing away the tightening skin and at the same time providing instructions for the coming last round.

I couldn't believe that the referee had not seen the foul, leaving me wondering if I had two opponents in the ring as well as the crowd on the outside tonight, making me more determined to get this fight over with as fast as I could. If the damage had been under my eye, Jacky would have stopped the fight, but after asking me what I felt like, it was decided that we carry on. I wasn't in any pain or distress, but eager to get on with the last round.

The last time I saw this small iron in action, which was used on our heavyweight, Terry Girdlestone, was during one of the last tournaments I fought in at the Doncaster Corn Exchange. These miniature irons are used to spread out the congealed blood and flatten out the swelling. I was in no serious pain, but very conscious of the tightening skin. I could see out of it OK at the moment and felt that if I could get in control early on then I could probably finish this fight before the end of the round. I needed to, anyway.

The referee, who had been watching the frantic activities of my skilful coach, walked over to inspect the damage and made enquires about my readiness to continue. Jacky reassured him that all was well and at the same time put in a complaint, asking that he keep an eye on my opponent's carelessness. He made no comment, turned away and walked across to stand close to the neutral corner in readiness for the last round.

The last few seconds of the break were used to discuss the way to deal with my opponent. "He will be instructed to come at you straight away. Move and catch him coming in," were my final instructions before the bell sounded and "Seconds Out", "Round Three!" bellowed out from the timekeeper, who was sitting with the judges below the ring apron to my right.

Jacky was right as usual, no sooner had I stood up for the start of this last round, than he was travelling like an express train in my direction with arms swinging wildly, even well before I was in range. His corner men must have been aware of my damage and certainly would have instructed him to make my left eye his main target.

A quick wide side step saw him crashing into my corner, but before he had turned around I was back in position and ready to catch him with a couple of good body shots, then stepping back sharply, avoiding his swinging punches before he could do anything about it.

I had never encountered anyone so fiercely determined to win at any cost than my opponent. He was like a predictable, but out of control, wild animal and at the same time extremely difficult to handle. His powerful swings and forward momentum were better avoided rather than blocking. His most unorthodox style of fighting leaves me with little choices other than stepping back sharply, or to one side and then counter-punching and not getting in the way of the almighty swings.

Our plan for the early part of this last round was to let him tire himself out with the efforts of his heavy swings and by not making any physical contact, it would be extremely strength-sapping for him.

I need to change the tactics slightly if I want to bring this fight to a quick end. It's time to stand and hover close, not allow him any forward motion but present an enticing in-range target. Teasing out the swinging punches is leaving him with no alternative but to punch and use his energy up fast, in effect, forcing him to punch at a target that evades contact. I can see the frustration in his eyes as well as his fatigued slumping posture.

I could feel my eye slowly closing, which I continually kept covered with my left glove at every opportunity to hide from the referee as the round progressed. I was becoming increasingly worried that if he could see the now almost closed condition my eye was in, then I would be in jeopardy of losing the fight through stoppage, which would be listed as a TKO. Is this how my opponent has gained such an impressive reputation?

My new tactics are working, by just using sharp left jabs, which are disrupting his robotised swinging attempts at catching me. In, jab and out fast enough to avoid the violent swings. He is running out of steam fast, gulping air in from his exerted swings, and unable to launch any more of his wild attacks, but my eye is now closed and time is running out before the referee will be forced to bring the fight to an end. I desperately need to stop him and quickly with less than a minute remaining of this last round.

I need to steer him into a position where I can double up with power and connect with a punch that will do the trick. In that split second as this thought comes into my mind, I am presented with the golden opportunity I was looking for, of using the ropes to my advantage. From the centre of the ring, I had launched a sequence of punches that connected heavily, backing him on to the ropes and, as anticipated, lacking in ring craft when being pushed back and through utter tiredness, he came bouncing straight back towards me like a rag doll, without any substantial guard.

It was as if time had stood still, providing a slow motion opportunity for that split second and giving me all the time in the world to deliver a perfect right cross to an unguarded target. The impact created by the catapulted speed with which he was coming back off the ropes and the power of my well-anchored straight right punch was more than anyone was going to cope with. I knew it was over before he crumpled face down to the canvas. I had felt the impact right down my arm, through my shoulder and even into my back. I knew that even if this one hadn't finished him, it wouldn't take much more to bring the fight to an end.

The referee suddenly grabbed me by the shoulders and almost dragged me off my feet, as he spun me round and directed me with a shove towards the neutral corner.

Standing in the neutral corner, I had to turn my whole head round so that I could see Jacky out of my good eye; he had responded to my look with a raised clenched fist in a triumphant salute.

My opponent wasn't counted out by the referee, that wasn't needed, because both my opponent's corner men had jumped into the ring to deal with him where he had landed. Two or three minutes later, he was walked over to his corner and helped down on to his stool like a drunken puppet.

The tournament doctor had been sent for and jumped up into the ring to check him over. You could have heard the proverbial pin drop in the hall as I observed the very subdued crowd to my side of the ring, looking out at them with my good eye.

The bright arc lights positioned about ten feet or so above the ring were beginning to feel more like heaters than lights and seemed to be scorching the top of my head while I stood waiting for what seemed like the best part of fifteen minutes. I was mesmerised watching the frantic activities of the doctor, his two corner men and even the referee, when it suddenly sunk in that the fight was well and truly over and had been for the past three or four minutes.

From the corner of my good eye, I could see that Jimmie was heading across the ring to escort me back to my corner where Jacky was ready to set about the swelling over my eye again. I was ready for a drink of water as well as being sponged off and half expecting steam to be coming off the top of my head.

"I might have to nick this swelling to release the pressure," Jacky commented, bringing me out of my daydream. I had heard some time ago that a sharp razor blade could be used to cut the skin deep enough to allow the trapped, congealed blood to be released, which would effectively reduce the swelling. This was a much-used process in the professional fights, even during the fight if the swelling couldn't be controlled. A small nick would probably be better than a large swelling with congealed blood bursting to get out. This could never happen in the modern, protected, sterilised world of amateur boxing today and leaves me wondering at times, how the hell we ever survived all those years ago.

After more than ten minutes of waiting for the doctor's decision to allow my opponent to move, we were brought together into the centre of the ring for the official result announcement.

It's strange to be able to look clearly into his face at last as we stand facing one another and for the first time he made fleeting eye contact with me, as he offered his bandaged hand for me to shake. On closer inspection, I could see the results of that cracking right cross. The left side of his face, but higher than where I thought I had caught him, was badly swollen, mainly around the jaw muscle. Already a deep reddy blue and looking like the start of a wicked bruise that will increase over the next day or two. He will suffer for a few weeks with that. As for me, well my eye is completely shut now and painful, which will take some time to heal, I suspect.

My right hand was lifted by the immaculately dressed referee, as the announcer made it official that my opponent had been unable to continue and that I had won on a TKO. He wasn't counted out; in truth it was a KO, but a win is a win and the ghost of my 50th self-inflicted farce had been well and truly been laid to rest. How ironic was it though that he had been beaten on a TKO himself?

I made the usual gesture of walking over and shaking hands with his corner men, who, to be fair, did say "Well done!" and in the normal friendly gesture that is prevalent in this sport, shook my hand while my opponent waited to accompany me back across to my corner. Jacky sponged him down, asking him if he was OK, and was rewarded with just a nod, so I suspected that he would be finding it difficult to talk.

I was finding it hard, for the very first time in my boxing career, to feel any friendship towards my opponent. In fact, I can't say that I had any feelings towards him, indifferent or otherwise. He would have flattened me if I had given him the opportunity and he, in turn, had not shown any friendship to me at all. My opponent had a strange, unfriendly attitude that I found so off-putting, leaving me with a sense of not being bothered about any pain he might be feeling or the fact that he would probably be feeling badly about letting his home supporters down as well. Normally after any fight, I would make a point of making friends with my opponents and, without exception until tonight, we would become "out of the ring friends". I had never fought the same opponent twice, but would generally catch up with them during tournaments around the country.

We were escorted out of the ring and, with me leading the way, were directed to the prize table situated across from the front of the ring. As is traditional, I was given first choice of the prizes which had been donated by a company whose name had been given out during the initial presentation of the bout.

Standing to one side of the table was the biggest woman I had ever seen, dressed in a dark blue coat, which looked like a man's mac. She wore glasses and had a white flowerpot of a hat on her head, greying hair and was without make-up. She had the plump, rugged face of a boxer who had been hit a few times, but I suspected that she would be someone of great importance in the area. She towered over me as we shook hands.

I chose the large cut glass salad bowl with ornate silver serving spoons from the table full of prizes, which she presented to me, shaking my hand again and commenting on a cracking fight.

Our celebrity for the evening gave off an air of being someone rather special and after she had made a short speech of congratulations using the compere's microphone, she wished me luck for the future, most of which I couldn't fully understand because of her strong Liverpudlian accent.

Throughout my boxing career, I have been introduced to some very famous celebrities, mostly stars of bygone eras like Bruce Woodcock, the British and Empire heavyweight champion boxer from Doncaster, John Charles, the famous footballer, who was the first English footballer to make the grade in Italy, playing for Juventus before returning to Leeds as the record goal scorer of 42 in one season, and normally sports people from the area we were fighting in. One of my favourites while boxing in South Wales was the ex-world flyweight boxing champion, Jimmie Wilde, nicknamed The Mighty Atom. Not much taller than I was at the time, but he had spread out a bit around his belly over the years, making him barrel-like in shape and size; but what a great character, who spent some time with me after the fight, talking about his world title fights and the places he had travelled to around the world. I was mesmerised. I remember one of the spectators shouting out "Who's thy butcher then, Jimmy?" causing a huge roar of laughter from the packed crowd.

I had been told that the celebrity, who would be presenting the trophies this evening, was a woman MP called Bessie Braddock, whom I had never heard of before this evening.

A few years later, I made enquiries about Bessie Braddock. I had been intrigued by her size and what she might have done to warrant giving out the prizes during our tournament that night in Liverpool. I was told that she was a Labour Party Member of Parliament for Liverpool, nicknamed Battling Bessie, and was famous, among other things for having confronted Winston Churchill on one occasion after an evening at some function during his time as Prime Minister. She had allegedly said "Mr Churchill, you are drunk, in fact, Mr Churchill, you are very drunk." To which Winston Churchill had allegedly replied, "Bessie, you are ugly, in fact you are very ugly, but in the morning when I am sober you will still be very ugly." Ha, ha, I find that so funny and can well imagine that this story might well be true. It sounds feasible, having met her. She was not one for keeping her mouth shut, it seems, when she was involved in causes that she felt strongly about. She was generally on the side of the underdog. Bessie, who I believe was an amateur boxing fan, died in 1970 aged 71. There is also a bronze statue commemorating her in Liverpool Lime Street railway station.

The hall lights had been switched to full, making the room look larger than a few minutes ago and signalling the end of the first half of the tournament. I turned to walk back to the changing room, followed by Jacky, with his hands on my shoulders, but Jimmie was just ahead, making a path for me through the local spectators who were stood clapping and crowding around me creating a sort of tunnel. Many were patting me on my back as we headed all the way back to the dressing room, down the long walk through the avenue of chairs. It was difficult to progress at any speed but eventually we made it back. It's not easy having sight from only one eye and trying to walk in a straight line, but I would have to get used to it for a few days, I suppose.

Because there was a 15-minute break at this halfway stage of the tournament, Jacky had time to work on my eye again before he would be back in action for the remainder of the bouts.

The tournament doctor had had time to inspect my fully-closed eye and I was given two aspirins and told to rest up for the remainder of the night. It was agreed not to cut the swelling, but to give it chance to subside on its own with the help of painkillers and cold water compression.

The doctor informed me that my opponent had been taken home by his parents a few minutes ago, which meant that they had been in the crowd and would have witnessed him being crumpled up on the canvas towards the end of the third round. I must be public enemy number one.

If for no other reason than what had just happened tonight, we had agreed some time ago that my Mum shouldn't come to my fights. She had not been to any to date. Even though I hadn't been on the receiving end of a good hiding, it was easier for me to perform without having to be worried about her feelings; she would have been upset tonight, though, with the sight of my damaged eye.

Six fights to go and Jacky was back in action again as the second half got underway.

I was in no rush to leave the changing room, spending a good half hour in the shower soaking and bathing my eye in an attempt to soothe away the pain that had kicked in big style.

We were well up and leading seven fights to one when I went into the shower, eight to two when I emerged.

The heavyweights are always last on the bill and tonight were no exception. I managed to catch the light heavy contest which went right to the wire, with the fight going from one side to the other as they both made their skills count. It was a great fight to watch. A draw would have been the perfect decision, but in amateur boxing there has to be a winner. Our guy came second! No surprise there, then.

Last fight of the night was our big heavyweight, Terry, who generally wins his fights by knocking his opponent out or, on the other hand, he would end up on his backside for the count himself. His opponent, who is taller but slightly lighter, looks a real mean animal. It's always exciting to watch these big guys trading punches at one another, trying to land the big one as soon as possible. They usually end up fighting for breath after swinging Haymakers and propping each other up before the end of the round.

I have sparred with our heavyweights on numerous occasions in an effort to help them quicken up. It's great to be able to use natural speed and to punch these big men almost at will, normally getting in to deliver two or three punches before they can react, but making sure you're out of the way well before they deliver a punch back; otherwise you're likely to end up sailing out of the ring.

It was evident that this one wouldn't last long from the opening half minute. The two fighters were not inclined to size one another up at the start. They were hammer and tongs at each other right from the start of the first round; trading punches that almost guaranteed one of them was not going to survive.

Beyond all expectations, they both end up walking back to their corner at the end of the first round after a few scary moments on both sides.

Jacky was up and into the ring before Terry had arrived back to his corner and was sponging him down before he had sat on the stool. Jacky was working hard on relaying instructions to him for the next round, probably advising him to steady down and box his way into an opening before launching into swinging the right Haymaker.

The crowd was going wild within a few seconds of the next round as the local fighter launched a fierce attack, causing our man to wobble, but Terry managed to hang on to his opponent long enough to recover before the referee could prise them apart. This was turning into a right ding-dong of a fight as Terry, who had now fully recovered from the last onslaught, returned with his own two-fisted attack, completely reversing the situation by putting the local fighter on his backside.

The crowd was going mental, cheering and shouting for him to get up and beat the count, which he did by eight. As he got to his feet, the referee grabbed his gloves and wiped the resin dust clear and at the same time I could see that Terry was advancing from the neutral corner to be close enough to take advantage of the knock-down. The split second the referee moved away, Terry launched into a wave of two fist punches that were full of power, for the best part of half a minute.

The local heavyweight hit the canvas again and literally bounced. He was out cold. This time he didn't make the count and while he was being counted out I was watching Terry in the far corner. From what I saw it was a good job it was all over, because he was lying heavily on the ropes heaving in and out and looked as if he was having convulsions, trying to get the breath back into his lungs from all that effort. He probably would not have been able to stand up unsupported if the ropes were not there to lay his heavy frame on.

They were both applauded loudly as the referee lifted Terry's hand, with the announcement of the result and bringing the evening's tournament to an end.

We, as a team, had had a very successful tournament, winning nine out of the 12 bouts, and were rewarded with a standing ovation from the crowd. We had been invited as a team to stand inside the ring at the end of the evening's proceedings to be applauded, bringing the event to a close.

The crowd, which had started out the night pretty hostile, had eventually warmed to us all, showing appreciation for our club's talent, as the night had progressed.

Half an hour later, we were heading out of the hall and filing into our coach in a not so regimented fashion as our entrance a few hours ago, ready to make our way back to the hotel and a supper which had been booked for our return.

I was starving by this late hour of about 11.45pm, according to the coach clock, and wondering what delights we were about to be served for supper.

The journey back to the city centre was a noisy one, with nearly everyone in a boisterous mood, making their own contribution to the stories of what a great night we had had.

On our arrival at the hotel, we were met by the night porter, taken into the hotel bar and directed to a long table which was covered with a long, white table cloth. A couple of our senior guys beat the hotel staff members to the buffet table and revealed a feast of sandwiches, bun and cake, the like of which I had never seen before, and my very first sighting of a black forest gateaux. Free drinks from the bar rounded the evening off and for me my first taste of Mackeson Milk Stout

Ale. "Go on, get it down thy, itle help thy get some sleep," commented Jimmy in a manner that suggested I keep it to myself as he handed me the black bottle. So my first taste of beer was purely medicinal and after two bottles I couldn't even stand up straight. I was helped to our bedroom on the second floor, or was it third, may have been the fifth, you get the gist, I was sozzled and unable to walk in a straight line, but happy and without any pain from my eye as I finally fell, fully-clothed, on to that enormous bed and slept like a baby.

I woke early next morning and couldn't remember where I was for a few seconds, dry-mouthed and in pain from my eye or was it my first hangover from the Mackeson Milk Stout? Either way it was an uncomfortable entry into Sunday morning.

After searching for the bedside clock I could see, out of my good eye, that there was still an hour and three-quarters before breakfast at eight.

I was lying on top of the huge bed trying to blank out how I was feeling, when the phone on my roommate's bedside table shrilled out, waking him up. This was all posh and cosmopolitan to me, giving me a feeling of being part of a much different way of life. I just didn't realise that he had asked for an early morning call. Wow, bloody phones in our bedroom. I had never used a phone; actually I had never been in a phone box, only to take shelter from the rain.

We were on our way home after a whacking big breakfast of food that I had never seen or heard of before, including my very first taste of black pudding and grapefruit.

Not long into the journey, most of the gang was fast asleep and with a quiet coach after Jacky had returned to his seat, making enquiries about my eye, there was nothing much to do but look out of the window at the passing scenery and wonder how Mum would react to my damaged eye. It's not something that I am going to be able to hide. The mirror in the bathroom had revealed the unfamiliar, swollen, blue and deep red shut left eye which wasn't going to go away before I get home, probably would get worse. I could wear the eye like a trophy at school.

Even the cut glass bowl trophy would not take away the feelings I knew Mum would experience when I walked through the back door later that afternoon. It seemed to me that I had been a great trouble to her over the past couple of years, she had said on numerous occasions that she never knew what to expect whenever I came home. Oh hell what's she gonna make of this shiner?

I must have fallen asleep with the heavy drone from the wheels on the road, because all of a sudden we were passing the entrance to the Temple Hotel pub on Sheffield Road. The high brick wall of the bar mill and Ickles seemed to be following us all the way down the road to the Rotherham melting plant.

We would be shortly arriving at our gym at Ickles. I had decided, while on our way, that I would take the shortcut across the canal rather than bus it into Rotherham and walk through the town to our house in Masbrough.

I managed to get the trophy into my bag, wrapping my boxing gear around the bowl to make it comfortable to carry, and after we had said our goodbyes, most of the lads were standing waiting for a bus to Rotherham, with a couple walking in the direction of Bow Bridge and Canklow.

It was time for me to head off across the back of Steelo's blast furnaces, crossing over the internal railway lines on the slag-filled footpath leading to the Sheffield-Rotherham section of the Chesterfield canal. Not long and I have crossed the mainline railway lines and am heading up the wide cinder track, passing the side entrance to Millmoor football ground, the home of Rotherham United football club.

I was up and on to College Street before I had seen a soul. But walking down Brown Street, I met a couple of my mates, both inquisitive about the damage to my eye with comments of "Bet that bloody hurts, dunt it." Word will soon get round now, I suspect, without any further contributions from me.

My eye was still shut and feeling taut, as though it was about to burst open, by the time I turned round the corner of our terraced house in Holland Place and up the passage to the back door.

The whole family had been waiting patiently for my return and with no way of letting my parents know what time I would get home, it would have been no more than a guess to predict anyway.

It was impossible to hide my eye as I walked through the back door and was greeted with the initial normal reaction of "How have you done?" to a frozen stare from both Mum and Dad, once they had seen my eye.

I had had enough time to remove the cut glass bowl and spoons from my bag before the inevitable "My God, now what you done?" followed by the full blood and guts version of how it had happened, during which time both Mum and Dad had managed a full panoramic inspection of my colourful, closed eye. Surprisingly, the first comment, "That's you done for a while," came from Dad, followed by a more sympathetic "Are you in much pain?" from Mum. My brothers seemed just mesmerised by the state of my eye and didn't make any comment at this time.

A nice cuppa tea was what I needed and that's what I got from an always boiling kettle, which permanently hovered over the coal fire.

While going through the entire fight for the benefit of the whole family, who were rooted to the spot, I delivered the full story of not only the fight and the outcome but the experience of the hotel and its modern, but I suspect very expensive, four star rating, God, that was something else.

I wasn't allowed to attend school the following Monday, "not until you can see out of both eyes," and certainly no gym for the next few weeks until Mum was satisfied that I was in a fit state to look after myself. By Tuesday, the swelling was down considerably, but the colour was like Joseph's Coat, ranging from pink through a variety of blues, crimson to purple and a sort of yellowy green. Hell, it stood out like a sore thumb or should I say eye?

Mr Flynn, my teacher, wanted all the gory details when I arrived at school for my first lesson a couple of days later and, after I had gone through the explanation of how I had picked up the damage to my eye, I became a bit of a celebrity with my mates, but it only lasted for the rest of the week. Well after all we do live in Yorkshire and there's no resting on your laurels upt north mate.

The slowness of the recovery was a big concern; it was difficult coming to terms with the realisation that if all the experts were right, it would take over six weeks or more before the swelling and colours would disappear. I would never get through a doctor's examination, making it impossible to fight in the Yorkshire Schoolboy Championships, which were due to be held in just over two weeks' time in Leeds.

The following week I started light training back at the gym and, after many discussions about my eye and any possibility of being ready to pass a doctor's examination, it was decided that I go through the actions of training and at least maintaining my physically fitness, enough to be ready should it be possible to compete in the Championships.

I was gutted, but deep down I had come to terms with the fact that this year's Championships would have to be missed. Almost half-heartedly, I set about the training and during my first session back, while I was in the process of completing my last round on the heavy bag, I was approached by an old man who had been sitting on a chair close by. He had been watching me for the last half hour. I had seen him in the gym a few times over the past six months or so, without knowing who he was.

"That's a nasty looking eye young man, how long have you had it?" he asked. "Coming up to a week now," I said. "Mind if I take a look?" but before I could make any reply, Jacky had walked over to the bag and introduced me to my new companion. "This is Eddy." "Nasty eye," Eddy said again, but directing the comment at Jacky, who explained the manner in which I had received it. "Probably taken some of the bone off the brow, that's why it's slow to heal. You need to get some Oil of Origanum from the chemist," he said in an authoritative manner, as though he knew what he was talking about. "I'll write it down for you before I go," he said; "A couple of ounces should more than do the trick." He then explained that I should dab a few drops on to a cloth pad, secure it over the damage with a towel around my head and leave for as long as I could stand the pain. "Whatever you do don't let it get into your eye, it'll sting like bloody hell," he said, and walked back to his chair to write out the name for me. He handed me the piece of paper before he left, saying "This will work!"

I would have tried anything and Jacky's comments of "He's a well-respected cut and corner man with the professionals", gave me a feeling of hope. I couldn't wait to get home and tell my Dad of my meeting tonight and hopefully find the answer to my eye problem. It made sense that a piece of bone had broken off the edge of my eye socket at the brow, but where would the bit of bone be? I couldn't really tell, because it was far too painful to explore the contours of my eyebrow. Mum was asked if she could get the oil some time the following day, so that we could make an early start to reducing the swelling and get me back in action.

Neat Oil of Origanum formed the basics of the rubbing oils of the early 50s, I was told, it certainly had that really strong smell to it and was sold only by a chemist. This small, two-ounce, dark brown, ribbed jar was very expensive, my mother told me, as she gave it to me to save. I was told to wait for my Dad to come home from work before making any attempt to try the treatment out myself.

My eye by this time was all the colours of the rainbow, not as badly swollen but extremely painful to touch, making it impossible to even think about being ready for the schoolboy championships. No way on earth would I make it past the tournament doctors with an eye like this, unless this small bottle, which I was holding up to the light to get a better look at, contained some miracle potion.

Shortly after tea, we prepared for the first of the treatment; applying a small amount of the oil to a lint pad and, after placing it over my eye, I was rewarded in less than ten seconds with the pain of the century. Even ten minutes after removing the pad, the pain was still excruciating, it felt as though my left eye was on fire and I finally had to wash my face off to get any sort of ease. Two or three hours later revealed a marked improvement in the colour of the bruise, giving me some reason to feel optimistic that if I continued with the treatment, it might well provide the results I was praying for. It was agreed that the next application was to be to apply far less of the oil than we had used on this first attempt.

I was never looking forward to my twice daily treatment, but the results were astounding, making the pain well worth putting up with.

With less than a week of treatment, the bruising had almost disappeared, leaving only the painful lump of bone which was floating about inside the soft area under the brow.

With just less than five days to go, my eye was almost back to normal to look at, slightly sore to the touch, and even the bone, or gristle as it would probably be at my age, had just about disappeared by the Monday evening of the second week.

It was agreed at the training session on Tuesday night that, since my eye had healed, with only slight visible signs of the damage which I had incurred less than a couple of weeks ago, I would probably pass the doctor's examinations, by maybe using a spot of Mum's make-up to disguise any last discolouration if necessary, as long as I was prepared to take on the two or three fights that would be needed to get to the finals. Mum wasn't too happy about getting back in the ring, with the possibility of getting hit on the already damaged eye, as she put it. I know she wouldn't stand in my way of getting back in the ring if I was really ready. "It's up to you"

It seems that my name hadn't been taken off the fight list, but what would the chances be that the Championship doctor could be the same one as the fight doctor in Liverpool? How unlucky would that be?

All will be revealed, but that's another story, you're gonna have to wait to find out!

# CHAPTER 12

## The final 50 miles and another dream completed

It's time to leave the comfort and warmth of Dearne Valley College hall at Manvers if I am to reach Helen, the first of my last 50 mile crew, at Droppingwell by around 11 this evening. My fears of not being able to complete the challenge, which were with me for about six hours or so earlier during the day, have gone and are now replaced with positive thoughts of success. I can do this; it's only another 50 miles to the finish.

Have I just made a stupid comment to myself, my legs are refusing to function with any degree of what I need for walking never mind running? God, I am as stiff as a board, as I attempt to stand up. I have been inactive far too long while shovelling the food down me. Finally getting to my feet, standing up, moving away from the table and swinging the rucksack on to my back provide enough movement to kick-start my legs into action.

Don't think anyone has noticed that I probably look incapable of walking to the doors of the hall, let alone run another 50 miles. This is a situation that I have never been in before. Nothing short of extreme determination will get me mobile, but mobile is what I so desperately need to be right now. The minutes spent shaking hands with some of the athletes, and coping with hugs from Jacky and Vonnie, who are half lifting me off my feet, is providing me with sufficient time to slowly get my limbs moving, and actually making me feel half human again as I make my way to the door.

Shouts of "Good luck!" and the cheering and waving as I set off out of the hall have provided me with the mixed emotional feelings of "Will I manage to make the coming meeting times?" and "Will I be able to achieve this last 50 miles if my legs continue not to play ball?" "Come on, Ray, dig in and let's get underway, I can't let anyone down now; I am so close to succeeding."

I have got two hours and about 20 minutes to get to the first meeting about 12 miles away. Normally this would be more than enough time, but with more than 100 miles in my legs I will more than likely need the extra time.

I make one last turn around and wave back in the darkening night before getting underway out of the complex of the college.

Making my way into the night and at last feeling better as my legs slowly give way into relaxing, allowing me to jog and then into a steady run before reaching the main road and the first, well-lit roundabout. I am heading towards the footpath on the left of the main road which will take me past Wath Fire Station for the second time today.

It's probably a good thing to have been able to start the first mile of this last 50 miles on firm tarmac, it provides me with a level surface to run on with less of a risk of tripping and stumbling with tired and fatigued legs. The longer I run the easier it's becoming as effort becomes less demanding.

Surprisingly I am running quite comfortably at last, and as good as I have run for weeks. The pace feels about right and the stiffness has disappeared at last, which is settling me down and providing me with a great feeling inside.

The food that I have consumed during my last stop is lying a bit heavy in my stomach, but not causing any concern; I am confident that the discomfort will soon ease and the "fuel" will be put to good use as the miles pass by.

I am now running along the wide path heading towards the level crossings at Elsecar, the head light has been increasingly losing power until it is almost not worth leaving on but the natural moonlight is good enough for the time being. Trying to remember which pocket the spare batteries are in, thankfully I had remembered to pack a spare set of AA batteries in my rucksack. I will have a stop at the bottom of the hill, replace the batteries and have a drink before heading up the hill into the dark woods.

Head light functioning like a good 'un, it's time to make my way up through the woods and the decision to walk has been made, must conserve as much energy early on into this last circuit as possible. I feel that should I manage to maintain this steady pace, then my first meeting will be on time give or take a few minutes, which means that I have pulled back almost all of the time lost during the early part of the day, providing me with a tremendous boost to the mental system.

The brightness of the head light which the new batteries have provided is making the route up through the woods much easier and taking out a good amount of risk of stumbling on partially-submerged tree roots or slipping in the mud and pulling tired old muscles.

While making my way at a pretty good pace towards the top of the hill and out into the open path leading to the wood yard on the outskirts of Wentworth village, my thoughts are with all my friends who will be putting themselves out to meet me throughout the night, renewing my resolve to complete this challenge as near on time as possible.

The traffic is fairly busy on the main road, as I make steady progress up towards the village church and past the junior school just beyond the crossroads.

It's time for the lights again halfway up the tarmac drive, before the turn off to the open country path.

I have been able to maintain a steady run since leaving the village, but decide to walk down the narrow boggy path, which bears the scars of the athletes who have left their deep footprints in the mud throughout the day. This churned-up, narrow footpath is extremely slippery all the way down to the bottom of the fairly steep hill, making it fairly torturous on my back in this limited light.

My feet disappear under the quagmire of mud along the lower path before crossing the small bridge over the stream at the bottom of the hill.

The climb up to the village above is used to clear my feet of the thick black mud, by using the grass sods on the side of the path. There's a sudden chill in the night air as the wind picks up on the exposed, open land before reaching Thorpe Hesley. It's so important that I keep warm and comfortable throughout the night, especially before sleep deprivation and fatigue start to take effect. I have decided to take a short break to put on my wet coat and drink. The effect is almost instantaneous and before much longer I feel comfortable and ready to get underway again.

I am getting funny looks from a group of people who look as though they are walking up the hill to spend an evening at the pub on the outskirts of Thorpe Hesley village. They are ordinary civilised people going about their normal business. I must admit that I am not your ordinary looking person out this Saturday evening. The shower that I would have taken at the college if all had gone right would have been great, but it's better to be here at this time, even though I am looking like a poorly-dressed tramp, than playing catch-up and risking picking up another injury. I am surprised that I haven't been stopped by the police during my night running.

The well-lit footpath and steep steps between the houses give me a firm footing for a few minutes around the steel tube pedestrian control barriers. It's soon time to switch on the head torch again as I run into the open, dark countryside. The climb up from the houses in the valley proves to be another muddy skating rink, no matter which path I take. Passing the health centre on my right, the security lights are providing enough lighting for me to plot the best route up this greasy-like hillside. It's easier to walk up the hill to the trees on the ridge, taking advantage of a drink from my camel back and ringing through to Helen to make her aware that I am getting closer to our meeting time.

"Hi Helen, it's Ray," there's a good amount of excited background noise coming from her phone, making it difficult to hear her. She is with a group of Kimberworth Striders in the Green Dragon Inn on the outskirts of Kimberworth, which is just over a mile away from our meeting point; they are celebrating the club's success in the RRR. "I am pretty much on time and just coming into Scholes village, will ring again when I reach Keppel's Column, which should give you time to reach the pub car park before I get there." I make sure that the phone is switched off and safely stashed away in a pocket on my belt before moving off again; being able to contact my team is vital, must be able to let them know if I get delayed at all. It's time to get underway again.

The imposing 115ft brick-built Keppel's Column is silhouetted with the lights from the housing estate behind and soon looming high above me as I finally get closer to the safety of the houses. My feet are saturated from the boggy gorse grass up the hill to the housing estate and squelching as I run down the side road, making a rhythmic beat for me to run to.

Helen and Kevin have arrived and are waiting for me in the car park of the Effingham Arms pub as I run pretty comfortably down the hill on Upper Wortley Road toward where they are parked up, opposite Droppingwell Road. I have managed the 12 miles or so from the college in a more than satisfactory way and will be arriving at just a couple of minutes past 11, just over my predicted time. Twelve miles completed, or, as I have just decided while running down the hill to the car park, from now on the miles covered will begin with the true figure of 100. So, 112 miles, bloody hell, how good does that sound? It's as good as it gets.

I am well into new mileage territory now and continually running beyond into new PBs. Right, let's get that out of the way and concentrate on the miles ahead of me.

Helen is out of the car waiting to greet me in the corner of the front car park as I arrive in full flight. Kevin, who is sitting in the front, has pulled the front seat forward to allow me easy access into the back seat to relax for a while as I eat the first of my requested meals, jam butties and hot coffee. They are both inquisitive about the run and wanting to know how I am feeling, but both commenting that they can't believe how well I am looking. Very encouraging remarks and having the effect of bringing home the enormity of the challenge so far.

The weather forecast looks pretty good for the next 12 hours, I am told, which will help through the night, hopefully keeping the paths and fields in the same condition as they have been throughout the day.

It's time to make a move and before setting off, we have a couple of photos taken with me and Helen. Thanks guys, it's great to have friends who are prepared to give up their time to make my challenge that much more achievable.

After expressing my thanks and a hug from Helen, my legs are surprisingly easy as I set off down Droppingwell Road leaving them behind.

Must not miss the turn off on my left, which is further down the road than I had thought, as I head almost freewheeling down the hill, but the track is easier to spot than I first feared and soon it's head lights on again and take my first steps steadily up the hill towards Hilltop. My running world at the moment is confined to just the distance the head torch reaches and takes me into another dimension that is created by my vivid imagination, with shapes that turn out to be nothing more than rocks or bushes.

The right turn off comes as a relief after the hard slog through the dark, dense tunnel of trees, which has left me sweating for the first time in ages, but as I head for Hilltop along the fenced-off grassy field, I am able to settle again into a good steady run.

The route takes me down between the houses on the signed footpath and on to the grassy path between the houses. Oh hell, I am tumbling head over heels having just tripped on a submerged stone on the grassy, rock-filled path. Amazingly completing a full somersault and ended up in a sitting position, I am waiting with bated breath to see what else is going to kick in and start giving me pain other than my big toe. This is bringing back vivid memories of an incident in the Sahara Desert when I broke my big toe during a sudden desert sand storm in March 2010.

At about 5km into the recent 100 kilometres desert race, while heading out on the first leg to Bibain, I felt the first wind hit me head on. It sort of sneaked up to start with and then, bang, almost stopped me dead in my tracks. That was quickly followed by the full force of the sand; it was like being shot-blasted. Survival mode kicked in and covering up became priority number one, with goggles over my eyes, mouth and nose covered with the buff I was wearing. It felt like stinging pellets to my arms and legs and I could taste the sand as it forced its way through the buff cover. Was I breathing too hard? "Relax," I remember thinking, control my breathing or I am heading for trouble. It's such a shock to the system and leaves you feeling very vulnerable and alone; suddenly, it's like your worst nightmare, you can't see your hand in front of your face and you question your sense of survival and ability to navigate, to be honest it was bloody scary.

I had made a mental note of the next flags located half a mile away and was confident that I was heading in the right direction and, while leaning into the storm, I had stubbed and broken my big toe on a partially submerged rock. The noise was like a twig snapping, which I heard above the howling wind. The pain was just sickening, the sort of pain that when you were young you would have wished your Mum was there to kiss it better. Yes, that sort of pain; I just knew it was broken.

I had gone tumbling over onto my back and in the process had cut my arm on a sharp rock. The blood, which was now trickling down my left arm, was soon caked in a layer of sand, which seemed to cauterise the cut and stem the flow of blood after a short while. I lay there cursing my stupidity for missing what turned out to be a trail of bedrock that I was running on instead of the soft sand of a few minutes earlier. I remember sitting up and waited for the pain to subside.

With my back to the storm, I swilled out my mouth, which felt so dry and was slowly filling as if I had half the desert inside. The throbbing started again and I remember thinking what's going to happen if I can't put any weight on my damaged toe? I had to blank out the pain and make tracks; I could have been out there for hours waiting for help. I remember getting up and putting my damaged foot to the ground and applying weight slowly. It didn't feel too bad. So I set off walking and then running, but compensating and trying not to bend the toe as I pushed off on the outside of my right foot heading off into the storm, hoping and praying that I was heading in the right direction, looking out for flags or any indication that I was on the right route.

I remembered that the wind had been hitting me not quite head on but slightly to my left, so setting myself up again I felt fairly confident that after the tumble which had left me a bit disorientated, I was heading in roughly the right direction.

A few minutes later I could make out a large dark shape to my left in the side of a dune, which turned out to be a photographer covered over with what looked like a tent, with only the lens of the camera sticking out. He must have been sitting there for ages waiting for runners to pass. I knew then I was heading in roughly the right direction. It was a great feeling knowing you were not lost in this wilderness, just hope the cameraman wasn't feeling claustrophobic in his little shelter.

I soon came across a large flag that had been flattened by the storm, which I tried to erect for the benefit of the runners coming at the back of me. It was extremely difficult because of the strong wind. I remember thinking later that it was a stupid thing to have attempted; I had been in danger of being airborne at any minute, with visions of paragliding across the Sahara Desert in the wrong direction. Eventually I did manage to erect the flag and felt better knowing that the runners behind me would have had a target to aim for.

The sand was being blown off what I later found out was an ancient nomad trail which for most of the year was deep in sand, but was being exposed because of the wind leaving this rocky bed stripped of deep sand and which I had missed due to half closed eyes and lack of visibility. The storm lasted for the best part of two hours.

It's OK, seems as though I have nothing other than just the pulsating pain from my right big toe, my half-filled camel back has saved my back from any damage. Getting to my feet, I don't feel any the worse for that tumble other than the dull pain in my big toe, just glad there's no-one around to have seen that dramatic dive, ha, ha. What a good thing that all my bits and bobs were safely stashed and zipped up in my rucksack, could have easily lost important items. Remember, and make a mental note for the future, it could happen at any time.

Back on the 150-mile challenge in Rotherham, I am finding it easy going down the hill to the first road and then onwards down the steep path on to Meadowbank Road below. I switch the head light off to conserve the batteries, as the busy Meadowbank Road is well lit and providing a clear view of what's in front. It's more comfortable to be running on the tarmac causeway than the last couple of off road miles, as I head towards Rotherham, crossing over just before South Street, on to the wide grass verge, and locating the half hidden path just beyond the TDE warehouse, that will take me down to the river path below.

Lights on again and it's wise, I feel, to use the additional hand torch down this dangerous path. With full light it's easy to see that there have probably been athletes who have lost their footing down this first section of the path by the looks of the skid marks on the stones.

It's important to make sure of my footing and even more important to tread carefully over the steel railway bridge, which is also proving to be slippery on the smooth, worn down chequer floor plates. Hanging on to the handrail for dear life, I slowly make my way down the two flights of steel chequer plate steps to the safety of the river bank path below.

I am heading towards Sheffield along the canal bank now with just the hand torch, which is providing me with enough light to see the dark path upfront, skirting around some of the deeper black, muddy pools before reaching the bridge which crosses over the river and leads up to the split section of the canal. The path is full of deep, muddy footprints from earlier athletes.

Soon the lights from the roads and streets around the Tinsley area are making it easier to navigate as I run out of the towpath, through the barriers and on to Sheffield Road. I am still running very comfortably and feeling pretty good even at this stage of the run, leaving the towpath at Tinsley and on to the tarmac at last.

These well-lit roads make a welcome change as I head up Bawtry Road past the boarded up Pike and Heron pub. I was once told that you could get almost anything you might want at this pub, from drugs to a knocked off Ferrari. If only half of what I was told was taking place here, then there's no wonder the pub has been closed down.

I have been very conscious of drinking regularly, I know the value of hydration, and it has paid dividends up to now. I have also been nibbling on dried fruit and nuts throughout the night. It's so important to maintain the energy levels that can only come from food and drink. I had estimated that I would probably need to consume more than eight gallons of water to keep me topped up, hydration is just as important as consumption of food. I will have to service something like 35,000 calories, which should provide me with the energy I will need during this 150-mile challenge. But during this last 50 miles, I feel the best way of providing energy will come from solid food, rather than relying on energy gels. My feelings are that I need to keep my body functioning as naturally and normally as possible over this last 50-mile stretch, using my digestive system to break down solid food, which should, if I have got my calculations right, slowly release the natural fuel into the system and provide the energy I will need. I have fortunately always been able to consume solid food and run at the same time, so I should be OK.

Isn't it strange how your mind stores information without really knowing that it has? Mine has just kicked in and reacted, sending a cold sweat down my back as I reach the entrance to the industrial estate after passing the school on my right. It's creating a sort of fear and bringing back memories of the pain that had suddenly kicked in at this spot just over 13 hours ago. I had actually forgotten about the problems of yesterday over the last 15 miles or so, but nevertheless I am determined to get past this point as quickly as possible and set off down the road heading for the far end at a faster pace. It comes as a relief to complete the length of the road without any recurrence of the hamstring problem I had suffered for more than six hours during Saturday.

After coming to a stop before climbing the stile at the edge of the main Brinsworth-Catcliffe Road, I decide to contact Glynn Hookbody, my next contact and team member, who will be meeting me at the Treeton Cricket Club car park.

Glynn had offered his help and services without hesitation more than two months ago when I had mentioned this challenge. He is the general caretaker, handyman, who sorted out most of the running day to day problems with plant and equipment at the gym in Parkgate, Rotherham, where I did most of my additional cross-training. Glynn, a pretty fit guy himself, has been an active member of the group who took part in my boxing workouts over the months leading up to this challenge. This additional boxing training without a doubt has helped me to achieve the extra fitness that makes the difference between being fit and being fit enough to take on and complete this challenge.

I am feeling pretty good, other than tired through lack of sleep, but can't see any real reason why I shouldn't be able to make the target time.

Catcliffe is soon visible from the path leading to the Parkway dual carriageway and soon I'm reaching the steps which take me underneath the concrete bridge and into the housing estate. The streets leading slightly downhill on to the main road are well lit and then it's flat again as I head towards Orgreave.

It's just turned 12.30 as I leave the tarmac road and turn left up the banked soil path heading towards the Treeton Dykes. The head torch provides a pretty good white light along the wide rutted path, which is a bit rough underfoot and uncomfortable to run on because of the oversize stone and brick rubble, which makes for a flattish but potentially wobbly ankle-turning problem for about a quarter of a mile.

Crossing the river over the steel bridge brings relief as I slow down to a walk through the pedestrian control barriers and on to the well-packed soil path beyond, leading to the steep steps of the railway bridge and the housing estate alongside the second checkpoint.

Glynn arrived a couple of minutes after I had made it to the large gates of the cricket club car park; he had been misdirected with the sat nav, but I was in fact three minutes ahead of our pre-arranged time of 12.45. I used the time to re-adjust my clothing and shoes just before he pulled into the entrance.

I declined his offer of a seat inside his car, opting to use the roof of his car as a table to set out the chicken soup, bread cakes and coffee; all we needed was a tablecloth to make it look like an official party. It's great to see Glynn and even better that I am back on track with the timing after all the trauma of earlier, I couldn't ask for more.

We stood leaning on the car while I consumed the food and watched the rushed activities of the late arrivals home. It's amazing the number of taxis that were coming onto the surrounding streets, dropping off mainly young women during the 15 minutes or so that we had been here, probably night clubbers coming home, it's about 1am now, but it is Saturday night, sorry, Sunday morning, after all, so is that normal? Us old wrinklies are normally in bed by ten.

The weather was changing and beginning to feel cold and damp while we were stood talking and finishing the last of the tasty soup. A second cup of coffee was a great idea and thankfully received, but I need to be on the move again ASAP, I feel, before my legs start to seize up from the inactivity.

I am reminded by Glynn that my achievement up to this point is something out of the ordinary and his comments of how well I look have a great effect and sort of charges up the batteries for me, but while it's brilliant to have my ego boosted, it's also time to come back down to earth and get underway again. Cheers Mate.

I pass on my thanks and reiterate my appreciation to Glynn for taking time to come out and meet me with the food and drinks; it's the basics of my being able to continue with this challenge. I shout farewell and wave as I head off up the hill, making the turn to my right into the dark avenue of trees and on to the soil path above the cricket club tarmac car park, leaving Glynn to make his way home and bed. "Envy".

The head light is back in use again before long and soon picks out a strange scene in front of me as I make my way from high level down to the lower level of the lakes. There's an unusual, eerie vision down below with the mist which is hanging above the ground in the valley, but is only about four feet in depth, a bit like being in the clouds while in an aeroplane. But before I had reached the bottom of the path, I was having all sorts of problems with my head torch, which is bouncing the light back at me with more glare than looking into the sun. I had to stop just before reaching the path along the dyke; I just couldn't see through the mist and the light was making matters dangerously worse.

This rather strange and eerie sight ahead of me with the swirling mist all around my feet but not quite up to my waist looks alive and out of control. It would be dangerous to continue running along the path, who knows what obstacle I could be running into, it's just not worth the risk, as I set off walking across the narrow steel bridge, feeling my way with the side handrails.

By my holding it as low to the ground as possible the hand torch is providing a light of sorts. I find that the light is not bouncing back quite as much and is just about faintly picking out the path a couple of feet in front of me. The lakes to my right and the sudden drop in temperature must be the cause of the mist.

The mist is starting to clear as I reach the terraced houses just before the main A57 dual carriageway and has totally disappeared for the time being as I leave the last cottage, allowing me to pick up the running again as I cross over the now quiet dual carriageway and down the path by the side of the joinery works, heading towards the viaduct a couple of miles away.

No sooner have I reached the low-level paths than the mist is back swirling in front of me, causing problems again , dense to start with and then intermittent, slowing me down and giving cause for concern about being late for my next meeting at Harthill with Andy Squires.

My eyes are stinging from the glare of the dense mist. Trying to get the light to work through the mist is frustrating; finally I come to the conclusion that it's better with the light off and just come to terms with walking and being very slow at times. The glare, which bounces back when I get the beam direction wrong, is blinding, it's best to take it nice and steady if I don't want to end up in the deep muddy puddles. I am going to have to be patient and use the slow pace to relax and rest as much as possible.

Zipping up my coat to the neck and putting on a pair of gloves creates the warmth that will be needed over the next few miles, until I can get clear of the low-level ground mist and back to running. Hopefully the mist will disappear before too long.

The viaduct, which has been silhouetted in front of me for a good few minutes, is finally reached and shortly after passing through the fifth arch and the last of the flat terrain, there is the challenge of a sharp uphill turn and the main dual carriageway road above, which makes a welcome change. The road above, which is clear of traffic, has provided a welcome relief from the misty path. The tarmac of the well-lit road provides a good running surface, even though it's only for a short spell before turning sharp right back down on to the black soil path on the other side of the railway track. This low level path will take me alongside the fenced off railway line for a few hundred yards before turning left up the bank side and through to Rother Valley Country Park, but at last the mist has dispersed.

I am starting to feel weary and it's becoming increasingly difficult to concentrate, as the path opens up on to the wide tarmac road which will take me through and out of the park. My eyes are stinging because of the glare of the mist and probably with lack of sleep over the last 42 hours or so since I last got out of bed.

The long drag out of the park on this never-ending road is having a negative effect on me; fortunately the slow climb on this monotonous road is fairly flat and smooth, allowing me to close my eyes for about ten seconds at a time in relative safety while still running; it is helping to soothe and take the strain out of my eyes. Although I am wandering about like an intoxicated idiot, there's little chance of being hit by traffic at this time in the morning, before reaching the park exit and the right turn on to the main road leading to Norwood.

I could do with a break to fuel up and the wall just inside the entrance to the drive off the main road to my left makes as good a spot as any to sit down for a minute and eat some dried fruit, a slice of malt loaf and drink electrolyte water.

I need to get my head in gear and focus on the next two or three miles for my meeting with Andy at the shops car park in Harthill. An extra couple of Jelly Babies, a segment of a Mars Bar and another good drink of water should be enough to provide a boost of energy for the coming few miles.

It's time to get underway again up the drive and past the magnificent new stone houses to my right. These imposing houses are set with landscaped gardens, tennis courts and large fish ponds that are fed from a derelict canal which runs between the drive and a private fishing pond to my right.

Before passing the top pond to my right, the head light is needed again as the damaged wooden stile comes into view at the end of this uneven path. The rickety stile needs careful negotiating for safety and just lifting my legs in a high arc to clear the top bar is proving difficult. My legs feel tired and stiff while crossing the grassy field to the higher level path by the side of the M1 motorway.

The walk up the hill on the narrow field path to Woodall village gives me time to recover and the energy boost from the Jelly Babies has started to kick in before it's time to turn off the road by the side of Todd's Cottage, between the houses on to the very narrow ploughed path that will take me past the pylon in the middle of the field and down the valley in the bottom.

Harthill is quite visible on the horizon as I make my way over the bottom stile, which I had nicknamed "the torture chamber" after a quite painful episode during the double lap a couple of years ago when my foot shot away on the muddy plank. I had come down on the hard ground with a jolt and my right lower leg muscles locked up solid. My calf had looked so deformed, almost as if I had had a tennis ball implanted under the skin where my calf should have been, and the muscle in my shin looked like a solid steel rod which was pulling my foot into a deformed cramp. The pain was really horrible, excruciating. I remember the cold sweat and the sickening feeling in my stomach. No amount of massaging would make any difference whatsoever and cursing for all I was worth didn't work either. I knew that I would have to be patient, relax and just wait for the muscles to settle, which seemed like hours, but in fact probably only took just a few minutes. Oh the relief as the muscles slowly started to ease back to their normal shapes, it was better than winning the pools as they say, but I felt that I had reached the limit where parts of my body were about to rebel and refuse to keep going at this 75-mile distance. This was certainly a new experience for me because I am this so-called tough guy who never has any problems of this sort. I remember hoping and praying that this was just going to be a one-off. I remember having to dig in deep to get my mind into a positive state as I set off walking up the hill to the Harthill checkpoint, nursing my right leg as though it were broken.

I shudder as I relive the memory and cross over the stile with extreme caution.

There's enough light from the village street lighting for me to pick out the route fairly clearly as I make tracks around the play area, across the car park between the house and through the pub snicket after passing the club house and event checkpoint. I am meeting Andy 100 yards down the road toward Kiveton Park in the off road car park.

My watch is showing 2.45am, slowing down to a walk as I reach the shops, "how good is that?" as I reach Andy, my predicted meet time is due in five minutes at 2.50.

The one and only car, which is parked in the middle of the car park with a tired-looking Andy at the wheel, is providing a very welcoming sight. The timing has been like clockwork and so satisfying for this very weary athlete up to now. "Ey up mate, been waiting long?"

The success of my challenge can only be achieved by having these close friends who have so willingly and unselfishly given up their sleep to come out to meet me on time. I feel a sense of duty to make the connection on time, or as close as possible These mates are giving up their beds to help me, but arriving too early and having to wait any length of time for their arrival would result in becoming cold during the night, partial hypothermia may be possible through inactivity, which could result in tight, damaged muscles and God knows what else.

Andy has been waiting for about ten minutes or so for my arrival, having travelled all the way from Rawmarsh, the other side of Rotherham.

The passenger seat is warm and comfortable with plenty of room to spread out, making it a welcome change from the cold night.

While eating my honey and banana mix from the Tupperware container, it's good to be talking to Andy after all the time on my own; filling him in with a short version of what the past couple of days had been like for me has passed on a good ten minutes. But once again it's time to make the increasingly more difficult decision to make a move, knowing that if I don't get underway soon I will become stiff.

I think my brain has gone to sleep, because I am finding it increasingly more difficult to carry out any meaningful conversation or make myself move. But I have to get back on track and think about the others who will be coming out to meet me throughout the morning.

Topping up the camel back and thanking Andy for all his help, it's time to go, ready or not.

My legs are as stiff as a board and reluctant to become mobile as I make my exit from the car. The night air is chilly; it's like stepping into a fridge, creating a bit of a shock, after leaving the warmth of the car. There's a need to warm up, like I would do before doing any exercise, it should save possible muscle damage. Exaggerated movements while walking for a couple of minutes are working and the stiffness gone before too long, leaving me feeling full of running again. I can't remember if I thanked Andy enough for his help, and felt a sense of guilt if I hadn't, but it's too late now if I didn't. No point in worrying, although I am sure I must have, what's going on, my brain is all over the place or gone to sleep.

The steep concrete path, which will take me up to the fields above Harthill, needs to be carefully negotiated in the damp night, and takes my mind off the earlier problem.

Harthill is now long behind me as I head out across the long field towards the large silos of the farm in the distance. My thoughts are about Maureen and hoping that she has been able to get some sleep, I know that she will have been worried about me since we last met at Maltby and hopefully the call I made at about 9.30 will have put her mind at rest. I have also been picking up good luck and well done messages from my daughter Karen and grandsons Adam and Ryan throughout the night, who have been keeping in touch with my progress and passing on the information to the large group of friends who have been monitoring my movements on Facebook and Twitter. Karen and Chris, my son-in-law, will be picking Maureen up to take her to the college in a few hours' time.

The gap in the hawthorn hedge seems to have been widened since I came through yesterday afternoon, making it easier to locate and pass through, as I leave the farm and start the long downhill trek over this sea of mud.

By the time I have reached the steel pylon in the middle of the field, I am running out of energy, feeling cold, uncomfortable and, to be brutally honest, bloody miserable. My legs have slowed down to a sort of slow-motion action over this sticky mud, just as though I have shackles on my ankles and dragging steel weights over this obstacle course. I feel absolutely drained for the first time since starting out. This is probably about the time when it's easier to give in than to keep going. I realised that I had not eaten or drunk anything for the last four or five miles since coming out of Harthill. God, I really am letting myself down. I feel close to meltdown, mentally and emotionally struggling.

Standing in the middle of this never-ending field I decide to switch off my head torch and just "Scream" "Haaaaagh", into the pitch black night. It's the only sensible thing to do really.

Oh hell, I need to sort myself out and get these negative feelings out of my head. Analysing the situation in the quiet of this field, my thoughts are that I am burning up far more energy than I am putting back. Baby food is the answer I think. Yes, you have read it right; I have a couple of 250ml bottles of SMA follow on baby milk in the bottom of my rucksack. Packed with everything I need to get into my depleted body, it should deliver a speedy boost of calories and get into the system quickly to provide the energy supply I so desperately need right now. But the cold creamy milk tastes foul; don't know why babies love it. A slice of malt loaf and a small portion of Christmas cake, together with a good drink of water, will do the trick, but it will take a few minutes for the food to kick in and convert into energy. I have obviously miscalculated on the hydration and my calorie needs for these last 50 miles.

There is much misinformation about hydration and fuelling from so-called experts who claim that we need to consume from between 200ml and 2 litres of liquid during marathon activities. Blimey, what a huge difference, so who's right? Well considering that my stomach is only the size of a large orange, which will expand to take in huge amounts of water, (something I would never do because, don't forget that it's also possible to over hydrate, where the excessive amounts of liquid in the body could create all kinds of problems for the athlete to deal with, even death).

Certain minerals for the body to function efficiently need to be present, and the body is always working to create the right balance of sodium and phosphorous, so one major problem with drinking too much water is the fact that you could throw off the electrolyte balance within the body. There are so many equations to take into account during long distance running and for me the knowledge and familiarity of my own individual needs feature above all else. It's more about knowing your own body, the sweat and work-rate intensity, which does vary drastically over distance, even different weather conditions and, in this case, time on my feet and sleep deprivation. Hey guys, I am certainly no expert on the subject and don't profess to be, but my advice is to listen to everyone and then make your own mind up.

When I was trying to work out my food intake for this event, which was always going to be difficult because of the compounding miles to energy usage, together with the overall time without rest or sleep adding to the equation, I did feel that this baby milk could become my secret weapon and possibly get me out of unforeseen difficulty.

Stride after stride I am feeling better as the miles pass by and soon the blip I had experienced while coming down the long field is just a distant memory. I am looking forward to taking on the rest of this challenge with enthusiasm. My secret weapon has well and truly worked.

Netherthorpe Airfield is brightly lit up with the security beams focusing on the parked-up planes to my right and is as quiet as it should be at 3.45 in the morning, as I make my way through the farmyard beyond.

The small village on the outskirts of Thorpe Salvin provides a tarmac surface in which to clear a good amount of mud from my shoes before turning right after the crossroads on to the grassy path leading to Turner Wood.

There's a hint of moonlight as I leave the slightly-raised grassy footpath before running on to the narrow tarmac road into Turner Wood.

Crossing the stone bridge over the Chesterfield Canal, the floodlights are activated again, creating an almost daylight effect around the outbuildings and gardens of the first terraced cottage. I make an exaggerated wave for the benefit of the camera; Diane and Mick will see the video film in a few hours. They are aware that I should be coming through at about this time and will be pleased that I am still making headway and with reasonably good timing.

This tranquil little hamlet, quiet now at this time in the morning, would have been a hive of activity during the 1840s, when stone from Anston quarry, produced less than a couple of miles away was shipped into London and used to build the Palace of Westminster. The soft, sand-coloured material was chosen after the architect Charles Barry, together with a leading stone carver, chose the Yorkshire stone because of its ease of cutting, also because it was probably cheaper and could be supplied in blocks up to four feet. It's debatable whether the rows of cottages were built to house the workers at the quarry or those working on the then newly-laid railway, but one sure fact is that my old friend Roy Warboy and his parents have lived in Turner Wood for well over a century.

Woodsetts is my next target as I leave the railway lines and run on the raised path above the relief dyke towards the farm buildings.

The moon is flitting in and out of the clouds as I reach the top of the hill and for the first time in this last 50 miles I am feeling a twinge in my right calf that is not going away by just willpower or even by talking nicely to it. "Told you I was probably mental, well there's no-one else to talk to." I reckon it's OK talking to yourself, as long as you don't answer yourself back and create a one-sided conversation that you can't win or control.

While taking part in any endurance race, there is always this constant, subconscious dialogue taking place and sometimes it needs to be verbal, especially at times like right now. I really do believe that above all else you have to become great mates with yourself; you're on your own, hour after hour in your own company. Imagine what it would be like if you didn't like yourself? I am expecting worse to come before it's all over; I need to activate the power that makes the difference between failure and success. There is always a price to pay, very few long distance athletes will escape the pain, and the bigger the challenge, the bigger the price you have to pay. At the time of thinking about running these 150 miles, I did realise that once I had mentally accepted this challenge, there would be times like this and the hamstring during yesterday. There's maybe even worse to come, but I felt then, that I would be strong enough to get through any of these negative blips. Ultra distance running is a very individual sport, even though you may have dozens of other athletes around it's a very lonely event, because it's all down to you and your ability but I know that whatever comes I am confident that I will be ready to meet the challenge.

More electrolyte and a vigorously good massage has worked with the calf, but it is still on the tight side as I run down towards the crossroads at Woodsetts and my next food stop.

I had received a text message ten minutes previously that my good friend, Tony Parkinson, was already waiting at the village shops. I had arranged to meet him under the good street lighting outside the village shops on the right as you leave the village towards Worksop, rather than down the dark private road at the Scout hut. It was always going to be easier for me just to turn the corner, knowing that there was plenty of light from the street lamps, rather than meet down the dark lane off the main road. He has been there for more than 20 minutes now, although I am just over ten minutes late at 4.40am by the time I arrive.

It's tempting again to take a seat in his car, but I have decided to decline his offer and by opening the passenger door on his 4x4 Land Rover as wide as it would go I manage to half sit, half lean inside the warm cab stretching my calf muscles. Tony had been keeping up with all the Tweeting and text information throughout the day and night, telling me that he was always confident that I would make our arranged meeting on time. God bless him!

I could smell my meal well before Tony had taken the tin-foil package out of the carrier bag. What a brilliant sight it was as he opened up the foil to reveal two thick juicy lamb chops in mint sauce. Tony burst out laughing as I tucked into the first chop with gusto. A couple of small bread cakes, half a mug of hot chocolate and a piece of fruit cake had been set out on the dash board for me, as good as any first class restaurant.

While discussing my food requirements during the meeting we had had a few weeks ago, I had requested the lamb chops and when I told him that I would supply the chops if he would cook them, his comments were, "If you are gonna eat bloody lamb chops after running all that distance, then I am buying. Lamb chops on the menu during a long distance run!" Unheard of, I suppose, but my thoughts were that by this late stage I would be in the need of some fat inside me. Luckily I am able to run after eating solid food. God, these are cooked to perfection. The chops taste great. I have decided to just eat the one I am devouring right now and take the second one with me to eat in a couple of miles or so.

The light-hearted banter which I have been enjoying for the last 15 minutes has left me feeling full of beans and relaxed. Tony, always the comedian, has one of the best supplies of jokes around and without a doubt should be earning a living on the stage rather than wasting his time in the warehouse at Tesco. Thanks, mate, not only for the supply of food, but also for the enthusiastic send-off and the supply of jokes that will keep me going and chuckling for many a mile. "Well done Crack-pot I know you're gonna make it; see you soon mate" shouted Tony as I left the warmth of his car.

My side are aching from laughter as I head off towards the edge of the village - or is it the food?

Just before heading down the cinder track towards the open fields, there's a toot on the horn as he comes past me and disappears into the night. Wow, I am running well, feeling pretty comfortable and hoping to pull back about ten minutes or so to bring me back in line with my predicted times before I reach Firbeck and another one of my good friends, Ray Silcock.

I am in overdrive now and running without effort. The moon has been kind for the past half hour or so, providing me with enough light to be able to switch the head light off as the miles pass by without any real incidents other than severe lower back ache that has been with me for two or three miles. I was hoping to run it off, but a couple of Paracetamols and a good drink of electrolyte should eventually take care of the pain.

I have been mentally entertaining myself with some of the jokes that Tony had told me. I had promised myself that I would remember all the great jokes and hopefully be able to provide a good rendition of them all, but by the time I had reached Langold I couldn't remember one. Typical, never have been able to remember great jokes that could be so useful for breaking the ice when doing the motivational talks.

The low-level moonlight is creating a picturesque image across the large Langold Lake as I emerge from the woods behind the old, redundant open air swimming pool.

It's time for a short break before reaching the woods, and the remaining lamb chop, which is still warm in the foil and oh so tasty, the mint sauce which has soaked into the meat and fat provides the mouth-watering magic.

I am beginning to feel the change in the air and realise that it won't be long now before dawn, as I reach the edge of the woods which will take me through to the open fields. It's strange how the atmosphere changes in the air just before dawn arrives.

My back is starting to rebel again and has been troublesome for the last half hour; it's not going to go away unless I take another couple of Paracetamol tablets. I feel like a pill popper, but it's the only way I am able to continue with my day-to-day activities.

It's starting to become lighter as I emerge from the small wood and out on to the Dinnington to Oldcoats road. I can see my next target just under half a mile away in the valley below as I steadily make the best use of the wide downhill path before climbing up from the ford on the gravel drive to Firbeck and my next pit stop.

Ray Silcock and his wife, Margaret, are waiting as I emerge from the darkened path into the bright light from the street lamp on the corner across from the Black Lion pub. I realise that another mate, John Clark, whom I haven't seen since yesterday afternoon, has also come out to meet me. It's just after 6am and I am on track again, having pulled back a good ten minutes over the last few miles, can't explain just how pleasing that is.

I am keen to get underway and keep up the momentum of being back on time before the stiffness sets in during the inactivity while drinking the hot coffee, and although the offer of company for the next four miles is tempting, I must decline Ray's offer for much the same reasons I had to decline Vonnie's company last night. Unless they have drastically dried out, the fields across to Maltby are boggy and difficult to deal with. Even though I have pulled back the ten minutes that was lost between Harthill and Woodsetts, I am still on the edge of the time limits that I have set for myself. I am never going to make it for 10am if I can't maintain the discipline of hitting the checkpoint locations on time. Sorry Ray, just can't take the risk of anything going wrong with something that I can't control, but a massive thanks to you and Margaret for coming out to meet me and providing the food and drink. They must have been up since before 5am, can't thank them enough for all their help.

Leaving the well-lit street behind, I make the right turn on to the grassy path behind St Martin's Church. It's a toss-up whether there is any advantage to using the head torch as the partial natural daylight is just beginning to make the difference between night and day. Although dawn has not yet quite broken, I plump for putting the head light away while slowing down to a walk for a few minutes and patiently wait for better light.

I am on my way home! What a great feeling, Maureen is waiting for my arrival at our cottage on Church Lane, Maltby, with a change of footwear and socks.

The soles of my feet are starting to feel sore and somewhat tender; especially my left foot, which has become increasingly more painful since I came down heavily on a rather sharp stone just before Firbeck. I had decided to change from running shoes to my lightweight walking boots to give me some extra protection and comfort over the last 12 miles or so.

Dawn at last, the light filtering over the edges in the distance sort of signals a new day, even though for me the day is almost six and a half hours old, but all of a sudden I can feel a new surge of energy, providing a real boost to the way I am feeling. This challenge is nearly over; and just that thought brings a massive grin to my face and a fantastic glow inside.

This challenge is now filling me with a profound sense of emotion, it feels so important that I complete this 150 miles for every runner who has been associated with me over the past few years, for my close family and every mate who has given up their time to help, support and encourage me, it's so vital for me to uphold my part of this commitment.

John is waiting in the old St Bartholomew church car park to greet me as I emerge through the old lichen gate. This guy must be psychic, there's a hot mug of coffee waiting on the roof of his car.

I really don't remember much about the last few miles since leaving the ruins of Roche Abbey, but the pace must have been pretty good, because I am a few minutes earlier than my predicted time of 7.15am, seems I can switch off and still maintain a good pace. Must be the familiarity of the last four miles, but I don't recommend running in this fashion without being in conscious control.

Taking the coffee across the road with me to our cottage, I can see my boots are waiting outside near the garden bench and Maureen is waiting with a clean pair of padded walking socks. It's a smart idea, leaving my change of footwear outside; I am filthy with literally half a field of mud attached to my legs and feet. There's no way on earth am I getting into the house in this state.

While changing from what loosely resembles a pair of running shoes and socks, I am able to fill Maureen in with a short version of my night's experience.

The sheer joy of foot comfort is drastically underestimated. Wow, what an amazing difference the change of footwear has made as I stand up from the bench! I am experiencing comfort far beyond what I thought could be possible this far into the event.

It's time to say goodbye to Maureen, we will be meeting in about two and a half hours when I arrive back at the college.

John is waiting with his bike at the ready, as I cross the road to hand back the mug.

There is no way that John will be able to keep up with me over the muddy fields and some of the worst terrain of the challenge to come. I know how keen he is to provide me with company, but I haven't got either the time or energy to help with the bike over stiles and deep mud areas. We agree for him to accompany me up to Micklebring, where we will part company. I will continue on the route, he will turn off along the main roads to Ravenfield and meet up again at the Old Denaby checkpoint with the rest of the guys to complete the last three miles on relatively flat easy terrain along the towpath

A brisk walk up past Maltby Grammar School, and my legs are back feeling as normal as they can be, this far into the challenge. With John riding alongside, I manage to break into a jog until reaching the top of Addison Road. The conversation is a bit of a one-sided affair I must admit, with John doing most of the talking, but I am sure that he understands, I must concentrate and continue to maintain the discipline.

It's time to phone through to let Phil and the gang know that I am on target and will be arriving at Old Denaby at our pre-arranged time of about 9.15am. They will then accompany me to the college and be with me at the end.

Progress is being maintained, but with less verbal contact from me as we head out on to the quiet main Braithwell road and we are shortly heading for Micklebring village full of expectations.

I have felt a degree of guilt by not contributing much if any to the conversation for the last mile, but I am sure John understands. I don't seem to have the energy; I am feeling weary, tired and uncomfortable with slight pains in my stomach that have been creeping up over the last couple of miles – maybe cramp?

We reach the edge of the village and it's time to part company as John waves farewell, heading back towards the main road and Ravenfield. I turn right towards Edlington and then make a left turn after reaching the last house in Micklebring, and head off down towards the motorway on the narrow grass path to the bottom of the field.

Just before reaching the wooden stile at the corner of the field, the deep rumbling in my stomach forces the quick decision to come to a full stop and drop my shorts. There's a distinct call of nature, well not so much a call, more like a scream as my bowels uncontrollably erupt. Thank God there's no one about as I am forced to remain in this most uncomfortable, exposed, squatting position at the bottom of this field for what seems an eternity. My thigh muscles are locked and on fire by the time I get the confidence to move, but try as I might it's impossible to stand erect, my legs don't seem too willing to bear my weight.

Looking around for something that I can use to help get me upright, I realise that the stile, which I can use as a ladder to get back upright, is about eight feet away in the corner of the field. There's nothing I can do now, only fall forward on to hands and knees. Crawling on all fours is the only way to reach the stile, where I can pull myself upright. Laughing out loud seems to be the only sensible thing to do in this situation. Is this funny or what? Probably would be to watch, but the pain from my legs says not. By the time I reach the stile my hands and knees are covered in a thick layer of mud. This is so embarrassing!

I need to pull myself up to the lower plank of the stile, which makes a seat for a few moments, while punching and massaging both swollen, locked thighs. "Ha, ha, I know what you're thinking," but all's well, I do carry a biodegradable toilet roll in my bag for just this situation, last needed in the Sahara Desert. It's time to collect my thoughts, before trying to lift myself over the stile and make some sort of progress. "Come on legs stop acting the goat and get moving".

I am absolutely lathered with sweat from that episode and feeling exhausted; just the simple action of forcing my legs over this low-level stile has required a larger amount of energy than I seem to possess and feels a bit like juggling razor blades at the moment. My legs are still burning from that extended squat, stiff, painful to touch, and feel as though they weigh a ton.

Slowly, almost crawling along the edge bottom to the next stile, it's easier to force my way through a gap in the hedge after breaking off a few branches to the left side of the stile, rather a few scratches than using depleting energy. A couple of Jelly Babies and a good drink will hopefully make enough difference before moving on to the next and last stile.

At last my legs are slowly coming back to near normal, but I am beginning to shiver and stiffen from the inactivity over the past few minutes. I decide to make use of my wet trousers that are stuffed into the bottom of the rucksack to increase my body temperature and hopefully provide heat to my shaking legs. It's fairly awkward getting tired and stiff legs into trousers, but while using the stile to keep me from falling flat on my face, I am confident that the extra effort I am using will reap the benefits that I so desperately need right now.

It's slowly working as my legs come back to life, but I decide to walk for the next mile or so and get some food inside me before any attempt at getting back to running and recovering some of the recent lost time.

Thankfully I am mentally back in control again after a spell of not being able to focus on the main issues of the moment. But fatigue is taking its toll, and taking all the effort I can muster to keep alert. Unfortunately I can't afford the luxury of stopping to rest and recuperate, must keep moving forward if only at a snail's pace.

Oh what a relief, that scare is thankfully over, some food and plenty of determination not to fail has got me back running again.

I am soon leaving the boggy path which winds its way down from the high ridge above Firsby Hall Farm and managing to clean off the mud from my boots on the grassy track just before reaching Hooton Roberts and the Rotherham– Doncaster main road where Holly and I parted company, "was it a week ago?" Well, it seems to be that long, but is, in fact, only just over 36 hours ago. I feel as though I have been on the go for ever, but the great news is that the energy is slowly returning and I am feeling more and more comfortable as the miles pass by, the food and electrolyte water have well and truly kicked in.

At last, all the climbing is over as I finally stand at the top of the hill surveying the panoramic horizon and down into the valley which will take me to the Old Denaby meeting point. It's still boggy, but I make the decision to just go for it and plough on down to the bottom of the field through the mud. My thighs are burning again well before reaching the gate at the bottom of the hill, but it's easier to run than to try to slow down, probably couldn't stop the increased momentum I had gathered anyway.

The change I made at home, from off-road running shoes to boots has proved to be a good move, not only are my feet dry but they are also still feeling pretty comfortable as I reach the road. I am slightly late due to the forced pit-stop an hour ago, but surprised that there is no-one here to meet me. John has probably gone ahead thinking that he will have missed me and perhaps Phil, Adele and Richard are still coming towards me from the college, they could well be feeling the effects of yesterday's 50-mile run in their legs and are taking their time. It gets worse over a couple of days, the muscle trauma takes a good week to settle down if we give way to it and rest instead of further exercising to relieve the muscles of the lactic build up. Sounds brutal to be stretching and working sore and fatigued muscles after 50 miles of running, but mark my words it's better than painful stiff legs and not being able to move for a week.

My plan of reaching the college for 10am can only be achieved if I get underway and try to pull back some time over this last three miles. Oh yes, just three miles to complete this challenge, hell, I could crawl from here if necessary. Ha, ha, well, I did have some practice a few miles back didn't I, but don't recommend it though, it's hard work on the knees.

With just three miles to go, it's almost over, and all of a sudden I feel full of running, the fatigue, aches and pains have gone, subconsciously I am now into that zone when I have mentally taken full control, it's a bit like breaking free of the shackles that my body has had to cope with for a good few hours and has suddenly given way to providing full co-operation as I get back up to speed.

Passing the entrance to the Manor Farm pub on my left I am able to run down the road at a good pace, turning left down Ferry Boat Lane to the railway level crossings and on to the canal towpath, mentally thanking whoever made these level crossings, rather than having to climb up and over on the pedestrian bridge that we had to use some years ago.

I am expecting to bump into John or the guys at any time as I increase my speed along the level well-trodden soil towpath, in an attempt to reduce the delay that I had incurred during the enforced pit stop below Micklebring Village.

The concrete fish is passed, marking the left turn off from the canal. Soon the tunnel leading to the railway platform is behind me as I descend onto the narrow river path which becomes a bit of a drag and seems to go on forever this morning, but at last I am out on to the tarmac, having just passed the concrete storage tank to my left away from the riverside. The bridge by the side of the industrial estate is now facing me; normally it slows runners down to a walk, at about the 48 and a half mile mark during the event, but today it looks like a mountain that needs conquering.

I have been continuously running more easily since it hit home that there were only three miles to go, more like I was at the start of this challenge, comfortable and, incredibly, without any tiredness in my legs or body. This feeling is great and confirms my theory that it's all about being able to control the mind. I must be subconsciously filtering the fact that I am less than a mile and a half away from finishing the challenge into my brain, which in turn is allowing my body to perform, even though it must be fatigued and wanting to call it a day.

Leaving the industrial area behind and crossing the bridge just past the Phillips factory, there is still no sign of my friends but I still need to press on, I am on time now and confident of reaching the finish line at my predicted time as long as the skids don't come off over this last mile and a bit.

The steep steps down from the bridge above, to the housing estate in Swinton, remind me that I am in fact on the end of a good old distance as my thighs tighten up again and provide an uncomfortable couple of minutes of running into the small housing estate at Swinton.

All of a sudden as I turn the corner into the estate, my friends Phil, Adele, Rose and Norman are in front of me and making a proper fuss. But there's no sign of John or Richard.

It looks as though Phil and Adele are recovering from the effects of yesterday's RRR, but Richard, who is struggling to move, a very common effect of running 50 miles at the sort of pace that he will have maintained, has decided to wait for me at the finish.

Time is passing and, although I have pulled nearly a quarter of an hour back since leaving Old Denaby, I am still on the edge of time to make it to the finish for 10am, with a need to keep moving towards the college guys.

Questions are being fired at me about how I am feeling, comments about how spritely I look and even a comment from Phil who suggested that "Well at least look as though you've just run 150 miles, then," as we drop down out of the car park of the Ship Inn pub onto the old canal towpath.

Rose is informing everyone who comes close to us about the distance that I have just completed, making me feel like a proper celebrity.

The college is close, it is time to get the Union Jack out of my rucksack and unfold it out to its full size, ready to use. Adele is ready with her camera as we make our way down the wide cycle track through the pedestrian barriers and then the brilliant view ahead of me reveals a crowd of friends waiting for my arrival on the grassy bank alongside the fenced-in pitches.

My watch shows half a minute past 10. Oh hell, half a minute outside of my predicted time of 10am. How can I feel disappointed with that result? It's almost over; I can see Maureen and my daughter, Karen, in the group of friends who are waiting a couple of hundred yards away. But I am suddenly aware of this strange sensation, not really what I was expecting, part of me doesn't want it to be over, I am not wiped out.

With the Union Jack flying above me, I make the last few yards' run in to the cheers and shouts of "Well done!" It feels as if I am floating along without my feet touching the ground as I run across the grass to finish my challenge.

I feel a mixture of elation and deep satisfaction that I have been able to conquer the 150 miles. It's over but my emotions are mixed, do I laugh, or release all the pent up feelings and cry like a baby? Holding back the tears that are ready to burst out is probably harder than just letting go, but I am that hard man who finds it difficult to show my emotions. I know that this distance has not taken me beyond my capabilities and I suppose I should feel happy with my performance. It did feel so good coming in at the end, but I could have gone on further if needed, leaving me feeling disappointed that this challenge has not taken me to the edge of my ability. Although I am left with a confident feeling that there is still more, part of me wanted this challenge to be the one that flattened me, my ultimate challenge.

So now what? Well, it's time to recover first and take stock of the lessons that have been learnt, but first of all it's time to celebrate with Maureen, Karen and my friends, above all else, to thank every one of them for their support and help, because without them, this challenge would have been almost impossible to achieve – we did this as a team and I feel proud to have fulfilled my side of the task.

They have all made time to be there, with the confidence that I would make it back to the college at Manvers on time, where it all started from about 38 hours ago. And to top it off, Rose and Norman have just presented me with a bottle of champagne, what a fantastic gesture and very much appreciated, I will pop the cork later on. Thanks, guys.

It's time to say goodbye and make tracks for home, but before we leave I have just one more important thing to do to complete the challenge. I need to go up to the large sports hall of the college where my challenge started from. Making my excuses to visit the toilet alongside the hall, I set off jogging up the drive to complete my challenge. It's just a small thing, but it is all about being true, the 100 yards may seem insignificant to most people, but to me it may as well be a mile. "It's finally done," as I reach the entrance to the hall, 150 miles has been well and truly achieved. Only thing I can't figure out, where my mate John has got to?

My final task before heading for the car is to pass on my thanks for the fantastic reception at the finish to Maureen, my daughter Karen, and son-in-law Chris, Glynn and his wife Lynn, and how lovely to see his grandchildren, Regan and

Reece, Vonnie and Andrew, Rose and Norman, Adele, Richard, Mick and Sue, with their son, Matt, and daughter, Vanessa, together with Sean and Maria and my old friends, Ken Chapman and Phil Haigh.

Vonnie and Andrew are coming back home with us to join Maureen, Karen and Chris for a meal together, before it's time for them to make the long journey down the M1 back home. After a well-deserved shower, the vigorous use of the toothbrush and a clean set of clothes, I am feeling half human again, surprisingly bright really, free from any aches or pains and ready for some solid food and a pint. It's about 12.30 and while the well-rehearsed practice of tea drinking is underway, it's giving me time to settle down for a few minutes before we are all ready to drive up to the Stockyard pub for a value-for-money carvery.

There's a knock on the door and John has arrived, explaining his reason for missing the run in. We must have just missed him by a couple of minutes, but it's just good to see him safe and sound. My invitation for him to join us for dinner is declined, because of prior arrangements. John leaves for home with my thanks for all his help over the last few days, as we all head for our cars to drive to the industrial estate for Sunday lunch.

The overflowing plate of food is great and the company even better, as I tuck into the first hot meal for some time and a pint of Foster's.

Time flies and like all good things that come to an end, all too soon it's time to say our farewells and pass on our wishes for a safe journey for Vonnie and Andrew, who will travel all the way back home to Cobham, south of London. They leave with my thanks for their friendship and massive support over this weekend.

Karen and Chris have to leave for home and all too soon the event seems to have come to an end. It's difficult to remain still at home while filling Maureen in with the main details of the challenge, but the inactivity and quietness of our cottage soon provides the perfect background and sleep, for a very weary me, finally takes over.

# EPILOGUE

I am blessed, and feel incredibly lucky that I have been able to complete this 150-plus mile event, which has lasted for a total of 38 hours, without any serious problems other than the six hours or so of hamstring pain. I have been able to cope with the distance, both mentally and physically, and pleased that I did get the food and drink intake just about right. I can apply that vast amount of knowledge for future endurance events. I feel confident that I will have the ability to maintain the strength of mind that is needed to overcome fatigue, enabling me to make it to the end of even longer and more demanding runs. I have put my body through a massive challenge and come through with a greater understanding of what makes me tick.

I was prepared to put myself onto that pedestal to satisfy a personal whim and be open to adverse comments should I have failed, but then it is a fact that I have always been prepared to venture into the unknown. I dared to stand on the start line, happy and content in the knowledge that I did my very best to become the best that I am capable of becoming. Many more questions were answered over those 38 hours.

So what are the plans for future challenges?

For a couple of months, I have been hatching plans to run across England on the Alfred Wainwright's Coast to Coast route, which starts in St Bees, just above Liverpool, crosses over the Lake District for about 70 miles, through the Yorkshire Dales and North York Moors, finishing at Robin

Hood's Bay, just above Scarborough, a distance of about 192 miles over three consecutive days. I particularly like the tradition of dipping your toe in the Irish Sea at the start and then the North Sea at the finish. Unfortunately the logistics of servicing three days of food for the running would be a big problem to overcome, as I feel it would be unfair to ask for a backup team to travel all that way for me, so I will look to make different plans for this event!!

The ultimate and, I guess, the one challenge that should take me to the edge of my capabilities will be to complete 75 ultra- marathons in 75 consecutive days in order to complete a total distance of over two thousand miles, and finish with a day off on my 75th birthday. This one has been hatching in my "to do" list for a few years and won't go away. Not only that, this challenge could only ever happen once in anyone's lifetime. So I reckon the only way of getting shut of that little elf on my shoulder is to just do it. It might well be worth writing about? So watch this space!

If you like to run and enjoy running, ask yourself what it would take for you to Love running!!

# COMMENTS FROM THE 100KM
# LONDON TO BRIGHTON GROUP

## Kerry's account of his 24 hour London to Brighton off road challenge

The reality of the situation is that on June 9/10, I undertook a 100km walk in which to raise money for Blind Veterans UK. I completed 72km (44.75 miles) of the course in 18 hours. I was accompanied for the first 30km by my guide dog, Pedro, who I then retired because the heat was getting a bit much for him. From that point onward I was guided by Darren Murphy, my best friend of over 25 years. With us the entire way was Ray Matthews, a 71-year-old ultra runner. I was also supported en route by my physiotherapist Lt Col (Ret'd) Stuart Patterson MBE, who served in the Army Physical Training Corps and Royal Army Medical Corps for 37 years until retiring a couple of years ago; Stuart came out at 10pm on the Saturday, having driven 60 miles to treat me at the 60km mark. Stuart has been my physio for a while, having started treating me after I underwent major orthopaedic surgery last September to repair the three primary ligaments in my left ankle and graft part of my hamstring into my ankle to reinforce it. The surgery became necessary after my abortive attempt to walk the Wainwright Way 192 miles, Coast to Coast, last May!

I withdrew at the 72km mark because of injury and, while it was enormously disappointing at the time, it undoubtedly prevented further injury. I developed a problem with my left hamstring (the one that had been part harvested for the graft last September) and Stuart is likely to be working on me for a few months yet to get me sorted out again. Looking back on it, while it may have been disappointing at the time, it was definitely the right call (to stop).

As I have been told more than once since the event, 72km in 18 hours mostly cross country is no mean feat without even considering that I am registered blind, a stroke survivor and did more than half of it without my guide dog, necessitating the ground to be described to me virtually every step of the way, and less than nine months ago I was in plaster following surgery.

Without Darren, Ray and Stuart supporting me I would not have made it as far as I did, that Darren and Ray completed the course gives me a sense of pride at being able to call them both friends.

On the fund-raising side of things, I have so far raised £1,300, Darren has raised £1,200 and my employer (BP) will match what I have raised, bringing the total contribution to almost £4,000 of the £75,000 that the event has so far raised. There were 269 participants and only 165 completed the course, 100 of them in 24 hours or less (I think they're the right numbers, this makes no mention of the sponsorship that Ray brought to the event.)

All in all, not a bad day's work!

Looking ahead, I am seriously considering doing it again next year and Ray has mentioned that he is keen to get me on a 100k race across the Sahara, which I am not discounting the possibility of! But before then I have a week of skiing to get through, organised by Blind Veterans, in January.

I have been told that I set my sights too high and on this occasion they may have been right but next time it won't beat me; but I must conclude by saying that without the support that Blind Veterans has given me, both practical and emotional, I would not have had the inclination or motivation to even attempt it. I must also make mention of the support of Guide Dogs for the Blind in providing my ever present companion, Pedro.

## From the account of Jo Newton

Reading that has made me feel really emotional as I was there! I am the Jo in that little team who battled and battled to complete what was for me the hardest challenge of my life. When the blisters burst just before the finish, it really felt as if someone was holding a lighter against my little toe, it was absolute agony. I would never have thought to take off my socks, I would have thought that would have made it ten times worse but it helped massively, that and the fact that Ray told me to lean on him after putting my shoe, without the sock, back on and offered me his shoulder and so far into the challenge was willing to shoulder my pain, too, was the final motivator I needed to cross that finish line. The feeling as we crossed the line, together, and under Ray's Union Jack was amazing. Of course, I did the only thing possible and burst into tears. It was wonderful that Kerry was there with Pedro to meet us too (although slightly disappointing that after all we had achieved, my little girls just wanted a photo of the dog!)

Since the challenge, I have thought a lot about my experience and can honestly say that it was one of the best experiences of my life. I am pushing 40, a slightly overweight harassed mum of three, and yet I did it, I walked from London to Brighton and didn't stop or give up no matter how much I wanted to. The feeling of achievement is worth all the pain and without wanting to sound too melodramatic, the experience is a life-changing one. I've never had to push myself before and I think to be honest, I thought I was a quitter, but I'm not. When I felt low, exhausted and in pain, there is a bit of me that keeps going, that and the fact that I didn't quit is making me look at my life in a completely different way

## Vonnie's account

This 100k walk from London to Brighton seemed like the perfect challenge for me; I felt comfortable, even though it would be a big challenge, but also confident that I could achieve it. This was a personal challenge for me to start something and see it through; I had attempted to run the London Marathon a (childhood dream) and because of injuries, I was not able to compete... leaving me feeling "let down" and a strong sense of determination to do something and finish what I started!

Then just ten days before the event, I was rushed into hospital and had an emergency operation to remove my appendix. It was amusing afterwards talking to the surgeon and his many assistants who were all looking at me with astonished expressions while I explained that I needed to walk 100k in ten days' time!

Once home recovering, I knew that I would still go ahead with the challenge, I arranged for my family to meet me at various checkpoints, this was more to pacify worried friends who thought I needed to be locked up! I knew mentally that I was good to go the distance and I had trained well, so felt fairly confident that I wasn't going to be putting myself in any harm or holding back my walking partner either!

The lows!

Well, I remember hitting a seriously low point while following Ray and Darren across yet another field, we had all become slightly separated and it gave me a few moments to get my head back into the zone, we were heading to our checkpoint at Plumpton, can't remember how many hours we had been walking, probably 20-plus?

I was exhausted and in so much pain from my swollen knee, my feet were so sore and blistered I just thought when we get to the checkpoint that's it, I'm done.

Then I gave myself a serious talking to and reminded myself why I was doing this. A sore knee is nothing to the disabilities or illnesses many people endure every day of their lives, my pain would get better and be forgotten. I had to finish what I started; imagining going home and saying I had almost finished: for me just wasn't an option!

I learned something about myself that day and I liked it, this was the start of something for me.

Sorry for the silly question Ray, but have to ask ... how do you keep the sand out of your shoes when you're running in the desert?

## The thoughts of Bernadette and Jane

Our challenge started at Richmond Rugby Club on Saturday morning at 11.15. After months of training, we set off walking along the side of the River Thames with a large group of athletes, who were soon strung out on the flat terrain which took us through Old Malden, Ewell and all the way to our first check point at Nonsuch Park at about 25 kilometres into the challenge for a much-needed comfort break and refuel on food. This first section had taken us 3hours 16 minutes. After a short rest and refuelling, we set off out of the park heading towards the A232 and our second leg, which saw us walking mainly on our own, encountering the first of many golf courses, where we got a mouthful of abuse from the golfers who were waiting to tee off. We found ourselves apologising and at the same time running across the permissive paths. After leaving the grounds of the golf course, we crossed over the A217 to yet another golf course, but this time without any abuse, we then headed towards the A2022, which took us through to our second check point at Oaks Park. We had now covered 30k.

Leaving the busy park after fuelling up, we made our way on our third leg, which took us in the direction of the A23 heading towards Coulsdon Railway Station. The route took us over the railway bridge to cross over the tracks and as we did so, the station master announced that the next train to stop at the station would be heading to Brighton. How cruel and soul destroying was that announcement, knowing we had probably another 18 hours to go. We left the station and headed towards the M25. Here we met up with three people, but soon left them as we realised they were probably struggling and not in a hurry. We soon reached Godstone, our third check point, which had taken us just under three and half hours since our last checkpoint, and we had now covered about 45 kilometres.

We were ready for a break and after a much-deserved stop and a cup of pea soup, we soldiered on towards Felbridge and our halfway point, where our partners were waiting to meet us with fresh clothes and a much-deserved hug. This leg took us through fields, with many stiles and kissing gates, on our way to Horne Park Golf Course. The terrain was brutal but not as bad as we were about to experience on our fifth leg. We managed to catch up with five men, one being partially sighted and a member of the Blind Veterans UK, at about 8 o'clock on Saturday night. After walking for nearly five hours on our own, we realised that it would be a good idea and comforting to stay with these five men, Ray, Rory, Darren, Kerry and John, to see us through the night. We reached Felbridge just after midnight – Sunday morning after a tough, just over four hours of walking. Felbridge marks the 60 kilometres point of the challenge.

The fifth leg took us all through the most difficult terrain we had experienced up to now, as we negotiated deep trenches and sharp inclines. The fields were getting longer and hillier, as well as muddier and deeper, and there were more stiles to climb and kissing gates to open than we could have imagined in the dark. Four of us went ahead of Ray, Darren and Kerry in search of glow sticks that had been placed on trees, fences and posts as navigational aids in the night. Reading the route directions through the night was causing us to lose valuable time. As we found each glow stick, we would shout instructions back to Ray, Darren and Kerry about any obstacles that would be difficult for Kerry to tackle and wait until they caught up. We finally reached Sharpthorpe around 3am on Sunday, 70 kilometres into the challenge, some 3 hours 54 minutes from our last stop. WE WERE SPENT. Here we lost Kerry (the partially-sighted guy) through some long-standing injury and John because of exhaustion but gained two ladies, Yvonne and Jo.

We set off after saying our goodbyes to Kerry on to our sixth leg, taking us over 12 stiles and more fields, but as the morning got brighter and the birds started singing, we realised that we were into a new day and the finishing line was very close. Well closer than it was 16 hours ago, anyway. We reached Scaynes Hill at the 85 kilometres mark, around 7am, for a well-deserved bacon butty just under four hours later. Once all blisters were tended to, we carried on to our final check point at Plumpton before heading towards the finishing line.

Our seventh leg was mentally the toughest leg of all. We were tired, fed up and sore, but somehow, somewhere, we managed to carry on, it's at times like this when you remember all the good wishes – "YOU CAN DO IT" – "YOU WILL DO IT." Pulling out was not an option at this late stage. Getting to the penultimate stop definitely was a challenge. As we headed towards Plumpton, we could see road signs – Plumpton 2½ miles. Great, we were nearly at the last but one stop. Oh, how wrong were we? Our route map and instructions took us on a soul destroying two and half hour detour around numerous fields, probably just to add the miles on to make up the distance, before reaching the seventh check point just under four and a half hours later, bringing up the total distance now to 95 kilometres.

After a short stop, we were told by one of the event volunteers that we had about 8.2 miles to go, which involved some very nasty hills that we would need to climb. We didn't care at this point. We were nearly finished. With a new lease of life, we attacked the hills on the way up and ran down them on the other side, only to be confronted with three more nasty hills on the horizon. We attacked each one for about two hours before fatigue set in and our brains switched off and we just followed Ray through the torrential rain. The last leg saw us reach Brighton and the finishing line in four hours – making a grand total of 29 and a half hours and 105 kilometres for the challenge, how we managed to smile at the end, we do not know.

One gentleman we walked with, Ray, was 71 years old, he was such an inspiration to us all. He was our guide and mentor throughout the walk. We did eventually run in over the finish line, flying his Union Jack, which he carries everywhere with him during his endurance races.

In three months' time, he will be trying to break a record which he already holds, by running the circumference of Rotherham (150 miles) in less than 38 hours. We wished him well.

Rory, to the left of the picture, did this challenge last year but pulled out after 75k. God he could talk! The lady holding the flag had her appendix taken out ten days before this challenge. How she finished is anyone's guess. The gentleman to the far right of the picture is Darren; he was the main guide for the partially-sighted Kerry and had the patience of a saint. We thanked each and every one of them for getting us through to the finish line of this extreme challenge.

My most memorable moment was when we met up with Ray, Darren and Kerry. Jane and I had been on our own for five hours when we joined them, it was a godsend because it was getting dark and we knew we didn't want to go through the night without any company. I couldn't believe how they accepted us into their already-formed group and allowed us to continue this adventure together. What was more overwhelming was that we were encouraged to run over the finish line holding Ray's Union Jack. I felt that at the time, every one of us was looking after each other and we had only just met. It was very surreal.

Fascinating comments from ordinary people doing extraordinary things, it's what makes the world go round.

# What the Papers Say...

# Ray runs rings Round Rotherham three times

*Article and photos printed with kind permission of*
*Worksop Guardian*

SEVENTY-ONE years old, 150 miles, five pairs of trainers and just one little blister – Ray Matthews is a running inspiration.

The Maltby grandfather completed an almost unthinkable challenge at the weekend, running the 50-mile Round Rotherham race THREE times.

A retired structural engineer, Ray has previously written a book (Me and My Shadow) on his extreme running exploits, but he told the Guardian this was his toughest task yet.

Setting off from Manvers College at 5pm on Friday, he crossed the finish line at 10.01am on Sunday morning, just a minute after his predicted time.

And he was delighted to come through it unscathed: "It was just amazing; it all went according to plan." "I have no aches or pains, no injuries, just a blister on my little toe." Of the three sets of 50 miles, Ray pinpointed the middle race – when he joined the official Round Rotherham event – as the hardest.

"About 70 miles into my run, 20 miles into the race proper, I felt like I had been shot, my right hamstring seized up and I had to walk for a while." "I got really down, that was a low point for me because I had people giving up sleep to come and meet me through the night and I didn't want to miss the times I had arranged with them." "But I realised I just had to go for it, and it was as if someone touched me and the pain just cleared."

"Having been down and lost two hours, I was able to pull all the time back and just about made every meeting time."

"The help I got from all those people running with me and meeting me was fantastic, I couldn't have carried all that food and drink and I felt so supported."

Friday's first six miles were a real highlight for the Maltby man, when he was joined by his beloved granddaughter, Holly.

The 17-year-old accompanied him on a previous ultra running challenge, and he admits her presence is a boost. "It's a great feeling running with her, she's such a lovely girl and a great athlete herself," he said. "It really set me up for this; it was like I was floating along."

The support of his family clearly means a lot to someone who dedicates himself to extreme running, particularly his wife, Maureen. Ray added: "These things couldn't happen if it wasn't for her. She thinks I'm a lunatic but she supports and looks after me." "The whole family support me, my daughter Karen and grandkids; they were all tweeting through the night trying to get people to support me."

The 150-mile slog wasn't just about a personal achievement however; Ray is hoping to raise awareness and finance for two good causes. He set up a donation page for the Blind Veterans UK charity, and wants to donate a specially adapted trike to the Newman School in Whiston.

"There are many disabled children at the school and I really want to get one of these trikes for the kids but they're about £800, so I want to get one and present it to them."

# Amazing Ray goes round – and round – and round --- Again

*Printed with kind permission of Doncaster Free Press*

HE conquered the Sahara Desert at 70, but at the age of 71, Ray Matthews has again done the almost impossible!

The granddad has just completed the 50-mile Rotherham Round Race three times over, and was still whizzing past the 50-milers as he approached his last lap.

Ray set off from Dearne Valley College's Manvers campus at 5pm on Friday, then ran through two nights to make the finish line on Sunday- half a minute over his target time of 10am.

And on Tuesday, Ray told the Times that although he suffered some hamstring trouble that forced him to slow down for a while on Saturday, he is now totally free of aches, pains or niggles, and at the 150-miles finish could have kept on running if he had needed to. His training base is Energie gym at Parkgate, and many of his gym pals turned up to cheer him on.

"I had no fatigue....in fact other runners were asking me to at least look like I was struggling as I ran with them," he laughed.

"But I couldn't have done it without the volunteers who gave up sleep to be my pit stops. They were amazing."

Ray's run was a sponsored feat to raise cash for an adapted trike costing £800, for pupils at the Newman School, Rotherham.

He now faces an enforced rest for several weeks following an urgent hand operation.

"It will be hard not to exercise but I do appreciate how privileged I am to be able to do what I do," he said. "Perhaps the six weeks' rest will do me good."

*With kind permission from Rotherham Advertiser*

# Runner Ray sets new challenge

DESERT-running septuagenarian Ray Matthews has set himself a new challenge - and is seeking others to join him in the ring.

For his latest feat, that will benefit local charity the World Aid Foundation, Ray goes back to his first sport - boxing, and a 15-round metabolic work out.

The qualified boxing coach, a former ABA boxing champion who won his first title aged 13, said: "This will be a tough workout, but I challenge others to get up and join me for 15 rounds, and raise money for a worthy cause".

Rounds will work up from a two to five minute intensity, with one minute between each stint.

Several others have enlisted already for the test, to take place on Decem-

**by Sally Burton**
editorial@dearnetoday.co.uk

ber 15, from 11.30am at Parkgate's Energie gym.

Ray, 70, is shortly to release a book telling how he battled across the Sahara Desert then began a new career as speaker, author and national representative.

He returned recently from the 26th Venice Marathon then wrote of that experience, from its 5am start, taking the water bus up the Grand Canal to Piazzale Roma, to moving 20 miles inland to begin the race that took in the five kilometre Parco San Giulliano bridge leading in to Venice.

One memorable feature of the race was the presence of rescue teams, said

Ray, in the form of specially trained dogs that lined the route along canal banks - but on this occasion were not required to perform.

Ray completed the marathon in 5.09.27.

Along with the December 15 date in his diary, he then aims to undertake the 100 kilometre London to Brighton 24 hour challenge, to benefit the charity for blind ex-servicemen.

And he is organising a Three Peaks Challenge bid to take place in April next year, also for charity, should anyone wish to join the group.

For more information on any of the above, or for sponsor forms for the Boxing Challenge towards helping the World Aid Foundation's East Africa Appeal, contact Ray on 07778 858586.

*Sahara Desert Sand Storm*

# Photo Gallery

*Louise, Joanne, Ray, Fay, Helen & Hope, after last training run before the RRR 150 mile challenge. There's more to this running malarkey than meets the eye*

*Ray in 1953*

*The start of 150 miles, with kind permission Worksop Guardian*

*Ray spreading out the Union Jack coming in to finish the 150 mile challenge*

*Ray Kerry & Darren at the start of the 100k challenge*

*Ray*

*Louise & Helen just after Wentworth as the dawn breaks on*

*Ray with Rony Robinson at Radio Sheffield's interview before the Blind Veterans 100k 24 hour challenge*

*Through the night across the South Downs Kerry & Darren on the 100k 24 hour challenge London to Brighton.*

*Ray today out training, Photo by Dave Poucer*